Area of 92nd Infantry Division Italy Campaign, 1944-1945.

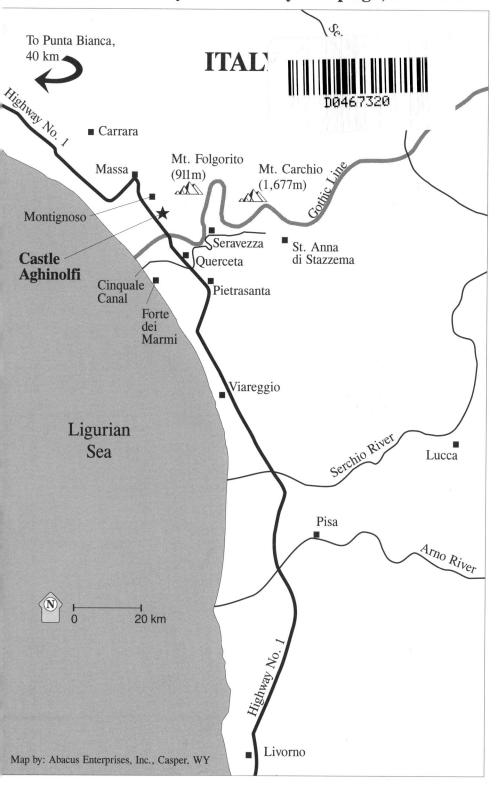

To Punta Bianca,
40 km

ITAL

D0467320

Highway No. 1

Carrara

Massa

Mt. Folgorito
(911m)

Mt. Carchio
(1,677m)

Gothic Line

Montignoso

Castle Aghinolfi

Seravezza

Querceta

St. Anna
di Stazzema

Cinquale
Canal

Pietrasanta

Forte
dei
Marmi

Viareggio

Ligurian
Sea

Serchio River

Lucca

Pisa

Arno River

N

0   20 km

Highway No. 1

Livorno

Map by: Abacus Enterprises, Inc., Casper, WY

LASTING VALOR

To Jake. You will be a
great American

Vernon J Baker
CMH

LASTING VALOR

Vernon J. Baker
with Ken Olsen

Foreword by General Colin L. Powell, USA (Ret.)

Genesis Press, Inc.
Columbus, Mississippi

Grateful acknowledgment is made to the following for permission to reprint previously published material:

Esquire Magazine, quote by Sally Kempton, reprinted courtesy of Esquire Magazine and the Hearst Corporation.

Harcourt, Brace & Co., excerpt from Bring Me A Unicorn: Diaries and Letters of Anne Morrow Lindbergh 1922–1928, copyright 1972 by Anne Morrow Lindbergh, reprinted by permission of Harcourt, Brace & Company.

Harcourt, Brace & Co., excerpt from Dearly Beloved, A Theme and Variations, by Anne Morrow Lindbergh, copyright 1962 by Harcourt Brace & Company and renewed in 1990 by Anne M. Lindbergh, reprinted by permission of the publisher.

Harcourt, Brace & Co., excerpt from The Life I Really Lived, copyright 1979 by Jessamyn West, reprinted by permission of Harcourt, Brace & Company.

Little, Brown & Co., quote from The Complete Poems of Emily Dickinson, edited by Thomas H. Johnson, copyright 1929 by Martha Dickinson Blancht; copyright renewed in 1957 by Mary L. Hampson, reprinted by permission of Little, Brown and Company (Inc.).

Prima Publishing, quotes from the book Speaker's and Toastmaster's Handbook, Prima Publishing, Rocklin, CA, copyright 1990 by Herbert V. Prochnow, reprinted by permission of Prima Publishing.

Stewart, Tabori & Chang Publishers, quote from I Dream A World: Portraits of Black Women Who Changed America, copyright 1989 by Barbara Summers, Brian Lanker, reprinted by permission of Stewart, Tabori & Chang Publishers.

ISBN: 1-885478-30-5
Library of Congress Catalog Card Number: 97-75283

Manufactured in the United States of America
First Edition

Dedicated
to my grandfather,
Joseph Samuel Baker,
and
the brave soldiers of the 92nd Infantry
Buffalo Division who fought valiantly in Italy during
World War II—especially the men I left behind.
Well done fellows. We did it.

All children, don't let your souls get used to waging such enormous wars, nor use your strength in fraternal wars.

—Virgil, *Aeneid*

FOREWORD

When twenty-five-year-old Lieutenant Vernon J. Baker led his platoon in an impossible charge three miles behind German lines in northern Italy, I was eight years old. That day, April 5, 1945, was my birthday. While I enjoyed a special day with my family and my Kelly Street friends in the South Bronx, Vernon Baker's platoon was helping to pierce the once-impregnable Gothic Line in a harrowing battle that cost them dearly.

It would be fifty-two years before I met Lieutenant Baker, and fifty-two years before his courageous deeds from that April day would be recognized.

Vernon Baker came to the Army in a time when most schools were segregated and Jim Crow ruled buses, restrooms, restaurants, and drinking fountains. He served under Southern white commanders who had no regard for the black soldier, no confidence in his ability. He persevered because, above all, he was committed to his country.

I stood on the shoulders of men such as Vernon Baker. When I graduated from college in 1958, the only place a black man could go all the way to the top was the military. I have never failed to recognize the inspiration that gave me the energy to do my very best. Looking over my shoulder, I knew that in World War II more than one million black men and women served their country. Blacks like Lieutenant Baker.

My Uncle Vic served in the 4th Armored Division. He brought me home a souvenir from those battles—a helmet from the German *Afrika Korps*—that I treasured for forty years. His contribution,

Vernon Baker's contribution, and much of the more than 200 years of military service and combat courage of black Americans are nearly a national secret. Consider the fact that this book is one of the first full-length biographies of a black World War II infantryman.

This book may prompt people to see Vernon Baker as a celebrity. It is vital to remember that he is something much different. Vernon Baker is a national inspiration, a national role model. He is a role model because of the quiet dignity he portrays. He is a role model because he never shirked his duty but quietly went about his life, believing in his country, in service to his country. He didn't give just one day in combat, he gave decades of service.

Vernon Baker never bragged of his deeds nor complained of his lot. Many of his closest friends first heard of his heroism in 1996, when news reports belatedly broke the story of his deeds. Even now, when prodded to talk of those combat days, Vernon Baker speaks of his men and not of himself. He quietly advises others, "Give respect before you expect it. Treat people the way you want to be treated. Remember the mission. Set the example. Keep going."

This from a man who endured decades of some of the worst this country offered 20th century black Americans.

That Lieutenant Baker finally has been recognized doesn't take away the indignity. It doesn't wipe out history. This country is still struggling. We must continue the struggle. We owe it to the young people coming behind us to conduct those struggles with the same quiet determination that fuels Vernon Baker.

When we see somebody like Vernon Baker, we see a soldier whose love for this country never wavered; we see a man who still carries himself with dignity despite the many onerous battles and legions of scars. We see a man who cares more deeply about helping our youth, the soldiers, sailors, nurses, engineers, parents, and leaders of tomorrow than he cares about medals, war stories, ceremonies, and accolades.

Lieutenant Vernon Baker will continue to inspire me. More important, he will inspire generations of younger Americans.

—General Colin L. Powell, USA (Ret.)

ACKNOWLEDGMENTS

Writing a book is a battle in its own right. There are a hundred individual skirmishes, seemingly overwhelming odds, and dozens of soldiers who contribute to the victory. Several of them deserve credit.

Craig Buck is friend and photographer extraordinaire who fed us, helped us, and gave us the faith to keep going. Our debt to him will never be fulfilled.

Winda Benedetti, Lisa Loy, and Dena Marchant devoted considerable time, thoughtful critiques, moral support, and vision to this book. Caroline Paul was inspirational and had extraordinary insight into what makes a story, one reason she is such a magnificent writer. Julie Sullivan—also a gifted writer—was reader, friend, and gentle coach.

Photographer Jesse Tinsley generously lent us his equipment and moral support. We owe Jess Walter and Stephen Lyons—also extraordinary writers—much more than mere words of thanks. Mike and Linda McCarty cared for the dogs during numerous trips to research this work and gave encouragement at every turn. Dick and Lil Shanks have never stopped giving and, along with Valerie Benecke, kept the fires warm and the pipes thawed so we could write another day. Heidy Baker always faithfully supported this effort. Thanks also are due to Ken Sands, Steve Massey, and Craig Welch for reading and listening.

A special "Hooha" goes out to Captain Mark Jackson, who contributed both his intuition about people and his knowledge of history; to Captain Leslie Jackson and the staff at Walter Reed Army

Hospital; and to Wendell C. Warner, Keith Gates, Richard Gooch, Lisa Beach, Jason Luhrs, Donald Lehr, Lisa Weidenbush, and the fine women and men of the 437th Military Police Company. Much of this would not have come together without them.

Michelle Bernard and Joe Johns opened their homes and their hearts to us. Steve Scharosch, cartographer and friend, provided maps and understanding on short notice. Gen. John W. Mountcastle, Mary Haynes, and the rest of the staff at the Center for Military History gave excellent assistance. Andrea Wales of the Army Reserve Personnel Center Public Affairs Office was critical in confirming dates and finding medal citations. Fellow Buffalo Soldier Harry Cox was tireless. The staff of Father Flanagan's Boys Town— formerly Boys Home—also helped with this effort.

We are particularly grateful to the people of Italy, who provided the warmest, most generous reception of anywhere we traveled in the world. Our hearts go out particularly to the partisans, to the staff of *Il Tirreno*—including editor Sandra Bonsanti, co-editor Claudio Giua, deputy editor Nino Sofia, Massa bureau chief Giuliano Fontini, and American-based Italian journalist Umberto Venturini— whose kindness and assistance were invaluable. Historian and author Giovanni Cipollini kept an eye on our Italian facts with the help of Mario Costa. Francesca Carboni translated, was liaison for questions, and is a great ambassador for her homeland.

We are deeply grateful to agents Charlotte Sheedy and Neeti Madan, who were resilient, upbeat, and always had faith no matter what the crisis. Many thanks to publisher Wil Colom, Cyrana Mott, and the staff at Genesis Press who had the skill to recognize the possibilities. Editor Karla Hocker knew how to polish the words. Our appreciation also to Linda J. Shepherd for excellent text design on a moment's notice.

Our gratitude to the hundreds of other people who made this possible. We remember you in our hearts and regret if we have overlooked you on these pages.

One final note about this book. Every effort has been made to meticulously reconstruct the names of people, the towns where the

Buffalo Soldiers fought, and the events of individual battles. The confusion of war and the passing of fifty-two years make that an incredible task. The problems are heightened by the loss of Army personnel records from World War II in a fire in St. Louis in the 1970s.

Because of these challenges, there may be errors and omissions we cannot catch. Nonetheless, the spirit of this work is to convey the experiences of one black infantryman's life in World War II and in 20th century America. To that end, we feel confident the reader will find the truth.

—Vernon J. Baker and Ken Olsen

PROLOGUE

There is a pain—so utter,
It swallows substance up,
Then covers the Abyss with Trance,
So Memory can step
Around—across—upon it.

—Emily Dickinson

I am haunted by the memory of nineteen men; men I left on a ridge in northern Italy five decades ago.

I still hear a German commander scream *"Feuer,"* howitzer shells whistling in, followed by the whish, whish, whish of mortars, the trees around us shredding. Wounded and dying men screaming. My only medic killed by a sniper as we try to withdraw.

A film of burned cordite covers the roof of my mouth and cottons my tongue. It's April 1945 in Italy's Northern Apennine Mountains and my men and I have been trading bullets and grenades with the German Army for so long that the air is more spent powder than oxygen. I know, as soon as this taste bites my tongue, the images will follow.

I gather dog tags from my dead comrades, time after time, figuring their bodies probably never will be recovered, that their families deserve to know where and when they died. I see the living wrestle rifles and spare ammunition from the dead and mortally wounded, taking from those who have given everything, so the rest of us can live and fight a little longer.

I hear, over and over again, my company commander telling me he is going for reinforcements. I stare long and hard at Captain John F. Runyon as he gives me that story. He trudges away, disappearing forever into the late morning haze, the haze of exploding shells, bodies, and blood. Yet today, I cannot remember a detail from his face, except that it was a white man's face, whiter yet, nearly translucent, with fear.

Blame? Rage? Perhaps. I am angry and aghast that he never returned. But more likely this memory lapse is habit. There was no reason to memorize anything distinguishing about Runyon or any other white commander. A white officer in charge of black troops could ask to be relieved of his command at any time and that wish had to be granted immediately.

The rest of us were black Buffalo Soldiers, regarded as too worthless to lead ourselves. The Army decided we needed supervision from white Southerners, as if war was plantation work and fighting Germans was picking cotton.

Harsh as those words seem, I can't work up much bitterness anymore. Yet, I cannot forget the faces of the men who died beside me, nor can I stop wondering if, as their platoon leader, I am responsible for their deaths.

I am haunted by what I cannot remember. Everywhere I go, people ask me to recite the names of those nineteen men I left in the shadow of Castle Aghinolfi. No doubt studio audiences and readers would be more satisfied if I could give dramatic discourse about how several men, closer to me than brothers, died agonizing but glorious deaths, with twists of heroism that stir *God Bless America* in every soul.

I cannot.

I cannot remember the names of the men of my platoon who fought with me and died at the castle or the dozens of other villages and canals, ridge tops and mountain valleys. I only remember bringing back handfuls of dog tags.

I cannot stare down those battles in search of every emotional detail. I now realize the mistakes I made, the recklessness of my bravado, the myth of invincibility that only existed when I was young and naive—which is why we send the young and naive to fight our wars. If I put fifty-two years of knowledge and perspective next to the names and the memories of the men for whom I was responsible I court insanity.

After the first combat death splattered blood across my face I realized there is no glory. I numbed myself in order to go on. I divided my mind into compartments, putting emotion into one, soldiering into another. I lived and worked from the compartment of soldiering. If I made the mistake of getting too close to somebody, I forced myself to forget about it after his face exploded or his intestines spilled. I didn't dare sit and mourn. I had to keep my wits about me or I would end up being carried out on a stretcher or left for the vultures and blowflies.

Fatigue at first disarmed me—making me more vulnerable to grief. Soon fatigue was my friend, helping to deaden my brain and the part of my soul that wanted to well up, overflow, and drown me with grief. Occasionally I could not quell it and ended up heaving my guts out, first with bitter gushes and then racking, dry retches. It felt horrible, not so much for the stomach spasms or bile rushing out of my mouth as for the fact that I was losing control.

I never feared dying. I always feared losing control.

It's not that I don't love these men and mourn their passing. It's not that I don't count the ways I might have prevented their deaths. That's the luxury and the damnation of having the time and opportunity to look back. That's part of the haunting. But gunfire, mortar rounds, artillery shells, and booby traps don't allow any perspective. I focused on the desperate need to survive that moment, capture a few hundred feet of hillside, a trench, a machine gun nest. If I survived one minute, I figured out how to deal with the next.

After years of trying to forget, of regretting many deaths, I have been handed the hero's mantle. I wear it uneasily. People have considerable expectations of heroes. We are not to falter in the spotlight; we are not to have made many mistakes in the past. Being a black American raises the ante.

"Black youth so desperately need heroes such as yourself," well-wishers constantly tell me, as if this is the ultimate compliment. It is not. It is the ultimate pressure to constantly re-examine memories long buried in emotional self-defense. It magnifies my shortcomings and my guilt.

I did not seek this final chapter to my life. I moved to a remote cabin in the backwoods of Idaho, with easy access only to good elk hunting, to escape attention. The Army came looking for me as part of its own self-examination. Its historians created this heroic image, and the media happily made additions. The public added another measure.

Once handed mythical stature, I have not been allowed to step out of the spotlight. Even if the mantle fits me as sloppily as a father's shirt fits his infant son, I am expected to stroll about my stage as if my outfit was tailor-made. If I ask for something more my size, I will be cast as ungrateful. And with enough hype, media attention, time as a poster boy for this cause or that, I have magically grown into the shirt, this stature. At least in the eyes of the public.

I am not an icon for any ideal. I am an old soldier, a loner, a man more fit to fight wars than deal with peacetime society. My mistakes are as numerous as any man's. My regrets likely loom larger than most.

My hero's mantle has been crafted out of carnage, the senseless sacrifice of young men and my mad-dog desperation to outlast the enemy and disprove the fiction that black soldiers were afraid to fight. It is not cause for national celebration nor the incarnation of heroes. It is reason for us to mourn our losses and question our motivations.

I love those nineteen men like no other souls. I cannot give their names, but I carry their faces in my mind with nagging clarity. They visit me in the night, or when I'm sitting on a downed tree awaiting an elk, or when some other small event triggers a memory of what we shared. The faces say nothing. They only stare at me with the final look they gave death.

These men, these faces, are the reason I am here today, the reason I was selected for the Medal of Honor. They are the heroes.

ONE

All that troubles is but for a moment. That only is important which is eternal.

—Inscription in Milan Cathedral

Summer 1944, Northern Italy

The August air wore itself Louisiana thick and heavy as we picked our way across the Arno River on the remains of a bridge demolished by the retreating Germans. The jagged shards of concrete rose and dove in the muddy channel as if they were razorback tombstones rather than a passageway. This awkward jumble was the only option. We were in too much of a hurry to wait for the engineering corps to pull together a pontoon bridge. The river was all that stood between us and our crack at the shooting war.

The Arno runs at a pleasantly slow pace from the mountains of north central Italy, through Florence, down to Pisa and on west to the Ligurian Sea. It serpentinely traverses cultivated fields, grape arbors, and the ever-present olive groves that stood sentry even when legions from the Byzantine era fought Germanic warriors here 1,500 years earlier. The chocolate water added one more stirring contrast to the collage of hazy blue mountains, deep-green fields, dusky trees, and glassy, aqua ocean.

The wrecked bridge was a regular element of the German's insurance policy—delay or divert us as long as possible—often taken to hideous extremes. The Ponte Vecchio in Florence, an ancient, stunning structure that is part art, part bridge, survived only because a German commander defied Hitler's orders to destroy everything as his troops pulled out. No telling what *Der Führer* planned for Michelangelo's works.

Standing within squinting distance of the leaning tower of Pisa, our company—Charlie Company—proudly led the 370th Infantry Regiment as it traversed the obstacle course over the Arno. Much of what remained of the bridge was submerged, making the crossing more swim than hike. Sergeant Willie Dickens, the diminutive company comic, ended up neck-deep in water, leaving visible only his head, his rigidly upthrust arms, and the submachine gun he was trying to keep dry. He reminded me of a prairie dog who had just popped out of a burrow, holding its front paws high as if surrendering to the sheriff.

Dickens was a Southerner from North Carolina or Mississippi, the way I remember it. He was the youngest of a large family that had subsisted with a team of mules on forty acres so pathetic that no white man cared that they were black folk with property. There hadn't been enough side pork, biscuits, and red-eye gravy to go around when Dickens was growing up, so the family didn't wring its hands when he joined the Army.

That story was repeated throughout my rifle platoon. Poor, black rural Southern men with no other way to make a living, whose families had lived a Depression since the day they were freed from slavery. Poor, black rural Southern men with nothing to lose by being drafted into a segregated, racist Army and going to combat. The only exception among the enlisted men, in the rest of the 92nd Division, were members of an Army program that sent even black men to college to become engineers. When political uproar shattered the program, most went from student with slide rule to infantry private with rifle and sixty-pound field pack. The black officer ranks included a batch of second lieutenants like me—promoted from the enlisted ranks and run through Officer Candidate School because, unlike most of the rest of the men, I could read and write—or the occasional National Guardsman or ROTC graduate.

"Hey, Dickens, get off of your knees," the men hooted when they discovered that, for once, they could give the sergeant a hard time. Dickens always was dealing it out. So, faced with opportunity, we all joined in. "Yeah, Dickens, you're a soldier. Remember, the Army moves on its feet."

Dickens shifted his submachine gun to one arm and made a stroking motion with the other, as if he were leisurely doing the front crawl. He jutted his chin forward and upward, drew his thick lips and chubby cheeks to an exaggerated "O," and opened and closed his lips in a guppy-like pucker.

"You sorry soldiers just wish you could swim," Dickens retorted good-naturedly. That generated more catcalls.

"We just glad we not gonna drown pretendin'," Corporal Minor Martin sang back in his lyrical drawl. Martin grinned, surprised at himself for successfully getting a shot in at Dickens. His mischievous look magnified the cleft in his chin that women likely loved to run an index finger down.

Foolish as this clowning was, so close to enemy lines, we were lightheartedly enthralled. Dickens's antics defused the tensions we masked with bravado. He showed us that this was an outing, a lark. By the time we stopped to rest and pull slugs of tepid water from our canteens, we were giving the Germans three weeks to a month before they begged for surrender. Or skedaddled.

Dickens's humor also helped us feel less conspicuous in our stiff new field gear—not yet softened by sweat and months of nonstop use—that stood us in stark contrast to the weathered likes of the First Armored Division. No doubt an outsider would have seen similar contrasts between our fresh faces and the hardened, detached looks of the combat veterans.

The First Armored was our temporary home until the rest of the all-black 92nd Infantry Division could be rustled out of Arizona and dropped in Italy. Meanwhile, as the first black troops to go to combat for the United States in World War II, we were as awkward as boys in Sunday clothes meeting a girl's parents on the first formal date of our lives. Fidgety, goofy with pride, trying to wear it all under a poker face and failing.

Our first day in enemy territory passed with our company untouched, although we heard the distant percussion of artillery and mortars. Cockiness notwithstanding, this thunder got the attention of my men. Unlike our training days, I never again yelled to get foxholes dug. Whenever we stopped for the day, the clink of shovels against stubborn Italian soil became automatic. And it was astounding what a little excavating did for our peace of mind. We could sleep knowing we had a burrow. It didn't matter whether that burrow was an ironclad guarantee of surviving the night.

War is built on such illusions. The illusion of strength, the illusion of immortality, the illusion of easy victory with invincible weapons, or, from a shallow trench, the illusion of protection. Those early, bucolic days north of the Arno River strengthened our illusions.

Our mission was to push the German Panzer, paratrooper, and mountain expedition troops out of the northernmost third of Italy. We were supposed to accomplish this before winter with the help of the South African, Brazilian, British, Indian, Canadian, and free Polish forces strung eastward the width of the country. Never mind that a similar strategy failed miserably the previous winter, elsewhere in Italy, even before the Italian front was robbed of seven crack divisions and relegated to secondary status in the European war.

This strategic schizophrenia matched Italy's political shroud. Or perhaps was prompted by it. Fascist dictator Benito Mussolini, goaded by delusions of empire building, had officially joined forces with Hitler in 1940. By July 1943, the King of Italy and many of his subjects had had a bellyful of fascism and its chief fanatic. The king deposed Mussolini and, in early September, made peace with the Allies. Mussolini fled to northern Italy with his black-shirted loyalist troops and established a fascist enclave behind the German lines my soldiers now faced.

Encouraged by Mussolini's rapid departure, and by victory in North Africa and Sicily, the Allies pounced on southern Italy the moment the king's treaty was announced. They believed the German Army—now largely deserted by the Italians—would retreat at least to the Alps as soon as the Allies touched Italian soil. But this was the first Allied landing on the European continent and the Germans did not go quietly or quickly. They fortified Italy with their best soldiers and extracted a bitter price for every bit of ground.

American forces alone sustained more than 8,000 wounded, dead, and missing in the first month of the Italian campaign. With the help of the worst weather on record, the Germans immobilized American, British, and Canadian troops the winter of 1943–44.

The Allies broke through German defenses in spring. The German's destructive retreat and the Allies' destructive advance obliterated nearly every building, vineyard, farm, and orchard along the way. Rome finally was liberated in June of 1944. Barely a month later, we black soldiers had arrived in Naples, at the shin of the Italian boot.

All manner of half-sunken ships still tangled the harbor. Listing cargo boats jammed against wrecked fishing vessels. Some ships sat perfectly upright—and half submerged. Others left only a bow or stern poking precariously from the water. The jumble was so thorough that our troop ship could not dock but pulled alongside the most convenient hulk. Our path to land was a haphazard network of catwalks and gang planks that crossed several of the ruined ships.

Not only had the Germans clogged the waterway with these scuttled ships during their retreat, but they demolished every dock in the port of Naples. The city lay in worse shape than its harbor. The Germans smashed the city water and sewer system, fouled the electrical lines, and tore apart anything else they guessed useful to their foes. They also exacted revenge on the Italians, whom they considered traitors, destroying most of the museums and libraries. More than 200,000 books were doused with gasoline and torched.

The only public building left intact, the Naples Post Office, was rigged with a time bomb. A week after the Germans had departed, in October 1943, tons of explosives erupted during the busiest hour of the day. The blast had such force that the streets nearest the building heaved a tornado of cobblestones. More than a hundred men, women, children, and soldiers died. General Mark Clark, commander of the American's Fifth Army, barely escaped a similar fate. Soldiers discovered the 1,500-pound time bomb in the hotel he used for his headquarters shortly before it was set to go off.

Most of our brief stay in Naples entailed frustrating hours pulling our gear out of the ship holds and carting it over the precarious catwalk system to shore. And plenty of accompanying jokes about Army engineering.

We clamored into trucks and lumbered and jolted to an old volcano crater outside the city. The crater was rumored to be the traditional hunting grounds for the king. The bottom of this bowl afforded ample level ground for the 5,000 men of the 370th Regimental Combat team to set up camp alongside the newly arrived Brazilian Expeditionary Forces. And there was plenty of room left over.

A ring of rocky hills formed the perimeter of the crater and provided perfect terrain for Army busy work.

"Just like those Huachuca Mountains," the men grumbled as, day after day, we shouldered our packs for training hikes. "Up, down, up, down. Lieutenant," they asked me, "is this all we're going to do? We coulda stayed in that Arizona snake pit if we were just goin' to march around. We thought we were coming to fight Germans."

I had no answers.

This ritual persisted for ten days, probably to give Army brass time to decide where to send its first black combat troops. The only action we tasted was a German bombing raid on Naples, and that we heard more than we saw.

The infantryman's limousine, those huge, two-and-a-half ton trucks with the suspension of a concrete sidewalk and available only in dull Army green, finally reappeared at "camp crater" and gave false hope of ending our boredom. We repacked, reloaded our gear, and climbed on the trucks for an unknown destination.

"They find us another crater to climb?" the men joked. Again, I had no answers, but we all hoped this was it—our move to the front line.

Our convoy traced the coastline of the Tyrrhenian Sea on a narrow tree-lined road that passed war-gutted farmhouses, monasteries, and villages. These warnings of what was coming didn't register with us. The warm Mediterranean day and the rolling, green farm fields rushed our senses with a dash of euphoria about the notion of going to war. Everyone who longs to be a soldier should be blessed with the good fortune of such conditions, we decided.

Our journey ended near the small port city of Civitavecchia, on a gentle stretch of coastline that melded easily into the ocean. Another week of waiting included hours of checking weapons, C-rations, and munitions and learning to live with the taste of warm canteen water flavored with Army-issue purification tablets. My buddy, Harry Cox, hasn't chanced a drink of water since.

One night, while camped near Civitavecchia, we heard the non-stop rumble of Allied airplanes taking load after load of soldiers from Italy to join the invasion of southern France. We felt excitement reverberating earthward from that impressive airborne flotilla, not realizing we had lost seven top-notch divisions from our front to the French front, seven divisions sorely missed by the time winter hunkered in.

Eons later, new orders told us to whittle our belongings to the essentials of battle and pack the rest for storage. I went to my tent and levered open the big, old battered brown suitcase I'd dragged overseas. With great care, I folded and packed my pinks and greens, as we called our dress trousers and shirts, along with my few civilian clothes.

Many of the men lingered over the task, sorting through letters and personal belongings. Most of them kept something small to remember home or family—a special letter or the sweat-stained, creased black-and-white photograph that was bragged around the platoon a minimum of a dozen times. Most men tolerated others' stories and photographs because they wanted the chance to show off their own mementos.

I kept nothing. My family never had money for pictures, everyone but my sisters were gone, and Helen hadn't written a word since I'd left Camp Rucker, Alabama—much less sent anything I could carry as a keepsake of our bond. Helen was my wife, but my estimation that time and distance would strengthen her feelings for me was flawed. It was as if, in her eyes, I was already a combat fatality.

The Italian heat was mindful of twenty-five-mile forced marches in the Arizona desert with fully loaded field packs, and that staved off the inclination to tote much more than memories anyway. I soon put those away, in a place far off in my mind, in order to function in battle. Focus and fortitude, not sentiment and memories, propel the infantryman.

Officers received a kind of shoulder satchel, called a musette bag, instead of a field pack. I easily managed to fit in a spare olive-drab Class A uniform—our battle dress—my Eisenhower jacket, a pair of long johns, and a few field manuals. One of the perks of being a second lieutenant was that my bedroll and other essentials were supposed to arrive with the supply trucks each night instead of burdening my back. A rarely fulfilled promise. The worse the weather became, the longer the lag between the troops and these trucks. I saw far more of the Italian mud than I did of my bedroll. Often I borrowed a blanket from an enlisted man or relied on the generosity of an Italian villager.

A few months into our war, I lost a musette bag with several souvenirs, including a German Luger, when the jeep carrying my bag hit a mine. I didn't care much about the stuff. The death of the supply sergeant, Frankie Washington, and his driver, Zach Lewis, in that catastrophe ripped at my guts. It was an accidental friendship that began the first time I handed them my musette bag and Lewis ribbed me about its contents. Washington chimed in. We established a deep rapport and ate supper together and talked of home anytime we could. They were the sort of men I made the mistake of believing I'd spend time with after the war. Their deaths taught me to quit thinking about "after the war."

After several days of preparation at Civitavecchia, we piled into the ever present Army trucks and spent another couple of days grinding our way to the front. We rode with less anticipation, considering our weeks of disappointment. Well after dark that second day, the Army deposited us east of Pisa, on the south side of the Arno River, on the edge of our shooting war.

Despite the previous winter's failures and setbacks, our commanders expected us to do in a matter of months what better trained, more experienced troops had not been able to accomplish in a year. We were perfect to throw at the task. Few of us knew what had transpired at Salerno, Anzio, Monte Cassino, and the rest of Italy. And we hadn't spent enough time in Naples to fully appreciate that we were headed for the same menacing embrace.

Beyond running the Germans out of the mountains, our task was tying down maximum number of enemy troops so they couldn't be withdrawn and sent to other major fronts. Our commanders didn't share that part of the mission with us. But it may explain, in hindsight, why we were repeatedly thrown into senseless frontal attacks.

That came later. Early on, we deluded ourselves into thinking the Germans didn't know our position and that we stealthily tracked them for the easy kill.

At first our progress was an agreeable four or five miles a day, north from the Arno River. We marched up the gentle slopes of Mount Pisano feeling no more peril than a Boy Scout troop. We claimed the mostly abandoned German bunkers and observation posts for ourselves. It was disappointing. We expected to at least kill or capture some Germans. It would be cheap to waltz into Switzerland without a few harrowing tales to tell.

Harrowing for the Germans and never for us. We didn't even plan to bother with prisoners. On the voyage to Italy my platoon leaders and I had settled on a more simple course.

Officers had the privilege of bunking, two-to-a-room, in the cabins above deck on the *U.S.S. Mariposa*, the luxury liner turned troop ship that took us from New York to North Africa and on to

Italy. During the day I fought the inevitable boredom by dropping into the holds to visit my platoon. I hoped familiarity could breed trust and tried to build a feeling that we needed to hang together and fight for each other in order to survive. Keeping them occupied also kept them from gambling and other trouble.

My platoon sergeant and the four squad leaders formed a rough circle—sitting on their berths, sprawled out on the floor, or leaning against the columns of floor-to-ceiling bunks—and we talked hour after hour in the sweltering, stagnant air of the crowded hold. My men made a dashing lot, most with pencil-thin mustaches and jaunty smiles. All dwarfed my five feet five inches, one-hundred-forty-five-pound frame, and if I hadn't been strong, wiry, and self-confident, I'd have made a weak-kneed effort as a platoon leader.

Most of these men were older than I was. Most grew up expecting the racism that continued to shock and surprise me. In our lighter moments, they made fun of the way I talked, accusing me of having a strange accent, of mispronouncing my R's. The teasing over my Wyoming inflection felt fine. I took it as their indirect way of showing they accepted me.

The experience was easily more mystifying for me than for them. I had never spent so much time in close contact with so many black people. During my three years in the segregated Army I had kept to myself as much as possible, uncomfortable with a situation growing up in the rural West did not prepare me for.

My platoon sergeant, Jacy Cunigan, mostly sat quietly during our conversations, his eyes somber, his words measured and authoritative. I could see my grandfather in his serious ways and warmed to that likeness.

Corporal Martin was the opposite, both with his boyish face and his unabashed demeanor.

"Lieutenant," he asked, clasping and unclasping his hands as he rocked forward on his bedside seat, "when we get over there into the fightin', are we going to take any prisoners?"

"No, corporal, not if we don't have to," I replied.

The other men nodded in agreement, voicing their approval. In our minds, we had already overwhelmed enemy lines; we were immortal, untouchable, and too busy crushing our foes to be burdened with taking custody of whoever miraculously survived our perilous onslaught. We loved war, as only men who have not experienced it can.

That seemed sage foresight as we moved from our easy overrun of Mount Pisano to a broad valley floor littered with the remnants of German tanks and trucks, and plodded through half-tended farm fields toward the Serchio River and the city of Lucca. It was a classic medieval north-central Italian city. Narrow cobble streets that refused to allow two vehicles side-by-side. Clay-tile-capped white, gray, and pink adobe buildings crowded so tightly together that a toothpick couldn't find a space between them. At least the buildings that were standing.

The Germans had reduced most of the city to rubble. Our advance artillery did the rest. My platoon found practically nothing, not even frightened peasants, as we filtered building-to-building looking for any remaining Germans. Only a few startled chickens were flushed out.

We forged through the verdant Serchio River valley, toward Mount San Quirico and Ponte a Moriano, going as far as our feet would take us. Here the settlements were more typical topographically, hanging off hillsides where centuries of warfare had taught the natives they would best survive and repel intrusion. But we were not repelled. This was part of the German plan. In reality, they were observing our every footstep and eventually sucked us in, again and again, with the same tactic. They fell back, we advanced, and they closed in and kicked the stuffing out of us. Our progress depended upon whether the Germans were falling back or kicking us. Our best gain soon was measured in city blocks, if we advanced at all.

By some miracle, however, my platoon and my company were escaping casualties. War didn't feel deadly. We continued to be heady about this outing.

The U.S. Army came to Italy with other illusions. One was that the jeep, truck, and tank could take us anywhere. The other was that we could pound any German position to pieces, in a matter of hours, with enough mortars or artillery. We weren't prepared for the Italians' thick stone-and-adobe construction, perfected through centuries of invasion and siege. Our supposedly modern weapons carved numerous pocks in the outer layer of stone and rough adobe. Piercing it required a much more dedicated pounding, which made it that much more difficult to dislodge the Germans.

As for easy motoring through Italy, there were few "paved" roads in all of northern Italy, and they were heavily defended. The summer and fall dust was so deep everywhere else that we felt as if we waded more than we marched. If there was a road passable to tanks, top speed was a few miles an hour. Anything faster created lofty rooster tails of dust—a magnet for enemy gunners.

As we advanced up the mountain valleys, we found the circuitous tracks often too narrow for a jeep. When fall turned to winter, the legendary pools of dust became axle-sucking pools of mud. Mules, not motors, kept us maneuvering through the mountains.

This was workable but considerably less desirable. Not only were mules slower to resupply us than trucks, they hauled a lot less. The errant mule occasionally pitched over the side of a steep switchback, taking the rest of the train and our supplies on a one-way trip to oblivion. And a mule train loaded with ammunition was a skittering, unpredictable bomb when German mortar rounds and artillery shells found us. Ammunition trucks could be abandoned. Mules had to be controlled lest their panniers caught a spark and the frightened mule danced shrapnel from their exploding load through an entire company. Fortunately, most Italian mule skinners had the steel to unload their animals under the most withering deluge while the rest of us selfishly looked for cover.

TWO

How beautiful youth is,
which will soon disappear,
He who wants to be merry—do so,
There are no certainties for tomorrow.

  —Lorenzo de Medici, poet and ruler of Florence

Fall 1944, Northern Italy

As the Germans drew us back into the foothills, much of our job became patrolling. Our first company commander, First Lieutenant Montjoy—Montie to his men—endeared himself to us by violating Army regulations and accompanying us on our earliest outing. A medium man in every respect save personality, Montie earnestly wanted both to command and to be respected as one of us. This, too, was against Army standards, at least the unspoken ones, because commanders were expected to keep a certain distance in order to better maintain discipline. One of the few black commanders we would encounter, Montie was just too human and too effusive about liking people to keep that gulf. It didn't create problems. We respected him more for it and probably fought harder for him than white officers as a result.

A New Jersey area native, Montie pronounced "coffee" with an exaggerated "k"—"kaw-fee."

"Kaw-fee, Bake?" he invariably offered when I was summoned to the command post.

"Why, shore," I replied at the first invitation, unintentionally mispronouncing "sure" in my imitation of a Jersey twang—easily insubordination in the eyes of some commanders. Montie laughed instead of writing me up.

He earned his officer's commission through ROTC while attending a traditionally black college and had been around the military long enough to understand what it was like to be a black man fighting in a white man's Army. Montie taught me that a leader must understand exactly what he was ordering his men to do.

"You'll make smarter decisions," he said, "and your men will trust your judgment."

This was his reason for bucking the system and joining us on our first night patrol. He escaped without losing his bars, because we discovered nothing but boredom, and was satisfied to stay at his command post during our future forays.

Patrolling was a way of life. Battalion and division commanders selected an area in enemy hands that they wanted to know more about. They issued vague maps of the countryside and intelligence reports about known enemy positions. Both were worthless. Instinct rapidly proved more reliable.

If the work came to Company C, I gathered a squad or two of men and went for a look. We typically snuck to a certain point, sat in a circle with our backs to each other and waited half the night for any sign of enemy movement. Much of our observation amounted to making sure those who fell asleep didn't snore and give away our position.

In those first months, I freelanced patrols whenever possible. My night vision was sharp. I liked the feeling of night, liked the cover of darkness, liked the way anticipation kept my veins nine-parts adrenaline to one-part blood. Once we made our objective and sat down for the wait, however, it was damn near impossible for my men not to relax and fall asleep. Sleep elsewhere was rare at first, because of the giddy anticipation of kicking the Germans clear back to Berlin. Then fall rains made our foxholes cold, wet, miserable dens of existence and certainly not places we rested. Sharing the communal back-to-back warmth in a circle of GIs on a patrol stakeout was comparative luxury.

As the war dragged on, exhaustion erased any reflexive defense against drifting off, even in those miserable trenches. On night patrols, once we sat down for the prescribed period of observation, sleep was automatic. Inevitably, we settled in, started listening for the enemy and, in less than a minute, somebody's throat started snorting.

"Somebody shut that son-of-a-bitch up," came echoing around a split second later, in as loud a whisper as any one of us dared. If he was awake, the soldier nearest to the offending vocal cords likely had already given the man a stiff shake. If that didn't work, the snoring soldier received a more serious nudge from a rifle butt. We imagined a German platoon leader hearing our tonsils warble, stopping his men long enough to hone in on our location, and then cutting through the darkness to wipe us out.

The worst all-time offender, an angular private named Casey Emmett, earned all variety of unprintable nicknames for being the first to fall asleep, the hardest to wake up, and for bellowing the most disagreeable noises. It was verbal flatulence on the exhale, with a whiny off beat when he took in air. His gawky demeanor and inability to fight back only encouraged the harsher critics. I waited for the situation to settle itself, thinking it best for Emmett's self-esteem and his ability to gain the respect of others if he made a move.

Emmett, I believed, would have stayed awake and fought back if there was any measure within him. His embarrassment and inability to fight off his tormenters grew depressing. I finally stepped in and warned the members of his squad to stop. They at first defied me because enlisted men are certain that officers are the dumbest creatures on earth and that it is their charge and personal burden to educate their officers. At least until they see said officers under fire, and then their worst suspicions either are confirmed or forever quashed. I made a habit of rewarding any slight to my authority with miserable assignments. Extra night-sentry or latrine-digging duty transformed souls more rapidly than Sunday school. And thankfully so because absolute loyalty and obedience were vital to minimizing problems when we were creeping around in the dark.

Gathering information was one goal of night patrols. The other was ambushing the Germans who constantly probed our territory. The Germans had the advantage of having traversed much of this ground before. They used that advantage against us.

Patrolling created plenty of legends among our ranks. The most famous—and truest—involved Vernon C. Dailey, a friend of mine from Officer Candidate School. In retrospect, it should have been clear it would happen to Dailey if it was going to happen to anybody. He looked like lightning primed to strike on the calmest day. Five feet, eight inches tall, he came with reddish hair and had a few freckles. A few. We affectionately called him the "red nigger." He was tough enough to take it with a smile.

Dailey earned a Silver Star and about lost his mind on a patrol. He and six men struck out from a village called Barga and crossed our front lines with explicit orders to find the Germans. After slogging a fair piece, carefully scanning every rock, bush, and tree as they went, Dailey's patrol spotted what they thought was a German emplacement. He arranged for five of his men to cover him, grabbed a squat ripple of muscle called Sergeant Percy Banton, and together they inched the last two hundred yards on their bellies.

They stopped abruptly when they had wiggled to the fold that formed the top of the ridge. A helmetless German soldier, with his back to them, sat in the foxhole below. A wide trench on the far side of the foxhole led to a larger dugout, they reasoned. A sizeable and steady plume of smoke about fifty yards distant told Dailey and Banton that the adjoining dugout had a large contingent of enemy soldiers.

Dailey knew he couldn't shoot the German because it would alarm the entire enemy platoon. He leapt into the foxhole, raised his .30-caliber carbine like a woodsman with an axe, and clobbered the German soldier over the head. When rifle stock connected with cranium, the stock splintered. The German toppled, but the blow did not knock him unconscious and the sore-headed soldier started moaning for help. Dailey began beating him with the barrel of his rifle to finish the task. To no avail.

Seconds later, another German soldier crawled out from a small side tunnel, which Dailey and Banton hadn't spotted, and locked his arms around Dailey's leg. Dailey kicked his assailant in the face and dove to the side. Banton dropped into the foxhole and gave the Germans a dose from his Tommy gun. The two men scrambled out of the foxhole, barely clearing the lip as more than a dozen Germans from the adjoining dugout poured through the connecting trench. Dailey and Banton bolted down the hill, bullets snapping over their heads, managing to rejoin their patrol and backtrack to our lines without so much as a scrape.

As they tramped back into camp Dailey still clutched the battered barrel of his rifle, baseball-bat style, in both hands, catching notice from every soldier who saw him, yet mutely refusing to answer any questions. Banton also said little. Both men were jumpy for days. But Dailey's brute fighting force wasn't dampened. He went on to Korea, and he earned a Bronze Star for more gallantry. Lightning. You didn't want to be where he struck.

My personal patrol debacle didn't end as well. I led two full squads—a power patrol—into the darkness from a small village in the bend of a high valley where we had been camped for four or five days. I don't remember the name of the place. We moved so frequently that I lost track of the names of the towns, and the chaos and destruction of war made one community look like another.

We scaled a succession of small, steep, terraced hills and wove our way through the clumps of trees rooted in rolling land at the top of the final summit. Our job on this night was assessing German strength. Experience eventually taught us that "assess German strength" means "go out and see how badly you get shot up."

These were our early patrolling days and we trooped along carelessly, charged by the crisp night air and by our confidence. The

Germans allowed us to walk about fifty yards past their position before they sent blinding flares howling into the sky. We twisted around, arms flying up to shield our faces and tried to see what was happening.

A split second later I realized we were had. "Get down," I screamed. "Ambush! Down!"

My words were lost in the staccato of German machine guns and rifles puncturing the air, their tracer bullets adding deadly, glowing streaks to the debacle. We were cut off, in unfamiliar territory in the middle of the night, too far from our own lines to hope for reinforcements. Spots danced in front of my eyes from the flash of the flares, and I knew if the Germans were charging us, we'd have little chance to fend them off.

When the initial surprise turned to rage, I furiously started pumping rounds through my M-1 rifle. My men needed no encouragement. If we went down, we wanted the Germans to remember our final fusillade for years to come.

The flares eventually sputtered out—it seemed like an hour but likely was a matter of minutes. Gradually, the crescendo of German guns slowed until, finally, there was silence. The changing tempo, I recognized belatedly, had been the enemy gunners leaving one by one. Such a gradual withdrawal prevented our counterattack.

We lay hugging the dirt long after the Germans left, occasionally unloading a clip or two in their direction in case the German withdrawal was another ruse. Our will to get up was dulled by the shock of being so easily jumped by enemy soldiers, when we had been certain the Germans were such lousy fighters that there was no way they would do anything but run from us.

As the silence of night resettled, I became more surprised the Germans had left at all. They had us at such a disadvantage they could have killed all of us, even if we had outnumbered them two to one.

I called for my squad leaders to report. There were frightened mumbles, but nothing audible. I half rose and crab-walked around, moving but staying low, to check for myself. Two were dead. One was a private whom I didn't know well; he had been sent to us not long before we boarded the *U.S.S. Mariposa* for Italy. And Sergeant Edward

Richardson, fourth squad leader, who, like the private, had the misfortune of being at the rear of our patrol when the Germans opened
up. I knew they were dead after touching them, not getting a stir, and
then finding warm, thickening pools of blood on their backs as I
moved my hand over their bodies to check for any other sign of life.

We had been caught so unaware that I expected to find more
casualties. Finding only two dead was grim relief. My relief was so
immense that I managed to focus on our good fortune and forget
how close we came to being entirely annihilated.

This was my first face-off with death in combat and yet I was
allowed to avoid confronting the horror. I didn't really know the
men stiffening there in the night. The darkness masked their faces. I
wasn't forced to see which parts of these men had been peeled away
by shrapnel or bullets. But it was a close enough call to start a tinge,
a minor twinge in my gut, that war wasn't a game.

We clumsily packed up our dead, retreated into the darkness,
skittish both because of the ambush and with the unexpected relief
of being alive. We concentrated on forgetting the worst of the night's
experiences. Forgetting was part of our survival, part of the way we
kept fighting. Forgetting death was something I had attempted since
childhood.

The most powerful memory of my parents is seeing their caskets
in the front room of our two-story house when I was four. My
mother, Beulah, was small and beautiful, with sleepy hazel-brown
eyes. It's the only image I have of her. It comes from a trip she and I
took not long before she died. We were riding the train from
Cheyenne, Wyoming, to Omaha, Nebraska, to visit Great-Uncle
Than, who was a Union Pacific man, just like Grandfather.

Mother and I were sitting in the dining car, eating lunch, as the
train gently rocked and clattered past the sandy-colored pine bluffs
of southeastern Wyoming and dropped into the dry, mousey-brown
expanse of western Nebraska. At the end of the meal the waiter
placed thick-sided white china bowls of warm water in front of us. I
promptly picked mine up with both hands and drank the water. My

mother, gently holding my attention with those eyes, explained the water was for washing my hands, not drinking.

My grandparents and my mother had migrated to Cheyenne from the family cornfields outside of Clarinda, Iowa, at some unknown point, when my grandfather chose railroading over plowing and planting. Perhaps it was economic necessity. Grandpa had five brothers and sisters to share the land and crops. In Cheyenne, Joseph Samuel Baker became chief air inspector—which amounted to head brakeman—for the Union Pacific. It was unusual for a black man in the rural West to hold a job that included his own office.

My mind cannot conjure up an image of my father. I don't know whether he was short or tall, fat or skinny. I don't know if he ever spanked me, fished with me, gave me piggy-back rides, or taught me to catch horny toads. I never knew his last name was Caldera, until the Army asked for my birth certificate and then asked why I used the name Baker.

That same birth certificate told me Manuel Caldera was a carpenter from New Mexico. He likely came to Cheyenne to work for the railroads or at the Army post—Fort D.A. Russell—the two things besides state government that the people of Cheyenne lived on. I think he was only twenty-five when he died.

I remember it was a month without snow on the ground. Grandma and Grandpa had always lived with us. They summoned my two older sisters and me to their bedroom. This alone induced fear. If we were called to their room, something big was wrong, and we wanted to put a board in our pants to protect our butts.

Grandma sat in her wheelchair crying. Grandpa's six-foot, 200-pound frame rested wearily on the edge of the bed, the bib of his overalls slack as he bent forward, his pancake-size, farm-honed hand squeezing one of Grandma's arms.

"Your mommy and daddy have gone to heaven," Grandpa said gently. "They aren't going to be with us anymore."

Irma and Katherine—Cass to all of us—looked quizzically at each other and then stared at Grandpa. "What's happened, Grandpa?" my older sisters asked in unison.

"There was an accident. A car accident. They're not going to be with us anymore," Grandpa said. Anymore. His inflection signaled not only the end of my parents, but the conclusion of the conversation. I know nothing more. Back then, adults didn't talk to children about such things.

I couldn't make the connection between my parents and the two long wooden boxes intruding into the most ample room of the house. My grandfather and Irma, who was nine, tried to explain death with "these things happen . . . death's a part of life . . . long as you are living, son, people are always going to be passin' on." I think I felt a dull something that I couldn't put words and feelings around. But I'm not sure anything significant transpired in my mind beyond taking in the immensity of the caskets.

Grandma and Grandpa seamlessly assumed responsibility for Irma, Cass, and me after our parents died. They never officially adopted us. We acted as if our last name had always been Baker and this parenting arrangement was set from the start. My grandparents not only didn't say anything else about the tragedy, they told us nothing about my mother and father.

My grandfather didn't display his feelings, so while I assume the accident was difficult for him, he gave me no clues to gauge his emotions. My mother was their only child and her death devastated my grandmother. Not that we noticed much difference in Grandmother's already miserable disposition. Dora Lucas Baker gave new definition to the term "meanest woman alive." A light-chocolate Missouri native with a round face and short, severe gray hair, she had elephant legs, gnarled hands, and swollen knuckles—all knotted into a wheelchair. Rheumatoid arthritis stranded her in that wicker-back, wire-spoked seat twenty-four hours a day for twenty-two years.

If I cried, she rapped me with the cane she crudely clutched in her swollen hand and screeched, "shut up you little son-of-a-bitch." As I got older and made her mad, she called me worse. I hated her. It took me years to realize that pain, not spite, fueled her anger.

Grandmother ran the two-story, twenty-two room boarding house that we moved to about the time I turned six. The former hotel was a gray wood-frame building that looked like a Southern mansion, with a four-column front porch and a bay window on each side of the front door. A small hand-lettered sign on the door-jamb proclaimed "Room for Rent."

It was the only place in town a black person could get a room. We never advertised. But the traveling minstrels and other black entertainers—who worked at the ample, brick Plains Hotel, at 17th Street and Carey Avenue, as well as other less-respectable whites-only hotels and saloons in Cheyenne—always found us. They rented the three-dollars-a-night rooms for three weeks or a month and moved on.

A blacks-only boarding house was odd, considering the mostly unstructured and unspoken nature of Cheyenne's segregation. There were eleven other black families in our town of 20,000—the Horns, the Witts, the Rhones, the Greens, the Clintons, the Wests, the Smiths, the Settlers, the Caves, the Andersons, and the Mitchells. There was no black neighborhood. We were sprinkled through the town like peppercorns. The generous number of Hispanics, to my memory, also were spread throughout the town.

Our boarding house sat eight blocks east of the railroad station, on a quiet street nearly devoid of trees, and a mere four blocks from downtown. If you slipped from our house down to Capitol Avenue, you could look north and catch the gold dome of the capitol building, prettiest capitol building ever. Our neighborhood was all houses, except for the livery stable and the harness and leather-works, both on the other side of the street. We lived on the ground floor of the boarding house. I had one of the small sleeping rooms, and Irma and Cass shared one of the doubles. Grandma and Grandpa had the largest room—one with a bay window.

The other bay-windowed room was the parlor. Normally, it was dark and gloomy. The double doors were always closed and the curtains drawn, unless the room was going to be used for a special occasion, something on the order of Christmas, Easter, a visit from the Baptist preacher or other special guest. Otherwise, even Grandfather retired to the bedroom to read the newspaper when he came home in the evening.

The front room held great fascination for me because of the highly polished gray player piano with dark marble-like streaks, that was stoically poised along one wall of the room. I hankered to begin my musical studies by pumping the pedals of that magnificent instrument while a roll of perforated paper scrolled through a door above the keyboard, tripping levers that tripped keys, and made one a virtuoso strictly by reason of physical endurance.

My grandmother forbade such foolishness. Nor did she grant us entry to the front room, except by rare invitation. The ban was of such force we didn't dare sit in front of the bay window if we were outside. Even tenants shied from that part of the front porch.

Things changed marginally when we got a big Spartan cabinet radio, put it in the front room, and Grandfather discovered Amos and Andy. That gave me an opening to use the room—at least on the sly. Late at night I'd wrap myself in a blanket, sneak down to the front room, lie on the rug and listen to classical music in the faint glow of the radio dial. It was luxurious, not only for the stolen moments in Grandma's shrine, but because of the eloquent strains of Bach, Beethoven, Mozart, and Vivaldi floating out just barely louder than the hum of the radio's vacuum tubes. Grandfather occasionally slipped into the room, settled noiselessly onto the sofa, and listened with me. We never exchanged a word during those moments, nor did we talk about this midnight ritual at any other time.

We had no lawn. The house ran right up to the edge of the gravel lane, which didn't see paving until sometime after Grandma died in 1933. The backyard was a dirt-and-gravel spread that held the chicken coop, rabbit hutches, and our dog, a walnut-brown mongrel named Shep.

I cleaned up after the animals, raked and straightened the yard, and tried to rescue wandering neighborhood cats that Shep otherwise cornered and killed. He was a considerable dog. It took four men to put a collar on him. Grandfather always had to put Shep out back if he was going to take the belt to one of us kids.

Grandma and Grandpa bought the boarding house from a Jewish family named Veta. Mrs. Veta, a gray-haired, heavy-set woman who always dressed like a pilgrim—long, black every-thing—came around once a month to collect the payment. She and Grandma would sit in the front room and yakkety-yak about this and yakkety-yak about that.

I think the Vetas owned the whole block. She went door-to-door at collection time. They also owned a tiny all-purpose store around the corner at 17th Street and Bent Avenue. Spotless wooden floors, burnished by shoe leather, stretched out between crowded aisles of everything from Victor mouse traps to canned goods, soda crackers to matches and leather gloves. Mrs. Veta knew every kid in town. She called us by our first names when we ventured in on an errand or out of curiosity, gave us sticks of black licorice, and asked about our families.

When I say Grandmother ran the boarding house, I mean she was something akin to a commandant. She issued orders from her wheelchair, reading a book or the Bible while our tasks were under way. When the phone rang, one of us brought it to her, or, if she was close enough, she dragged it to herself with the hooked end of her cane. We were expected to be alert enough to know if she needed our assistance, no matter where we were in the house. Failing to catch on until after several rings of the telephone was a serious offense. Of course with Grandma, everything was a serious offense.

Irma and Cass cooked and cleaned, sometimes with the help of full-time tenants such as Miss Ester. When bills came due, the girls pushed Grandma downtown in her wheelchair. Grandma was known all over town, had good credit, and was respected. I could hear it in the greetings of the merchants. "Morning, Mrs. Baker. Fine to see you, Mrs. Baker. How's the boarders, Mrs. Baker?" It amazed me, considering her demeanor.

I chopped wood, carried out the ashes, stoked the stoves, and, when progress brought it our way, got up early to light the coal-fired hot water heater. I also swept the front porch, performed numerous miscellaneous chores and fought off boredom by dreaming of owning a bicycle and roller skates. The closest I got to any wheeled outfit was Grandma's chair.

Two of the ground-floor rooms stayed clean and locked for itinerant guests. The eight rooms upstairs, four on each side of the hallway, were mostly for permanent residents, including Miss Ester—a grand old lady—and her husband, a man we called Mr. Moses. He was the first freckle-faced Negro I ever saw. He cleaned out the locomotive boilers at the train yards and came home every night with his freckles buried under layers of soot. There was Mr. Cecil, a long, slim, ugly fellow in his late forties or early fifties. I don't know where he came from or what he did for a living. He went to work early in the morning, and sometimes he would dress up fancy and go out until all hours. All hours. That's something I learned from eavesdropping. Few adults talked to us children. And we were fed and hustled away before the tenants came downstairs for their meals, so it was difficult to get to know much about any of them.

One of the exceptions was a jolly-looking bass fiddle player with round, shiny cheeks who caught me watching his fingers fly across what I took for an oversized violin.

"You want to play, son?" he asked, motioning for me to come into his room. He was too easygoing for me to be intimidated by Grandma's rules against fraternizing with the entertainers.

"Can't," I said. "Don't know how."

"Who are you, boy?"

"Vernon."

"Well, step up here, Vernon, let's make you a bass player."

He showed me some notes, then stood me on a wooden crate so I could reach the neck and the fret board. He spent much of his free time trying to coax me into learning a song or two during the month his group was in Cheyenne. But I found it boring. It was nothing more than "Bom, bom, bom, bom, bom" over and over again.

My favorite renter, and the one I came to know best, was old William Ashford. Mr. Ashford and Grandfather went clear back to childhood in Iowa. When Mr. Ashford's children discarded him at the Cheyenne old folks home, Grandfather persuaded his friend Al Palmer to bring a car around—Grandfather never learned to drive and we never owned a car—and they fetched Mr. Ashford and Mr. Ashford's boxes.

About Grandpa's height, six-foot or more, Mr. Ashford was heavyset, with a long white beard and a moustache. While supposedly blind—his children's reason for dumping him—he washed and dressed himself every day and came down to the front porch in a union suit, pants, and suspenders. A white shirt was added on rare occasions, as was a coat if it was terribly cold.

He held court on the front porch, from the wooden bench resting under the bay window on Grandma and Grandpa's side of the house. I sat with him, hour after hour, while he recounted his adventures, some of them as a kid on the farm in Clarinda, some more worldly. By his telling, he was a lady's man. These days I guess you'd say he had a great sex life. He was my mentor.

"Did I ever tell you about the woman I met, oh, she sure was a fine woman, that woman that I met up at Buxton?" Mr. Ashford would start, winking and running his hand down his beard as if it would wrinkle if he didn't keep it smoothed down. "She was somethin'. A real pair of legs."

Mr. Ashford read a lot and loaned me several books. He also teased my senses with the little cook stove in his room. As a young boy I was puzzled by how a helpless blind man did so well for himself. Until I realized the blindness was not his.

Mr. Ashford died sitting in the front room when he was well into his eighties. I'm not sure why he had ventured in there that day. Grandma probably never was the same after discovering he had expired in her sacred room.

THREE

Opportunity wears many disguises, including trouble.

—Frank Tyger

September 1944, North of Lucca, Italy

"You Lieutenant Baker?"

I didn't look up until I finished pulling the cleaning rod through the barrel of my rifle. Not out of disrespect. I knew from the tone of the questioning voice that I wasn't dealing with a higher ranking officer, and I hated to stop a cleaning stroke midstream. I didn't want to leave a wad of cloth or a chunk of debris in my rifle.

The last of the rod came out of the top, with a tug. As I laid the cleaning rod on the ground beside the rock where I sat, I spotted his boots. There wasn't even a film of dust. The pants were so evenly tucked into the tops of those black-topped boots that it seemed a tailor had stitched the two together so the motion of marching wouldn't disturb the symmetry. My eyes followed starch-stiff creases up the legs to as crisp an Eisenhower jacket as I had ever seen, fresh out of a box or otherwise. Before I arrived at shoulder level, I knew I had misjudged, that I was sitting on my behind looking at an officer when I should be on my feet showing proper respect.

I dropped the rest of the cleaning gear, thrust the rifle up against the embankment, stood, and saluted. The man before me was stiff enough to have been ironed into this snappy uniform. His helmet was firmly held under his left arm, and his right arm made a forty-five degree turn into a salute.

"I'm Lieutenant Baker," I said. "My apologies."

"Sergeant Napoleon Belk reporting," he said.

I looked closer. Indeed, the stripes of a buck sergeant graced his uniform, and they looked brand new. Gawd. And his high-sloped forehead shimmered, not with sweat, but as if polished like the rest of him. Belk caught my double take.

"Is there a problem, sir? I believe I'm your replacement squad leader. If you are Lieutenant Baker and this is Third Platoon, Charlie Company, First Battalion?"

I shook my head dumbly. "No. Er ah yes, this is it and no, there's no problem and um welcome," I sputtered.

"Sorry, in all my time in the Army, and especially the last several weeks I've not seen anything as polished as you, Sergeant Belk," I explained. "I mean, damn, those boots, those creases. Did you fly in here? I get more dirt on myself getting dressed in the morning."

Belk grinned, stiffened even more, and pumped out his chest.

"I came in with a supply truck. And this is just routine, sir."

"Well, at ease," I countered. "You'll make these men think we're having a visit from the Inspector General."

I motioned to a nearby rock and settled back onto the one I had been using as a chair when Belk appeared.

"Where'd they send you from, sergeant?" I asked, holding my rifle to the sky and sighting through the barrel in search of any specks.

"Chicago. I worked construction."

"No, the Army. Your last outfit?"

"I came with the 370th, just like you, sir," Belk said, still standing rigidly at attention.

"At ease, soldier." I gathered my cleaning tools and shook the dirt off them. "Sit down."

"I'm fine here, sir," he replied, and it struck me that he didn't care to ruin his creases by perching on a rock.

"Where have you been?" I asked.

"Second battalion, sir. They have plenty of sergeants and they said you needed a squad leader."

I only nodded, preferring not to retell the story of losing Sergeant Richardson. Thinking about him brought that feeling of warm blood adhering to my fingertips.

"You see any action, sergeant?" I asked, thinking his clothes had already announced he had spent his brief career hermetically sealed in a museum showcase.

"Lucca," he said with enough bitter inflection to signal I'd been unfair, "Bangi di Lucca, Moriano."

He paused, contemplating whether to tell me any details, and I encouraged him.

"I had the belt shot right off of my body at Bangi di Lucca." Belk poked his midriff. "The bullet hit the buckle and it came right off my body." He shrugged, rapidly putting his guard back up.

Obviously Belk's outfit had been on the part of our line that had caught the serious German fire in those places. More serious than my platoon took. I had been unfair.

"Sorry, sergeant, I'm um. . . ."

Belk waved me off. "You're just like all of us other GIs, lieutenant. You want to know who's going to be coverin' ya."

"How'd there get to be so many sergeants in your platoon?" I inquired, wanting to change the subject. "Are you a field promotion?"

Belk cracked his first smile. "Sort of a field promotion, sir. It was at Fort Huachuca. I was a corporal on sentry duty. They left me at my post and forgot about me for thirty-six hours. They were so impressed that I stayed awake that they made me a buck sergeant."

Belk talked, I cleaned and oiled, checked and rechecked my weapon, a vestige of my grandfather's thoroughness. Belk was named by a Frenchman, he told me proudly, who was a close friend of his parents. His father was three-quarters Cherokee Indian, and his mother was black. I studied Belk's features and decided it probably was true. And he was too proud of everything to bother lying.

Belk was twenty-six, two years my senior, and a draftee who had taken his basic training in Camp Breckinridge, Kentucky, in 1942.

"Kin-tuck-ee," he said. "Nobody loved us boys in Kin-tuck-ee." But he smiled, as if that was just part of living.

With my M-1 rifle firmly back together, I stood and offered to show Belk to his squad. I couldn't stop myself from shaking my head and whistling at his outfit.

"If the lieutenant will permit, sir, I would point out a similarity?"

I laughed and looked down at my clothes, aware that I had long since quit worrying about my appearance unless I was going on leave.

"No, sir, not your uniform—no offense," Belk said. He was pointing to my rifle.

"Who else has fitted their rifle with a recoil pad?" he asked. "Who else could damn near shave in the reflection of their rifle barrel?"

Though he appeared overdressed for war and was downright forward about teasing an officer, I liked Belk. We could use his spark.

"All right, Sergeant Dandy," I said good-naturedly. "Follow me." He shouldered a field pack as clean as his uniform and we walked a few hundred yards back to the foxholes. I introduced him to Sergeant Dickens as "Dandy Belk" and never heard his real first name again. Belk complied by always looking haberdashery sharp, even when the mud and rain had the rest of us sagging. Every night he carefully removed his pants and shirt, folded them just so and slipped them under his bedroll to preserve the stiff creases.

Belk's arrival was good news for morale considering he came with the supply trucks. It meant the monthly liquor ration had arrived. Officers received a bottle of whiskey or the occasional cheap scotch. I paid little attention. I turned it over to my men without breaking the seal. My weekly carton of Camels or Lucky Strikes also went to my soldiers. Grandpa had easily cured me of any taste for tobacco.

It was the summer after I turned eight. Irma was a teenager and smoking Camel straights, looking all adult and sophisticated when she lit up. She spent much of her time holding the cigarette at a distance, admiring the way the ash formed on the end, and then tapping the ash off with false detachment, as if this was a custom from birth. I envied her affectation and started sneaking her cigarettes for myself.

My progress toward worldliness required quite a few tries. I could only tolerate lighting up and taking one puff. Then I sputtered, hyperventilated, relit the now-dead cigarette, and had another drag. With the second puff, my tongue swelled to choking size. I burned from my mouth to my lungs and dizzily ditched the cigarette. I kept trying, but couldn't get more than two puffs out of each cigarette.

My customary smoking room was an old Model T Ford, one of the tenants had parked in the back yard. One afternoon I was trying to get my shaking fingers to light a match and get it to the end of the cigarette before it sputtered out. I leaned toward the floorboards, pretending to inspect the pedals, thinking I was fooling the world.

Cass snuck up on the Model T, peered through the passenger side window and said, "Hey, Vernon, give me a puff."

I jerked back in surprise and barely missed crowning my head on the steering wheel. Anger at that near miss, plus sanctimony and stubbornness, clouded my common sense.

"Nope. You don't want one of these," I retorted. "These are my cigarettes."

"You little liar. Them are Irma's cigarettes and if you don't give me a puff, I'm goin' a-tell Grandpa you're out here smokin'."

I couldn't back down. I moved my head back toward the floorboards and struck a match, showing her I could smoke and she couldn't. Cass marched for the house and I foolishly disregarded her threat.

The back door of the house slammed open. Grandpa came right out, striding across the yard with his easy, long-legged gait. I stubbed out that cigarette and waved my hands around as if I could disperse the smoke before he covered the last ten yards.

"Vernon," Grandpa said, hooking his hands in the straps of his overalls. "Vernon, what 'ya doing out here?" His face was impassive and his tone flat. Yet, I knew his temperament from the way he addressed me. He only called me Vernon when I was in serious trouble. The rest of the time he called me boy.

"Nothing, Grandpa. Nothing. I'm driving this here car."

I put my hands on the steering wheel, uttered imaginative engine noises, and craned my neck to see out of the windshield as if I was on my way to town. Out of the corner of my eye, I could see Grandpa's nose wrinkling to assess the air.

"Boy, I think you've a yen to learn to smoke. You come with me now. I'll teach you." Grandpa reached over and opened the door so I could dismount from the Model T. It was his signal that I should follow him.

I tramped to the house, a few strides behind him, angry at Cass for telling on me, dejectedly wondering what my punishment entailed.

"Sit here," Grandpa ordered when we got to the porch. I settled on the second step from the top. He disappeared into the house and returned in a moment, palming a can of Granger Rough-Cut Tobacco in one hand and his pipe in the other.

He leveraged the bowl of the pipe into the can, packed it tight, and passed the pipe, stem first, to me.

"You want to smoke, boy, smoke this," Grandpa directed. "All of it."

He pulled a kitchen match across the bottom of his thigh and brought it, crackling with flame, to the pipe bowl. He protected the flame with his other cupped hand and said, "Start smoking, boy."

Grandpa rode herd while I gagged and gasped my way through every speck of that tobacco, which tasted worse than burned Brussels sprouts. Until then there had been plenty of time in between my two-puff cigarettes to regain my senses. This nicotine marathon left no time for my head to clear and my blood to detoxify.

"There you are, boy, that's real smokin," Grandpa said, taking the pipe I dizzily proffered after sucking it down to the last ash. "You like that, boy?"

I shook my head and leaned woozily into the steps. He left me, headache parachuting into my brain from the top of my head, my stomach spinning, and my mouth sticky and unquenchably dry. For the next two days I lay on the floor of my room. The coolness of the wood eased my headache a bit and stopped the spinning. I was nauseous in a way that throwing up didn't ease. If I moved, my head reeled. When I sat down at the supper table the smell of food promptly started me thinking about that pipe. My stomach surged like a downhill roller coaster car rushing the next uphill stretch.

Grandpa's remedy worked. The mere smell of tobacco turned my stomach for decades to come. Most nonsmokers in the Army redeemed their coupons for a carton of cigarettes and used them to barter for things they liked better. I didn't want to handle the carton for even long enough to work out a trade because my nose would later catch that tobacco whiff on my hand. It brought back a tinge of that roller coaster feeling.

FOUR

When the American soldiers came, the children asked,
"Who are these black people?" Their parents said, "They
are only American soldiers who wash their faces with
chocolate." And so the children wanted to kiss their faces,
because they thought they were covered in chocolate.

—Giuliano Fontini, Italian journalist

Fall 1944, Northern Italy

Our regiment spent most of its World War II combat career clawing through a forty-mile stretch of coastline near the top of the Italian boot. This coastal plain stretches endlessly north in the maritime haze, as narrow as it is infinitely long, a small slice of relatively level land between the arc of the Ligurian Sea and the spikes of the Apennine Alps.

Italy is two-thirds mountains and most of them seemed jammed behind the foothills that leap out of these coastal lowlands. The German Army polished the misconception by delivering daily doses of shrapnel, the magnitude of which suggested most of their mortars and heavy artillery were anchored in the Apennines.

The flatlands were checkered by farm fields and grape arbors, sprinkled with the ruins of shelled-out farm houses, and crisscrossed by drainage canals. Small towns squeezed against the foothills or were anchored in every tuck and fold of the mountain valleys. If we weren't patrolling, we were driving the Germans out of one of these little towns, ordered to pull back, and redirected to take another small town.

Simultaneously we were immersed in the Italian culture. My introduction was irresolute at best. I couldn't savvy my Army-issue Italian phrase book and threw it away soon after we landed in Italy. It didn't appear that accepting the local culture was going to be any easier after I had my first taste of Italian coffee. It was worse than the crap they served in Louisiana, heretofore the worldwide benchmark for bad java.

The Italian people were quite another matter. I rapidly grew to love them.

The Italians were slow to show themselves to us. When they shyly started appearing, it was strictly women, children, and elderly folk. The young men had been conscripted by Italian fascists or the Nazis, gone into hiding, or were fighting as partisans in the hills.

Most Italians never had seen a black man, and, outside of officers, that's all there were on the western end of the Allied front in north Italy. Mussolini conditioned Italians to consider black men savages. The Germans spread the word that we were "less than human." White Americans who arrived in Italy before us spread rumors that we had tails and ate people. Even white South African expeditionary forces treated us more kindly than our own countrymen.

Add this to the fact that we often went six weeks without a bath and it is little wonder we frightened a lot of people. One black American stopped his tank in a recently liberated village and emerged to ask if there were any Germans about—customary Army policy. The Italian woman was so terrified at the sight of the Buffalo Soldier that she tossed the infant child she was holding into the nearby bushes and ran away. Perhaps the goggles pushed back on the top of his head looked like the horns she expected to find on black devils.

Our relationship with the Italians changed easily. I'm not sure why. Perhaps it was because we gave cigarettes to the adults and chocolate to the children, although the chocolate often was basalt hard and not much of a prize. Perhaps the poor rural Italians, who had been repressed by Germans, could easily identify with poor, repressed rural black Americans. Perhaps it was because we were chasing the Germans, who extracted horrible revenge for the Italians' change of allegiance.

The Italians called us "buf-a-lo"—the best they could do with the double "f" of buffalo. They picked it up from asking about our shoulder patches—a brown buffalo on a green background that was supposed to be the morale-boosting mascot for the 92nd Infantry Buffalo Division. It was stolen from an old cavalry legend—a legend I was unknowingly born to.

Cheyenne had been home to black soldiers for decades when I arrived. It served as one of the Old West outposts for the all-black 9th and 10th Cavalry, formed by Congress after the Civil War. Indians called these black horsemen Buffalo Soldiers because their nappy hair and fierce fighting spirit reminded the natives of the animal they revered.

A Buffalo Soldier born not far from my home town, Sergeant Major Edward L. Baker—not my relation—earned the Medal of Honor during the Spanish-American War. His actions were suicidal. A wounded comrade was drowning in the surf off the Cuban coast, near Santiago. Although the enemy gunfire was punishing, Baker left his well-protected refuge and rescued the man. Black soldiers earned six of the 109 Medals of Honor bestowed during that war.

As I was growing up, I knew nothing of Sergeant Baker. I knew nothing of the Buffalo Soldiers, who had the lowest desertion rate and lowest alcoholism rate among the troops sent to settle the West after the Civil War. Sent west because it was good politics to keep black men with guns out of sight of white folks with votes.

That didn't quell all of the problems. Western towns greeted the black soldiers who protected them with contempt. White officers refused to command them. The arrogant George Armstrong Custer declined to take charge of an all-black cavalry division before he went to his doom at the Battle of the Little Big Horn. Black soldiers stayed anyway because, as miserable as it was, Army life was superior to civilian life.

I recall seeing black soldiers from nearby Fort D.A. Russell on the streets of Cheyenne when I was a child. A close family friend, Al Palmer, knew people at the fort and once took my grandfather and me to eat in the mess hall. All I remember is the food; heaped, steaming portions, and as much as I wanted. It was the best meal I ever ate.

Still, soldiers were an anathema in the community. "Soldiers broke up such-and-such a saloon last night," Grandpa complained. Or, "Those are ruffians, stay away from them."

Nobody talked of their heroics. They probably still don't talk about their heroics in Wyoming history classes. Or the fact that two of the three soldiers from Wyoming who have earned the Medal of Honor were black.

Perhaps it doesn't matter. This history wasn't important to our relationship with the Italians, only the symbol was.

Soon after they learned "buf-a-lo" and "you buf-a-lo," Italian villagers opened their doors to us when the inevitable shelling started. They offered us food, if we stayed for any length of time. And they shared our unspoken grief.

I was first touched by the Italians during one of our efforts to push the Germans out of a town in the foothills north of Lucca. We arrived at one end of the town in the fading light of evening. The town sat between two dry canals that converged at the opposite end of the community. That junction was our first objective.

Montie told me to take my men through the town and position them in the trees lining the top of the canal. There was a stone wall nearby. For some reason, I had my men stick with the trees. Unbeknownst to us, the Germans patiently waited and watched.

Sergeant Belk, Sergeant Cunigan, and I examined the bridge crossing one leg of the canal. It was the typical story. The Germans had demolished most of the structure before withdrawing. Although our soldiers could negotiate what was left, anything larger, like tanks or trucks, was out of the question.

I headed back to the command post to share my findings. As I reported to Montie, mortar rounds rained into the grove where I had left my men. Without so much as a departing salute, I ran out of the command post and sprinted through town, breathlessly visualizing the worst. I originally trained as a mortar man. I knew that when a mortar round hits, the explosion becomes a two-foot high tornado just above the surface of the ground, spreading shrapnel in all directions. Shrapnel wounds are much worse than bullet wounds. Quarter-sized pieces of metal are buried in places surgeons weren't prepared to probe. Neither X-rays nor surgery, especially battlefield surgery, were well developed then. A lot of World War II veterans who survived mortar wounds still pack around some of that iron.

My worry was for naught. Three men suffered minor wounds in the barrage. I pulled them back to the command post and returned to spend the evening with the remainder of my platoon. Jittery from the mortar fire, we squatted among the trees. Nobody slept.

At daybreak, Montie and I found a two-story warehouse with a view of the canal, the blown bridge, and the country beyond. From a second-floor window, we glassed the entire area, seeing nothing but a vineyard, a road, a grove of olive trees, and, a bit farther out, chestnut trees. Our blithely gawking out that window that morning was a death wish, a sign of our naivete about warfare, considering the German brilliance for camouflage. The neighborhood was riddled with the enemy. All that saved us, apparently, was the Germans' desire to coax us farther.

Montie told me to take my platoon over the bridge and then divide it into two groups. Two of the squads were to go as far as the curve in the road. We assumed the road led toward the German troops—troops some distance away. The other two squads and I would work our way up the canal, toward the vineyard.

We easily crossed the damaged bridge and split into our groups. Spread out we'd be a tougher target for mortars. I ordered two regular riflemen, armed with standard-issue semiautomatic M-1 rifles, and my Browning Automatic Rifleman—the so-called BAR man— to walk the slope of the canal. The rest of the men marched as quietly as possible up the path behind me.

A machine gun chattered. I looked to my right. The two riflemen on the canal slope dropped. Nothing dramatic. No Hollywood hands-to-the-chest, slow-motion twist and fall. They crumpled. They were gone before we'd had enough time together to have a simple conversation, or for me to know any identity other than their rank.

Eldridge Banks, stout as a timber—like many BAR men—pulled up his gun and threw a couple of bursts toward the machine gun nest. The German machine gun chattered again. Banks went down soundlessly.

My legs started me running toward the machine gun, the rest of me too crazy with anger to consider what I was doing. A rhythmic chink, chink, chinking added itself to the cacophony. Plumes of dust kicked between my legs. Shit. They were shooting at me from the vineyard ahead. I jumped sideways and screamed, "Get down!"

The machine gun continued, but briefly. Immediately the heads behind me started to rise as if my men thought it was safe to rush it. My hand frantically waved, "Stay down." We waited. Three or four minutes passed in silence.

Gunfire re-erupted, this time from the road, from about where our other squads were supposed to have stopped. They needed our help more than we needed to face down a machine gun nest. I rose to a stoop and signaled, "Follow me." Staying off the deadly path and above the slope of the canal, we ducked, dodged, and made for the road as fast as a panicked crouch allowed. Once on the dusty track, we ran harder, zigzagging in mild deference to tactics. At the curve, our fellow soldiers surrounded a pair of dead Germans and their light machine gun. I retraced their tracks and confirmed it was the pair who had ambushed us from the vineyard. They had been set up to nail us on the bridge or the path along the canal. They instead allowed me to lead some of my men closer to their nest, shot three of us, and ran off to rejoin their platoon without watching for my other squads. I shuddered and wondered why they hadn't killed all of us on the bridge before we split up.

I found my medic and asked him to risk more German fire to look after the men in the canal. He returned all too rapidly. They were, indeed, dead.

We pulled back to the other side of town, uncertain the machine gunners were the only Germans aiming at our chests and cognizant that mortar rounds might call anytime. I ordered my platoon to set up a perimeter, post sentries, and eat. Unsettled, I drifted through the streets on our supposedly safe side of the village. In my mind I heard a machine gun open up and saw three men fall in succession on that canal slope. It replayed over and over. There was no way to take my mind elsewhere. Nausea tiptoed forward, then retreated, tiptoed forward, retreated. I cursed myself, my judgment, the fact that I couldn't even throw up right but vacillated between settled and sick.

After a day and a night of quiet, we figured we could fetch our casualties. Jeeps and volunteer stretcher bearers went to retrieve the trio. Guilt, anger, and frustration welled up inside me again. I had sent those three men out on that slope, out in the open, without any cover. I wanted to believe I didn't order them to do anything I wouldn't have done. It didn't matter. They didn't have a chance, and I should have known that ahead of time, I told myself. Nausea crept forward and I fought to shove it back. Not now, not here, not in front of so many men, I told myself.

Three loaded stretchers emerged from the canal, went crosswise on the back of the jeeps, and were roped down. We turned and drove slowly back through town. Doors opened in the tall gray stone houses that crowded the narrow cobblestone street. The jeep drivers stopped as Italian women and children with armloads of flowers poured out. They made a procession, gingerly coming to our jeeps and putting their bouquets on the blanket-shrouded bodies of our men. Some of them gave a small bow or curtsy to the bodies after placing their flowers. All of them made the sign of the cross before turning away.

They reverently said nothing. Their eyes fixed only on their task. But we could hear their hearts.

FIVE

The basic discovery about any people is the discovery of the relationship between its men and women.

—Pearl Buck

Early 1920s, Cheyenne, Wyoming

Women made a profound mark on my life long before I stared into the sorrowful eyes of those flower-bearing Italians. It started with my sisters and my grandmother.

Irma was six years older, but small, delicate, and more like a spoiled younger sister. Her angelic features were a disguise for her more devilish propensity to pick at me and run. She loved to give my ears a stinging flick or grab and twist a fistful of the soft skin on my stomach. She had nothing to fear, even when I grew to more than her size. She could count on Cass to beat the hell out of me if I retaliated.

Irma was Grandma's favorite—cousin Mary Mitchell said it was because Grandma liked her lighter coloring. Grandma, who also was lighter skinned, was prejudiced, Mary explained.

"Irma was first and she's the prettiest color," Mary told me authoritatively. "Then came Cass, dark, and oh, your grandma cussed that. You, you were red when you were born. That was worse."

Mary told it with all seriousness, adopting the persona of a wise elder. I never was sure whether it was one of her sly games or useful family history.

Whatever the reason for her popularity, if Irma went to Grandma with any story, Grandma immediately seized it as gospel. If that story implicated Cass and me, Grandma never asked questions before meting out punishment. Cass and I became wary of Irma's princess-like behavior, eventually forming our own alliance. But none of it was ever more serious than the usual alliances and disputes among siblings.

Cass was a Tush Hog—stout and muscular. She had a sixth sense for when and where to rescue Irma, and always came with her thumb thrust between the knuckles of her forefinger and middle finger, took my head under one arm and rubbed it with that special fist until my scalp burned. Before Cass and I formed our pact, Irma and Cass were a team of tormentors. Add cousin Mary's older and more devious ways to the mix, and I was doomed.

One day Mary caught me crying because Grandma had refused to let me play the front-room piano. Mary was not disposed to sympathy, nor was she inclined to pass up any opportunity to tease someone.

"You little sissy, come here," Mary said, crooking a finger to beckon me. "I'll fix you."

I hesitated. She grabbed my collar and hauled me down the hall to Cass and Irma's room.

"Give me your clothes," she ordered.

"Nope, not going to do it," I replied, folding my arms across my chest to emulate the "forget it" stance I'd seen Cass and Irma adopt.

"Give me your clothes. I'm going to fix you," Mary repeated. I've always had a dangerous sense of curiosity, and she was bigger and stronger than I was. I complied.

Mary took my clothes, fished one of Cass's dresses out of the dirty clothes heaped in the corner and put the dress on me. Then she led me back down the hall to the front door and shoved me onto the porch.

"Go out there and cry," Mary said. "Show people what a little girl you are." She slammed and locked the door.

That cured me of crying in front of Mary.

As well as heckling me, Cass often assumed the role of mother and older brother. She happened upon more than one schoolyard altercation, where I was outnumbered or outweighed, and gave to my antagonists as good as she ever gave to me.

Fat Buddy Thorton lipped off to her during one such encounter—a fight over a school football I was using—and Cass slugged him in the stomach with the zest of a welterweight champion. He doubled over and sat down with an "uhf" that spoke as loudly of surprise as pain. Cass threw her arm over my shoulder and walked me home, beaming at her technical knock out. She wasn't a bit winded, nor the least bit afraid of Buddy coming back after her.

"Jeez, Cass, that was quite a pounder you gave Fat Buddy Thorton," I said.

Cass laughed and looked down at me.

"We Bakers stick together," she said.

I was simultaneously proud of Cass and mortified that word would get around that my sister had to stick up for me. Buddy Thorton was more embarrassed than I and never breathed a word of the incident. He avoided Cass religiously, as did the half dozen other clods who figured no girl could hurt them.

In one of her mothering moments, Cass did me a sizeable favor. "Come sit here," she commanded one afternoon, soon after Mom and Dad died, in the lull between morning and evening chores. I slid onto the hard pine chair next to hers, at the wide planks of the kitchen table, and she produced a tablet and pencil. Cass, who was seven, gave painstaking concentration to putting lead to the paper, drawing two angular lines and connecting them with a bar.

"A," she said. "That's an 'A'."

"What's an 'A' for?" I queried.

"It's a letter, part of the alphabet," Cass replied.

"What's a alphabet?"

"An alphabet. An," she emphasized. "Listen and watch."

With the tip of her tongue stuck up over the edge of her top front teeth—Cass's concentration face—she sketched out several more letters, pronouncing them for me as she went.

Each day Cass added more letters to our tablet. She made the sound, showed me the letter and I repeated it. Soon I knew the alphabet.

Cass then turned to whatever book she could find and started showing me how to sound out words. After a few days of basic words, however, we landed a new rush of boarding house guests and our lessons were interrupted.

"Cass," I begged, "more words today."

"Can't Vernon. Grandma'll have my hide tanned if I don't get those upstairs rooms cleaned."

Although I knew that Cass and Irma both were saddled with work and responsibility far beyond their years, especially when our boarding rooms were full, I pestered Cass until she snapped.

"Vernon," she finally yelled, shaking the fist she gave me head rubs with, "go find your own words."

I did. I first tried to apply the ABCs to photograph caption lines in books and cast-off magazines. One Saturday I found a Western magazine with a picture of a cowboy on the cover. He wore six guns, a white hat, and sat astride a handsome white horse. He was shooting at a guy in a black hat. But inside there were no pictures.

I kept looking at the magazine cover, wanting to know the details of this cowboy's adventure, and then repeatedly turned to the text inside, as if I could find the inevitable pictures. Finally I tried reading one line and then another.

Cass occasionally helped me sound out words, when I became too frustrated, and finally showed me how to use a dictionary. By slowly reasoning the meaning of the sentences, I discovered that words created pictures in my mind that were as vivid as the drawings and photographs. It took several days to get completely through the cowboy story—a Texas-sized tale of cattle rustlers, Winchester rifles, Colt pistols, fast horses, and the good guys winning in the end. But intrigue of the story and Cass's help were incentive enough for me to teach myself to read.

Much of my reading material inadvertently came from the alleyways of residential Cheyenne. On Saturdays, sometimes alone, sometimes with friends, I combed the trash cans behind each neighborhood house for Coca-Cola, Dad's Root Beer, and Orange Nehi bottles to sell at the Vetas' store or whatever other grocer was most convenient. If it was a group effort, we always gathered enough soda bottles to earn our admission to a Saturday afternoon Western at one of the three movie theaters—the Paramount, the Princess, or the Lincoln. Blacks were welcome and could sit anywhere in the movie house.

In addition to movie money, I nearly always came away from our garbage-can raids with a decent haul of Western magazines or Sears & Roebuck and Montgomery Wards catalogs. The latter provided my first look at partially-clad women, as fascinating to me as *National Geographic* became to my grandchildren.

Reading took a bonus turn when a carpenter purchased three shanties on our block. He replaced the one-room shacks with a brick workshop. On a table, by the big picture window at the front of his operation, he had all manner of magazines: news magazines, women's magazines, detective magazines like *The Shadow*, and my favorite—Westerns.

I poured over them for hours at a time from a stool at windowside, enjoying the words and the sweet scent of sawdust and shavings, while the carpenter joined and planed, sawed and sanded. Often he let me take a magazine or two home. I tried to take the occasional women's magazine for Cass when I was sure I wouldn't run into any friends who would accuse me of being a sissy.

Our tenant, Mr. Ashford, also entertained me with his personal library. Tom Swift, shoot-'em-up Westerns, "Tarzan of the Apes," and James Fenimore Cooper swept from the mysterious depths of his room to absorb me. Soon I was in trouble with Grandma because I was more interested in reading than in doing my chores. If she spied me in the backyard, curled under a tree with Shep and a book, she confiscated the book, heaped extra chores on me. Rather than deciphering Cooper's old English verbiage about the Mohicans or spinning through fanciful adventures with Tom Swift, I scrubbed wooden floors with a stiff brush and strong soap. If Grandma's mood was ugly enough, she arranged for Grandpa to administer some of the belt when he returned from work. But the lick always was lighter if reading was my mischief.

With enough sore knees and tired elbows, I smartened up. When I had an especially absorbing book, Shep and I walked out south of town, to the shade of a cottonwood on the lee side of a prairie gully, and I absentmindedly tossed a stick for him and read. He eventually tired, curled up close to me, and put his feather-soft muzzle on my lap. Shep's eyes pleaded for attention and I stroked his head until he went to sleep. We passed many a summer afternoon hour with him sleeping and me reading. If I giggled or let out too loud a "wow" at something I read, Shep came to with a start, barking at the sudden noise in alarm. I'd laugh, reassure him, and he settled his head back into my lap.

My early reading ability not only earned me—or stuck me with—the role of church deacon, it readily advanced my educational career. The first day of second grade at Corlette Elementary School I was summoned to the front of the room. My mind wondered what sort of trouble I could have gotten in this early in the year. The teacher led me down the hall and up the stairs to where the upper classmen—third, fourth, and fifth graders—received their reading, writing, and arithmetic. She showed me to the door of the third-grade classroom.

"You're going right to the third grade, Vernon," she explained. "You read too well for my class."

I hesitated, not wanting to enter the lair of older students who, to the last pair of eyes, were watching us at the doorway. The third-grade teacher came forward. My second-grade teacher turned me toward her and sent me her direction with an encouraging pat. My fate was sealed.

SIX

Fall 1944, Northern Italy

As fall deepened, my company shifted west, pushing from the
Serchio River valley northwest to the foothills that buttressed the
east side of the all-important Highway One. The 1,000-mile road
was started more than two hundred years before the birth of Christ,
under orders from Roman politician Aurelio Cotta, to link northern
and southern Italy. Good roads made good military strategy. It
allowed an emperor to rapidly dispatch soldiers to deal with threats
in the northern reaches of his empire.

In WWII, this barely two-lane highway remained the most
important north-south route on the western side of Italy. If we
expected to capture coastal points such as La Spezia and Genoa, we
needed to control Highway One. Unfortunately, the Germans dominated the nearby high ground—the foothills and the mountains—
making them strategic masters of everything from the highway to
the coastal plain and beyond.

Our first destination of any consequence on this swing was
Pietrasanta, a small city lodged between Via Aurelia, as the Italians
call Highway One, and the terraced foothills. The 92nd Division

fought its way into the city by mid-September. It was days before all of the few remaining residents made their presence known to us. They feared us as much as they feared the retreating Germans.

Pietrasanta was a postcard of Mediterranean architecture—whitewashed three-story buildings with red clay tile roofs—or the remains thereof—and the traditional watchtower left over from the days of earlier invaders. A few beautiful dome-topped buildings graced the southern end of the city. Before the ravages of war, vineyards spilled from the western edge of the community toward the coast.

Heavy defensive walls from the Middle Ages loped alongside parts of the town. An entrance with a half-moon top looked west from one wall. Once fitted with nearly impervious wooden gates, this entry was called "Porta a Mare"—"the door which looks to the sea." An equally intricate entrance once looked east into the mountains from the wall on the opposite side of the city. Although pocked and peeled by artillery and machine guns, sections of walls went missing more because of time and disrepair than because of war and purposeful destruction.

It was the only destruction in the city that couldn't be blamed on the war. Building after building was reduced to piles of stone or brick, either by the exchange of artillery or by retreating Germans bent on denying us cover. The ancient cathedral survived, and once a few Italian residents emerged, they found this cause for great celebration.

Architecturally, I could appreciate the massive marble walls and the building's domed top. Its stone lattice work was so delicate it appeared hand-carved wood. But I had spent too much time confined to Baptist-hard pews in my childhood to appreciate any religious miracle that the locals credited for their cathedral suffering only superficial wounds.

In my youth, Sundays were the unhappiest days of my life. Grandmother was determined to offset any foul influence Mr. Ashford or any other of life's evils had on me. She dragged me off to church in my special suit—a white shirt, tie, black coat, and black knickers with stockings that wouldn't stay up. Fair weather or foul, we'd march the seven or eight blocks to church, me in my stiff suit, pulling at my silly stockings; and Irma and Cass in their Sunday-only dresses, ribbons on the pig tails that stuck fashionably straight out from the sides of their heads as they pushed Grandma's wheelchair.

Grandpa never donned a suit, except for funerals, and never went to church. But he made darn sure I did.

Second Baptist Church was a white frame building, hot in the summer and cold in the winter. So cold, the preacher would take a break in the sermon to chunk up the pot-bellied coal stove in the center of the room. A Baptist preacher invariably was a passionate shouter. One would have thought his pay depended upon how well he could make that little building reverberate with the words of *"The Lord!"* Services ran the eternity of ten a.m. to four p.m.—and later if it was a significant religious event such as Easter.

I was baptized in true Baptist fashion when I was six. They took us down to the muddy, willow-clad banks of Crow Creek—which divided Cheyenne into east and west—on a cloudy, cold day. The rest of the great unwashed and I put on gray nightgowns, swimming caps, and watched while the preacher waded around for a spot deep enough to immerse the tallest among us.

At the command of his thundering voice we waded out and stood in a line beside him until each of us was totally wet, shivering cold, and spitting filthy water—all with the Lord's blessing. The preacher correctly predicted that it was a day I would *"Remember!,"* but not for the relief of redemption so much as the relief of finally getting out of the water and drying off. I didn't need divine guidance to know that it wasn't smart to go swimming in Crow Creek on a cold, cloudy day.

Despite my lack of piety, I was a deacon in the church because I could read. During Sunday services I sulked to the front, stood at the high wooden lectern, and read Bible verses. I didn't get "Third chapter of John, verse sixteen" out of my mouth before Irma, Cass, the Mitchell brothers—Robbie and Dunbar—or Wilford "Buss" Cave contorted their faces or pretended to pick their noses or made other obnoxious gestures. Inevitably I laughed, causing the preacher to reach over, slap me on the butt, and admonish, "You are in the *House of the Lord!*"

No one else got in as much trouble. When my sisters, the Mitchell brothers, or Wilford went up to read, I would make faces at them. Instead of them cracking up and getting their due, I got caught making faces and ended up catching hell again. Grandma slapped me, or, if the incident was serious enough, she called Grandfather aside when we returned home. A church offense almost always meant the belt, doubled up, and applied to my buttocks.

Church very nearly killed me. Or should I say it was the place of my literal resurrection? It was Easter Sunday when I was seven years old, one of those services that ran well into the evening because the preacher had so much to say. During a break from the hooting and hollering, we children were outside playing tag in the dark. I ran out into the street to get away from whomever was it.

I didn't see the car coming. The locomotive-sized front bumper knocked me out of my shoes. And it knocked me out. I woke up in the hospital with nothing more serious than cuts, scrapes, and bruised shins and was immediately allowed to go home. The doctor stopped by the house the next day to lecture me about how lucky I was.

"Young man," he said. "Young man, it is difficult for me to believe you are still with us. Do you know the seriousness of this? Do you? Do you know the scare you've given us?"

He went on, probably at Grandma's bidding. She was too shaken, for once, to deliver a verbal thrashing. Still, Grandma wanted no misdeeds—my playing tag at church and running out into the street—to go unpunished.

The fellow with the car, on the other hand, felt so bad about the accident that he stopped by later that same day with a basket of candy and fruit. His profuse apologies embarrassed both me and Grandma.

I hadn't bothered to reconsider my faith, based on that mishap, or the fact that fate sometimes deals us good fortune well beyond reasonable expectation. I didn't reconsider it based on the unscathed Pietrasanta Cathedral.

Pietrasanta also is famous for its poets and artists. Michelangelo came here to select the Carrara marble for his sculptures. I initially mistook the far-off quarries for something entirely different.

"Those mountains must be pretty tall," I commented to Joe West, a fellow second lieutenant and platoon leader, as I pointed at the sharpest peaks pressing the sky. "It seems like there must be snow on them year around. There was snow up there when I first saw them in late summer."

West looked at me and smiled. "That white? Is that what you're pointing to?" he asked.

"Of course," I responded.

"Well, that's not snow," he said authoritatively. "Those are marble quarries. If John Henry had been an Italian, he'd have been drilling rock up there."

Pietrasanta became famous among the Buffalo Division for less artful reasons—you don't think much on marble and Michelangelo when focusing on bullets and bombs. We dubbed the road from here to the mountainside village of Seravezza "Boulevard 88" because the Germans saturated the route and anything near it with highly effective 88mm cannon fire. We could count on a pounding at any time. The German war machine used this sort of firepower to keep us a few steps behind. Meanwhile, they cut a wide swath of destruction as they fell back to the heavily fortified bunkers, machine gun nests, mortars, and artillery batteries woven into the slopes, peaks, and high mountain valleys.

For months, the Germans forced hundreds of Italians to dig trenches and gun emplacements and make these fortifications invisible and impenetrable with logs, dirt, and rocks. Before being shipped to German prisoner-of-war camps, the Italian laborers also carved a labyrinth of escape tunnels that rendered our most intense shelling and bombing useless. The machine gun nests that laced the hillsides, for example, were covered by a thick cross-hatch of logs. The added German camouflage was so masterful that our artillery shells and bombs rarely scored direct hits. Even if they did, enemy soldiers sat comfortably protected in their caves, able to re-emerge, reload, and let us have it as soon as the smoke cleared. The Germans also excelled at always having a backup. If a machine gun nest or mortar battery was snuffed, the nearby second, third, and fourth emplacements easily kept the killing apace.

Some ruin comes with war. Yet, the carnage wrought to widen the German front lines and give her artillery spotters a better line of sight became the stuff of senseless rape and pillage, not simple combat. Years later, when I returned to visit the battlefields, I began to understand this marauding, although I didn't abhor it any less. And I realized the devastation was far greater than those of us in the middle of it had known.

Along this front, as nowhere else in Italy, thousands of Italians were caught between the German and Allied lines. The Germans assured people they had nothing to fear and no reason to leave. Then their villages became a jigsaw of no-man's-land laced with mines, cannon shells, mortar rounds, and bullets. We dashed into these villages trying to clean out the Germans and gain a protected foothold that would propel us deeper into enemy territory. The Germans leveled anything that might help, but went far beyond "strategic destruction."

The Germans searched house-to-house for men of military age. Anyone they found was forced to choose between joining the Italian fascist troops or going to a concentration camp. Many Italians hid in fear, further enraging the Germans.

In villages such as Strettoia, German soldiers plastered the town with posters telling the townsfolk to leave within twenty-four hours. They visited the parish priest, warning him to spread the evacuation order. The following day, this priest, Don Giovanni Dini, was delivering mass near a roadside wayfarers chapel, two-thirds of a mile up the mountain from the abandoned village. The liturgy was halted by a child screaming, "My God, the church!" Don Dini stared quietly as the tower and the church, built in the 1700s and practically brand new by Italian standards, disintegrated.

"I heard the people crying and sick, sick, sick," Dini wrote. "The church was only stone, dust, and fire that morning. After they got the sacrifice—it was our sacrifice—we all felt alone and with death in our hearts." The Germans kept working, systematically dynamiting house after house. The nearby village of Ripa also was razed, as were all of the olive groves, vineyards, and houses between the two towns.

In several Italian villages, the German terrorism became more personal, part of Field Marshall Albert Kesselring's policy of "scorching the earth" around resistance forces. The worst of the atrocities occurred as we worked our way up the coast toward the Arno River. A battalion from the 16th SS Panzer Grenadier Division, guided by Italian fascists from the likes of the Black Brigades and the *Decima Mas* converged on a string of tiny, high mountain communities around Sant'Anna di Stazzema. One group of Nazis arose early enough to kill a priest and his friends in Mulina, burn the priest's home, make the steep climb to Sant'Anna, and still arrive by dawn.

Under the direction of German Major Walter Rader, soldiers with flamethrowers destroyed several homes on the slopes surrounding the village. People not killed before their homes were torched burned to death. More than 130 other people, including thirty-two children, were lined up in the Sant'Anna town square and shot. The SS then removed pews from the adjacent church and stacked them like kindling in the middle of the town square. The soldiers heaped villagers' bodies on top of the pile and used their flamethrowers to ignite a massive bonfire. A few yards away, other German troops ate lunch and listened to accordion music.

The bodies burned, the band played on. A three-year-old boy's corpse cracked and swelled with the heat, according to eye-witness accounts, but his arms remained stretched outward, as if still pleading for mercy.

Afterward, the Italian men shanghaied to pack the Germans' ammunition up the mountain were dragged behind the church and shot, and the church was burned. Bodies of other victims lay strewn throughout the woods around Sant'Anna. The youngest was a twenty-day-old girl. She survived a bullet wound in the shoulder but later died at an aid station. Soldiers performed crude surgery on one pregnant woman, taking her baby before killing her. The final death toll was 560 women, children, and elderly. Military-age villagers, believing the Germans were on a mission to conscript them, had fled to the woods assuming their families would be left unharmed—as had been the custom.

It is difficult to determine who, among the victims of an atrocity, are more fortunate—those who die or those who survive. Sant'Anna is testament to that ambivalence. The oldest son in the Eugenio Battistini family was spared only because he was in a prisoner-of-war camp when Major Rader visited Sant'Anna. Battistini anticipated meeting his family when he stepped off the train in Pietrasanta some months later and was greeted with the news that his father, mother, and five brothers and sisters had been slaughtered.

Antonio Tucci, a Naval officer who had moved his family to Sant'Anna for their safety, had disappeared into the woods as soon as the SS entered the village. He rushed back at the news of the massacre and threw himself into the still open grave where volunteers were burying his wife and eight children.

"I am going with them," he sobbed as went into the grave. "I am going with them."

People from neighboring villages pulled him out and struggled to hold him back until the burial was completed.

A few people escaped the atrocity by sheer happenstance or with the aid of a sympathetic German soldier. Enio Mancini, six years old, survived with such help. The soldier sent to execute his family lined them up outside their house and told them to duck. Then the German fired several machine gun bursts into the wall over their heads and urgently whispered for them to run. Bewildered, they fled, half-expecting they were victims of a cruel joke and bullets would find their backs. They didn't.

Other survivors lived to help bury the dead, clutching a bit of disinfected cotton over their noses and mouths as they dug graves for the putrefying bodies under huge clouds of flies. Once the war ended, survivors commissioned a stone tower, on a high knob called "Col di Cava" that is visible even from the sea. They unearthed the bones and ashes of the massacred and moved them to the tower.

Upon my return to Italy fifty-two years later, I found a spare but powerful museum Enio Mancini runs in what used to be Sant'Anna's primary school. Inside, a single four-foot-long display case houses the mementos found in the remains of the crematory fires. There is a watch stopped at eight minutes before seven a.m., charred rosary beads, bloodstained coins, a solitary hat, a wallet with a photo of a man and a woman. The man was identified when his companion came looking for him and found nothing but a photograph of them together.

My heart surged. Couldn't we have moved faster up the coast and stopped this? Did this happen because of the days we spent on make-work and perfunctory marching, waiting for orders to move into combat? I thought of our departure from the Naples area, in classic Army hurry-up-and-wait style. Had we pushed north instead of scaling the slopes of that crater day after day, Major Rader's carnage might have been foiled.

The German genocide moved to other areas as we battled our way from the Arno River into the Serchio River valley. In the Versilia and Massa-Carrara area at least another 1,500 people were killed and many villages burned. The final toll across north Italy was much higher. It took us an entire winter to break the German defenses and get to the survivors.

Much has been made of the horrors suffered by civilians on other World War II fronts. Little attention has been paid to the hell the Italian people endured, at the hands of their own fascist countrymen, at the hands of the Germans. It had one beneficial affect for the soldiers of the Buffalo Division. The abominations helped meld leaders of the communists, right-wing sympathizers, and moderates into the "Comitato di Liberazione Nazionale"—the Committee of National Liberation. This secret committee directed the partisans, a 600-member citizen resistance that endured longer and remained stronger in this region of Italy because German brutality wiped out their sons, daughters, grandmothers, fathers, mothers, and friends.

Once our commanders learned to trust the partisans, they supplied them with arms and ammunition. The resistance fighters moved these supplies miles behind enemy lines and used them to torment the Germans with a guerrilla war. They scouted German positions for us, helped move civilians and escaping prisoners of war safely to our side of the fighting zone, and helped clear the way into many a town.

They did so at great personal peril. If caught, the partisans were treated as traitors and cruelly tortured in the nearest town square. Their spirit was inspiring. They only fought harder for every horror, every wronging.

Grandpa was such a person.

SEVEN

Silence at the proper season is wisdom, and better than any speech.

—Plutarch

Early 1920s, Cheyenne, Wyoming

"You know Lloyd Hammond, boy?" Grandpa asked.

"Yes sir," I answered.

We sat on the front porch catching the warmth of one of the false spring days that Wyoming teased us with every March. The sun pushed the mercury to sixty degrees one day—sweltering if you considered the recent bone-chilling fifteen or twenty degree weather. And invariably the wind blew in six inches of sloppy-wet spring snow by noon the following day.

I waited patiently for Grandpa to reveal the reason for his interest in Lloyd Hammond. He didn't rush. He never did. Grandpa was a man of few words and every one of them was counted out with authority.

"I work with Lloyd's father," Grandpa finally said, "down at the railroad yard. He tells me you've been sticking up for Lloyd with those bullies. His father appreciates that."

In those few sentences Grandpa conveyed his own approval as well as appreciation from Lloyd's father. The floor wasn't open for questions and the matter wasn't up for further discussion.

Lloyd Hammond was a scrawny little white kid, a grade or two behind me at the two-story brick elementary school. His smudged face always carried a smile bigger than his pale, thin body. Early that school year, when I was eight, I happened upon four or five older boys, the schoolyard thugs. They circled Lloyd, pulling at his books, punching him, and shoving him around.

"You a pansy, Hammy? We think you're a pansy. Hammy's mammy's pansy," they chided.

Lloyd was too timid to fight back, too meek to say anything while they tossed him around like a rag doll. They were so absorbed that they didn't notice when I walked on the scene. Without forethought, I reached past a beefy, freckle-faced sixth grader with greasy red hair, grabbed Lloyd by the arm, and pulled him out of the circle. The tough guys whirled around, automatically lining up side-by-side, unsure of who had caught them taunting Lloyd. They appeared ready to add a second victim to their circle upon discovering it was scrawny old me.

"We could even this up a bit," I said, raising a fist, red-hot angry and not thinking about the disadvantage in numbers standing before us. "Pretty tough, all of you picking on a guy like Lloyd."

Lloyd straightened a bit, as if he was now ready to throw a few punches. I shot the group my meanest look, took hold of Lloyd's shoulder. We turned and walked away. Perhaps they were stunned by my insolence or ashamed that they had been caught picking on the smallest boy in school. The bullies allowed us to go unchallenged.

From that day forward, I had a job. Lloyd waited for me by a big cottonwood tree on the edge of the gravel schoolyard. I walked him as far as my turnoff on Eighteenth Street—about two blocks from his house. The bullies taunted us at first but didn't come close enough for trouble.

It had become routine and I quit thinking about it. It also wasn't the sort of thing I talked about at home. Grandpa hated violence.

"Use your brains, not your fists, boy," he admonished many times.

Grandpa's approval of my protecting Lloyd meant all the more because I technically was going against his "brains, not fists" policy and still winning his appreciation. That's one of the things I loved about Grandpa—he put common sense over strict adherence to rules.

I spent as much of every day as I could with Grandpa. He woke me about six a.m. with a gentle shake of the shoulder and a "Time to rise, boy." While Grandpa shaved and dressed, I cleaned the ashes out of the stoves in the kitchen and ground-floor bedrooms, filled the wood box, and started a fire in the cook stove. Grandpa's morning rounds brought him to the kitchen by seven o'clock, ready for the heavy black metal lunchbox Cass and Irma had packed the night before. Grandpa wore an engineer's cap, blue cotton work shirt, pants, and Osh-Kosh-By-Gosh overalls every day. If it was winter, he added long underwear.

He rarely paused for coffee or breakfast. He hefted his lunch pail, nodded at whoever was in the room, and moved out the door. If Grandpa stopped at the kitchen table and treated himself to a cup of coffee, I sat with him.

"Can I have some coffee, Grandpa?" I asked, wanting to share everything he did.

"No, no coffee. Coffee make you black, boy," Grandpa said.

I asked again, many times, so we could laugh at the joke. In the evening, Grandfather returned to the house right before supper. While Cass and Irma finished pulling together the meal, Grandfather unfolded the evening newspaper and took it to his and Grandma's room. The rest of us understood not to touch that newspaper until Grandpa read it.

This was all the reading Grandpa did, and his writing was choppy and imprecise. Years later I realized he was only semi-literate. I found that puzzling. The schools in Iowa where he was raised were quite good. His formal schooling must have ended early.

I loved to go down to the railroad yard and sit all-importantly in the high-back wooden chair beside Grandpa's desk. It was my chair, as far as I was concerned. I watched him lean on his elbows, scribble notes in a record book with a pencil, and wait for the next train. Periodically he tugged on a rawhide tether to pull his watch out of the top right-hand pocket of his overalls. He left his desk before the whistle sounded and rotated his substantial arms and shoulders forward to loosen the joints as he walked to my chair.

"Boy, I want you to sit right here. Don't move 'tall."

I nodded. Next thing I knew, the train whistle sounded and Grandpa was outside moving smartly toward the tracks to meet it.

The immense rail yard held a thousand fascinations, including the smell of creosote, coal, lubricating oil—all the smells Grandpa wore. It was charged with the air of meeting important schedules, the pride of men who made the big trains run, and the exhilaration of hearing "All la'board" boom down the tracks. Whistles moaned, air brakes hissed, railcar hitches clanked. Men swore, baggage handlers grunted and scurried.

Because of the dangers of all the moving machines, I experienced the railroad yard only from Grandpa's side or through the window or doorway of his tiny office. I always was tempted to sample more but settled for being in the presence of such an important man.

Grandpa also had a strength that surfaced when the Depression hit Wyoming in the mid-1920s, after hard winters, agricultural failures, and an oil bust. Rail strikes followed and Grandpa kept working at his own peril. He was proud of his work ethic, even without the pressure of hard times to keep a man doing whatever he could find. Grandpa figured the railroad paid him regularly so he ought to work regularly. Period.

When the strikes turned sour, he stuck a pistol inside his coveralls before he walked out of the boarding house in the morning. Angry white strikers confronted him, calling him everything but a scab. Grandpa eased his pistol out from inside his overalls just far enough for the strikers to see it and informed them he'd be getting along to work. They scattered like frightened magpies.

Grandpa wasn't the sort of railroad worker to frequent saloons and settle scores with his fists. But he could be politely authoritarian when the rare moment commanded. So, while these men had to have known he avoided violence at all costs, they also must have recognized his willingness to use the pistol to protect an important point of honor.

He and his best friend, Al Palmer, eventually laughed about those tense moments, which is the only way I learned about them. Mr. Palmer, who lived a block north and a block east, also worked for the Union Pacific. While Grandfather had never altered his schedule or his route to work during the strike, Mr. Palmer left home three hours early to avoid the strikers. He shared Grandpa's aversion to physical violence but, being built more like a symphony conductor than a railroad hand, he didn't have Grandpa's bulk to deter challenges.

"I didn't have a gun to pull on those guys," Mr. Palmer said, probing Grandpa for the details of the encounter. I pressed myself up against the wall, trying to remain as inconspicuous as possible, knowing that if I was noticed the conversation would end or I'd be sent away.

"Didn't pull no gun," Grandpa replied. "Wasn't going to shoot nobody. I just acquainted them with one of my friends." It sounded jovial, but Grandpa wasn't smiling. He had noticed me and was trying to dismiss the topic quickly. The talk turned to the weather and prospects for hunting.

The fall before I turned twelve, Mr. Palmer, Grandfather, and I went out northeast of Cheyenne, onto the sagebrush flats, for my first hunting expedition. We rode out in Mr. Palmer's black car. The sky was scored with the deep blue of early fall, reaching to the far away horizon and then melding into the gray-brown prairie. A few clouds floated above. The air exuded a mixture of tart chilliness and the aroma from the fires in distant home coal furnaces.

I loved the reeling prairie, the pungent sage, the deep coulees, and the way it all ran headlong into the Rockies to the west. The added excitement of going hunting made me delirious. I dreamed of this day each time I eavesdropped on Grandpa and Mr. Palmer. During most of their conversations, they talked about the finer points of hunting, how a deer couldn't see you if you stood still in the woods, and how to lead a flying bird before shooting at it. I reviewed all I had heard while we drove. My vast accumulation of knowledge was certain to me by the time Mr. Palmer parked the car alongside a dry wash and we started walking to find sage chickens.

When we were a safe distance from the car, Grandpa pulled two shells out of his overalls pocket, tucked them one at a time into the chambers of the double-barrel .12-gauge shotgun that seemed pencil-thin compared to the arm over which it was cracked open. Shells firmly in place, he snapped the gun shut, checked the safety, and handed it, butt first, to me.

"Give her a try, boy, just to see how she shoots," Grandpa instructed. "Thumb the safety off this a way when you're ready," he added, giving a demonstrative flick of his thumb. "Front trigger'll handle that left barrel; back trigger for the right one."

Proud to show my prowess with guns, I pulled the heavy three-foot-long shotgun to my shoulder, sighted on some imaginary birds, and clumsily grabbed both triggers at the same time. The double recoil slammed my ninety-pound frame to the ground. I miraculously missed the prickly pear cactuses, instead imbedding only sand and dirt into my skull. It's difficult to say whether the recoil of the gun or the impact of me hitting the ground had more to do with knocking the wind out of me.

Grandfather laughed with uncharacteristic abandon, slapping his knee, nearly doubled over, his throaty guffaws spilling like water from a bursting dam.

"Boy's a hunter, Al. Boy's a hunter," he roared.

Mr. Palmer nodded vigorously, with half of his mouth in a smile and the other half uncertain. He generously didn't comment. He was as amused by Grandpa's reaction as he was by my mishap. I lay there trying to regain my pride and my breath.

"Get up, boy," Grandpa finally said, wiping his eyes with his sleeve, coughing, and laughing more.

Mr. Palmer helped me up, his face now offering a kindly smile, and then leaned over and picked up the shotgun. He fingered the triggers without pulling them, then opened the shotgun, extracted the spent shells, and talked me through the proper mechanics of handling a double-barrel.

"One at a time," Mr. Palmer said, holding the gun so the triggers were level with my eyes. "You want to work these one at a time. Otherwise the only thing you'll wing is you."

I was not admonished for my error. The throbbing black-and-blue patch forming under my heavy cotton shirt served as my reminder not to seize a gun with cocky assumptions about what I knew. Grandpa and Mr. Palmer and I resumed hunting and found no sage chickens that day. I think they purposefully avoided the most promising spots out of compassion for the pain another shot-gun blast, single or double, meant to my shoulder.

Come Christmas, Grandpa called me aside. He handed me a brand-new bolt-action .22-caliber Remington rifle, with gun oil still glistening on the barrel.

"This is yours, boy," he said, his eyes sparkling.

"Grandpa. Grandpa!" I yelled. He smiled and nodded, pleased with his choice.

A brand-new gun was a remarkable gift. Ours was a no-frills household. We had to pay for the boarding house, three children Grandma and Grandpa hadn't counted on raising, and numerous house calls by Grandmother's doctor. As the person in charge, Grandma squeezed every nickel until the buffalo hurt.

After teaching me to shoot, Grandpa dispensed .22 cartridges, one handful at a time. For every cartridge he gave me, I had to return a spent shell. And I had to have a jackrabbit or prairie dog to show for it. In his quiet way, Grandfather was teaching me not to waste.

"If you can't make the shot count, don't make it," he'd say, holding up a single shell for emphasis.

Having my own gun added new magic to Saturdays. Where before Shep and I had wandered up coulees to catch horny toads, to read and chase sticks, or just kick dirt clods, I now roamed them as one of the men of the house. We were raised on beans, jackrabbit, prairie dog, and the occasional deer. Now that I had a gun, I provided.

Hunting suited me. Gun in hand, I had a better excuse than ever to follow the banks of Crow Creek south out of town, into the sagebrush breaks, and find a sheltered cutbank in a dry wash where I could sit and think. Sitting in this shelter while the inevitable wind cut up from the southeast helped me relax. It gave me a chance to curse Grandma or stew about boyhood things and talk to Shep about my frustrations as he cocked his ears and earnestly looked like he understood. And I soon gained enough ability with my little .22-caliber rifle and enough knowledge of the jackrabbit dens and prairie dog burrows that I didn't have to hunt every moment in order to bring home food. I could relish an hour or two of solitude, knock down a few rabbits, and return home without seriously breaching my curfew.

"Always gut 'em out here in the field," Grandpa instructed as he turned a rabbit inside out with two strokes of his hands. "Wait to skin 'em at home—the meat'll get less dirt on it. Hang 'em in the cold shed as soon as they're skinned."

The cold shed stood in the shade created by the northwest side of the house. It was made of wooden slats, each spaced a couple of inches apart, to allow the wind to funnel through. Meat stayed cool here in the summer and board-stiff frozen in the winter.

Cass was kind enough to share my hunting pride. She made it a point to find me when I returned from my first few outings and admired the rabbits I'd brought for her to cook.

"Those 'er bigger than most of the ones Grandpa brings in," she said. "Giants."

"Really mean it?" I asked.

"Giants," she said.

I knew it wasn't true. Grandpa could rustle a handful of the biggest rabbits with less than an hour of effort. I still wanted to hear her admiration, her approval.

Turning twelve, lambasting myself with the .12-gauge, and then getting my own rifle gave life a coming-of-age flavor. But nothing like the first deer hunting trip when I turned fifteen.

Irma had married a tall, rough-cut ranch hand named Charles Franklin, who worked near Laramie. Bowlegged and slightly gimp-gaited, like any man who spent too many hours on a horse, Charlie was all the cowboy except he never wore a cowboy hat. He brought both a car and thorough knowledge of hunting to the family and was welcomed for both.

Grandpa, Charles, and I went on an expedition, driving 150 miles to Elk Mountain, north and west of Cheyenne. Charles took the Lincoln Highway, past mile after mile of prairie tentatively hemmed in by barbed wire. Every quarter mile or so a sign hung on the fence announcing "No Trespassing—Warren Cattle Co."

"Who's this Warren?" I finally asked, after several miles of squinting at the blue-and-white signs on the left side of the car.

"Largest rancher in this here county," Charles said. "This man Warren was the first governor of this here state and a United States senator for pretty near forty years. He's dead now, though."

No doubt Charles knew the Warren Cattle Company's stocking rate, whether they calved in the fall or spring, how many brood cattle it raised, and if the outfit bred its own horses. His knowledge of Elk Mountain was no less impressive.

Elk Mountain dominated the landscape long before we left Highway 30 at Wolcott Junction and headed directly to the majestic blue-green mass. Not because it was the largest pinnacle of the Rockies, but the lofty knob was the most impressive topography to interrupt the dusty prairie.

Snow already covered the top of the 11,162-foot mountain when we made our camp among the lodgepole and ponderosa pine. Charlie and Grandpa cut a ridgepole for Charlie's white canvas sheepherder's tent. I gathered wood for the sheepherder's stove.

When the tent was up, its guy-lines taut and walls staked down, Charlie started pulling things from his trunk that gave the term expedition new meaning. There was a bale of straw I spread along the wall farthest from the stove as a mattress for our bedrolls. His cook box was indicative of the fine meat, beans, and biscuits to come. Charlie even fetched along a dutch oven and cooked a sort of doughy cobbler, made with canned peaches, that spread sweet juice all over my chin and down the front of my flannel shirt.

When we had the camp in order, Grandpa sat on a stump, drew out his pipe, and repeated all of the things he had been teaching me: How to stalk, making every shot count, patience.

We got up in the cutting cold of four a.m. the next morning, ate, and walked to the meadows well before daylight. After hunting for three or four hours, we came back to camp, ate, napped, and headed out again before dusk. The outing alone was pleasant, with nothing but the wind and our footsteps to accompany our thoughts.

The second day out, after standing as still as possible for well over two hours in the late dawn of November, a four-point mule deer walked into in a meadow 150 yards away, turned broadside, and stared into the trees. I lifted my gun ever so slowly, not wanting to make a single mistake. I put the sights dead on the deer, held my breath for a three-count, and reached for the trigger.

"Squeeze it, boy. Don't jerk," Grandpa always said.

The rifle kicked. The deer dropped.

Grandpa crossed the downed timber and crackling dry meadow grass with me to check on the animal. It was dead with a single shot, just as I'd been taught. It looked like a giant to me. I grabbed an antler admiringly and looked to Grandpa for approval.

He smiled. "Good shot, boy," he said. And handed me his skinning knife.

EIGHT

The role of the rifle company was the worst in any division. Everyone out in front of you was trying to kill you.

—Capt. Harry Cox, mortar platoon commander,
370th Infantry Regiment

October 1944, Northwest of Pietrasanta, Italy

Somewhere in October, the glory of war began to dissipate in earnest throughout the regiment. Our mood darkened with the departure of the agreeable weather, the arrival of General Edward M. Almond to command the 92nd Infantry Division, and a rising number of casualties. Our regiment, the 370th, was reassigned from the First Armored Division to the 92nd.

To round out this cheery picture, we faced nothing but wet, slippery, steep terrain. That, combined with the impenetrable German defenses, stymied our attempts to press into the mountains. It took a month to move from Pietrasanta to Seravezza, four kilometers by way of a road the Germans controlled, and a hell of a lot farther sliding up and down ravines, terraces, gullies, and steep mountain passes to get around the Germans. Pavement hadn't touched the narrow, contorted tracks we attempted to use.

Attempted. Torrential rains turned everything to mud or something even more fluid and slippery that cannot be described but must be experienced. The beautiful old olive trees, supplanted by

71

chestnuts and stone pines as we moved higher in the mountains, were no longer welcome shade from the Mediterranean sun, but dripping reminders of the almost total absence of the sun. The grassy slopes didn't paint scenes of pastoral bliss as they had on clearer days. They yanked our sure footing and soaked us when we fell.

More and more of our energy focused on keeping our feet dry and our hands warm. Fires were forbidden. During the day the curling wisps of smoke alerted the Germans to our exact position. At night, the flames became even more efficient homing beacons for German artillery observers. Eventually my platoon learned to dig a special foxhole, with a deep pit at the front, and build a small nighttime warming fire that wasn't visible for any distance.

The fires were more psychologically heartening than physically warming. It was a small moral victory to outsmart both our commanders and the Germans. And anything that improved morale was a bonus.

I tried to look out for my men, tried to encourage them, tried to ease the resentment black soldiers felt when asked to fight for the 92nd Division's unappreciative Southern white colonels and generals who blamed the fruits of their poor leadership decisions on black privates, sergeants, and lieutenants. Our commanders made it clear that they considered black soldiers failures, no matter what we did, and they would ensure history reflected that. It was difficult to tell who the bigger racists were—the commanders behind us or the Germans in front of us.

That wasn't a shock that greeted us in Italy.

From the moment the Japanese bombed Pearl Harbor, nearly three years earlier, the black soldiers I knew yearned to go clobber the enemy. Many of them came from a tradition of fighting, a tradition that extended clear back to their slave kinfolk helping defend the colonists from Indians before the American Revolution. We considered our homeland imperfect and still considered it the best country in the world.

Blacks had to fight for the right to work in the war factories. President Roosevelt issued an executive order in 1943 prohibiting discrimination by government contractors. That stirred anti-black riots that killed more than thirty blacks in Detroit. Black political leaders, meanwhile, were arguing black men should be allowed to go to combat. Instead we had drilled and trained, drilled and trained.

By early 1944, the tide holding blacks from going to war was receding. The United States was running low on young, combat-qualified recruits. White mothers were angry that their sons were dying while black men stayed behind. My old outfit, the 25th Infantry Regiment, was absorbed by the recently resurrected 92nd Infantry Division—the all-black Buffalo Division. Instead of imbuing our men with a sense of accomplishment—gaining the right to fight—it brought unrest.

Before I had gone to Officer Candidate School, we soldiers of the 25th had been a close group. Now we were broken up and scattered across a new nonentity, an amalgamation of every black soldier the Army could throw together in one spot. The bad actors—and the Army hastily drafted many into our ranks—diluted our spirit. The War Department added to our agony by deciding if it was going to have black combat troops, white Southerners had to be in charge. "They know how to handle those blacks," the conventional wisdom went.

During those last months in Arizona, when we were supposed to be finding cohesion as fighting units, we changed white company commanders like Mae West changed lovers. A month with one of our companies was a career for them, six weeks a lifetime. They came, marked a little time, and moved up the ladder. They made sure we saw their boot print as they climbed. White officers weren't dying to command black troops so the thirty-day wonders we saw at the 92nd often weren't Uncle Sam's brightest and best.

Black officers such as myself didn't enjoy any sense of inclusion. We weren't asked for our thoughts on reforming the division. The only real communication from the top officers centered on making sure we recognized our place. Officers' clubs were segregated just like everything else on the base. We knew that if we were summoned to division headquarters, we should call only at the back door. When we were summoned we knew to expect some phony assignment or a dressing down for reasons that were never made clear. We speculated that the chewing out was some sort of practice drill for the white officers.

Black draftees were sometimes a difficult part of this new division. Morose, unruly, and distant, they knew the Army didn't want them. And they didn't want to be there. Most came from the rural South and spent their lives taking crap from the brand of men the Army sent us as commanding officers. How could they get enthusiastic about going to fight for a bunch of white men whom they knew only as oppressors? Especially when they knew the cause they were recruited for was tokenism, not the fight for freedom.

The Army's response was humiliating. The 92nd Infantry Division commander, a Virginian named Major General Edward M. Almond, decided a mascot was the cure for the division's malaise. He brought in a sullen buffalo calf that some smart soldier named "Buffalo Bill," in honor of Buffalo Bill Cody. Cody was a white showman, not one of our honored cavalry legends from the era of the original Buffalo soldier. But like a small-town football mascot held holy by powerful people, there was no changing the name.

What was supposed to be a catalyst for enthusiasm was a catalyst for unrest. Buffalo Bill was disgraceful. He went to the bathroom at the most unfortunate times in the most embarrassing places. We could count on Bill stopping and plopping buffalo pies in the middle of the street wherever he went on parade, or taking a leak in equally uncouth circumstances. When Buffalo Bill was brought out on the field before one of our inner-divisional football games, the soldiers booed, hollered, and threw rocks and beer cans. General Almond similarly was booed when he appeared before a group of the black soldiers.

Outwardly, Almond pretended to ignore us and continued to try to win us over by inviting Joe Louis and other famous folk to entertain us. It didn't work. We needed respect from Almond, not black entertainment, to feel at home. He never delivered.

Late in the spring of 1944, all black officers were ordered to Almond's headquarters. Outside, in the always blistering Arizona sun, his chief of staff confirmed we would join the war within a month. A regimental combat team, called the 370th, was in the making, using the best officers and enlisted men from several infantry companies. They said nothing about where we were going.

"All these years, our white boys have been going over there and getting killed," the chief of staff concluded. "Well, now it's time for you black boys to go get killed."

I prepared to go to combat, experiencing, for the first time since joining the Army, a thrilling sense of anticipation. Many of the other officers transferred to the 365th Regiment or the 371st, hoping those units would never go to combat.

"Time for you black boys to go get killed," they said sarcastically when I inquired how they could pass up an opportunity to finally go fight. "If that's how they feel about us, to hell with them."

To hell with them. I knew that sentiment still burned with these soldiers when we squatted around those meager foxhole fires and talked about our frustrations.

"Put it aside, we've got a job to do," I advised, "and the best way to take care of each other is to fight smart and keep going." I believed it most of the time. The rest of the time I ignored the ample reason most white officers gave me to doubt my own philosophy.

While there wasn't harmony throughout the 92nd, I had no problems with my platoon when the shooting started. None of my platoon "faded away" or retreated, as newspapers alleged of the Buffalo Division. My men respected me, I respected them. When I went forward under fire, they followed.

Although I was younger than the bulk of my platoon, these men regarded me as a father. They came to me with their problems, and less often, their fears. We didn't speak much about fear. Dwelling on it was incapacitating. Instead, we taught ourselves to ignore it.

I didn't have profound thoughts for these men when they came to me for counsel. Mostly I listened and tried to say what I figured

Grandfather would say. Their confidences touched me and yet they complicated the job of war. I didn't want to get close to anybody.

I'm solitary by nature anyway. Here, trying to keep my distance was an attempt to protect myself. I couldn't be someone's buddy and send him out to get shot. I avoided picking the men who went on patrols. I told their squad leaders how many men I required. They made the selections.

It appears cold and impersonal. But enough already gnawed on me without going down the ranks, choosing men one by one. I felt personally responsible when one of my men was wounded or killed. And no matter how much training we had received, war was a learn-as-you-go proposition. To my horror, I often learned by losing men.

My efforts to make these men anonymous never totally worked. Living around soldiers day after day subconsciously imprinted their faces on my mind. I couldn't help worrying that the two jovial, care-free pals in Belk's squad that were known for their practical jokes would catch the brunt of an ambush on our next patrol. Or that I would repeat the kind of blunder that sent those three men to their deaths on that canal slope.

On top of that, even the most careful officer didn't outflank every casualty. Take Harry Cox, a paragon of caution, whom I'd known clear back in Fort Huachuca. Harry never allowed his mortar platoon to bring up supplies—even food—in the daylight, lest it make too tempting a target. All of that waited until dark, even though Harry's outfit was part of a heavy weapons company and always was located quite a bit farther back from the front than a rifle company such as mine.

Harry's outfit bedded down in a marble works, which appeared the perfect mortar emplacement because they could use slabs of cut stone to cover their foxholes. Well into evening, Harry crawled in his sleeping bag while his men finished unloading food and a fresh supply of mortar rounds. He began to doze off when a thunderous explosion, with enough force to shake his marble hovel, brought him awake.

He crawled out of his den and ran outside to find catastrophe. When the damage was sorted out, Harry and his men learned they had been the victims of a crafty enemy pilot who spotted them under the light of the full moon. The German, flying a light airplane, had cut his engine, glided in, and dropped a bomb in the midst of the unloading crew.

Miraculously, only one man died. But it shattered morale. We hadn't counted on an airplane silently appearing to dust our men. We could hear artillery shells coming and run for cover. We could hear a machine gun open up and shoot back, crawl for the protection of a rock, or go after it with grenades. Because we couldn't hear and couldn't see the airplane, we didn't have the satisfaction of fighting back, of releasing the anger at that nameless, faceless someone who was trying to kill us.

We learned to ignore that type of fear, the fear of things we couldn't do anything about. Hunger was a little harder to put aside for platoons like mine that relied upon their feet to get them from skirmish to skirmish.

Fighting our way around these mountain passes and valleys in the muddy season not only slowed progress, it also hampered supply lines. The mules couldn't keep up. When we outran our food, we bartered with the Italians or made the best of whatever we could scrounge. Most outfits had a guy like Dandy Belk, who could resurrect near cuisine from mere C-Rations and a few Italian ingredients. Still, no outfit gave as literal a meaning to scrounge as we did.

It was early October. We trudged through the olive groves and the occasional fields farmers hollowed out of a high mountain valley east of Pietrasanta. It had been weeks since we had been close enough to a road to have a hot meal courtesy of the Army—and that had been a gluey glump of mashed potatoes, gravy, something supposedly passing as meat, and gelatin. After being jolted up those mountain tracks in a jeep trailer, potatoes were remashed with gelatin, melded with gravy, and pancaked into the meat. A whole new version of awful. The rest of the time we were reduced to eating only the cold portions of our C-Rations, and even those were running thin.

As we passed through the edge of one olive grove, I saw a simple stone building in the middle of a field. We stopped and studied it carefully from cover of the trees. It appeared deserted. I took a portion of my patrol, and we moved slowly to the building.

It was perfect for a German booby trap. Soldiers often got lured inside these deserted country buildings by what appeared to be an enemy weapons cache and ended up blown to bits. My men tediously inspected the perimeter of the building, mindful that even out here a misstep could trigger a shoebox mine—small but capable of ripping the calf muscles right off the back of our legs. After considerable probing, the area appeared clear.

We entered this one-room hut with the same painstaking precautions. It was empty, save for an official-looking olive-drab box off in one corner. Once we finally made it safely to the box, we could see the letters W-Ü-R-M-E-R stenciled on the front. After another careful inspection for booby traps, we decided to open it. A dozen tall, shiny cans stood inside. I lifted one, set it on the box, and cranked the top off with my GI-issue can opener. The aroma was canned stew. The contents looked like the plumpest grains of cooked rice. I pulled my knife off my belt and dabbed out a taste with the blade. It was great.

We sent for the members of our patrol still in the trees and dug in for a feast. It was the most satisfaction our stomachs had felt in days. Later, with the help of a translator, I realized the less palatable truth—our gourmet meal was little worms called grubs.

Soon after this brush with living off the land, headquarters found new purpose for our lives beyond the constant patrolling. The commanders wanted our battalion to capture the next valley to the east, an attempt to find a new way around the solid defenses directly ahead of us.

High on one wall of this coveted valley, the Germans had turned a stone farm house into a machine gun nest and observation post. This two-story house, suspended right below the ridge line, controlled the upper end of the valley. Taking out that house was Charlie Company's problem.

We mud-slogged over mountain passes up the valley from the German positions, dropped down, and came in near Scolina, at the east end of Seravezza. The area had sustained a serious artillery-and-mortar pounding that severely damaged several buildings where we were trying to establish a line. The Germans were far from gone, as their rifle and artillery fire firmly attested.

Beyond our line, much of the village remained intact. Two- and three-story stone buildings pressed end-to-end on the scant level ground along the valley floor. Brush and trees took over as soon as the steep valley walls left the ground, taking this jungle to the sky. The valley was deep enough that the late fall sun never touched all corners of the village. The narrowness of the streets and the height of the buildings enhanced the canyon feeling.

The usual canal bisected the village. We came in on the north side of the canal at the upper end of the valley. The Germans ruled the south side of the canal and the rest of the valley. As usual, we scouted for ways to cross the canal and avoid or eliminate German positions inhibiting our crossing. Rumors said there was a German dugout at our end of the canal.

Lieutenant Montjoy, Second Lieutenant H. James Hansen—who commanded one of our platoons—and I found a nice-looking house at the edge of our side of the canal. We reasoned that if we climbed to the second floor we might be able to spot the dugout.

Before the war, this had been a substantial villa, considering the modesty of the rest of the homes in the area. Outside, stately trees and neat rows of bushes attested to once well kept grounds. Inside, a marble foyer led to a white marble staircase gracefully arching along the wall from the first floor to the second floor. Artillery had given the house a fairly serious drubbing. But the feature we needed most, the stairs to access the mansion's enviable view, appeared largely intact.

Montie and I climbed to the second floor without paying much attention to Hansen. We were absorbed in the particulars of spotting the German dugout—supposedly located in dense foliage on the opposite side of the canal. About the time we walked into the room promising the best vista, we heard Hansen's yell and a thunderous crash. I made for the stairs.

The outside half of the top two stairs was gone. Hansen was lying on his back, directly below, in a pile of broken marble. A halo of fine dust filtered through the air. He had been too much for the artillery-weakened top steps. When they broke, Hansen went crashing down. I couldn't help laughing.

"Shut up, goddamnit, I'm hurt!" Hansen roared, his pride in as much pain as his posterior. Montie and I walked down the stairs, rather more gingerly than we had bounded up, and tried to help Hansen to his feet. He couldn't stand. He had a broken ankle. We already had a casualty, inflicted by stairs, before the day's fighting started.

Once Hansen was dispatched to the aid station, hobbling between the broad shoulders of two privates, Montie and I returned to our second-floor lookout and studied the hill with binoculars, looking for the dugout and any other neatly disguised machine gun nests. We couldn't see anything, but by now we respected the Germans' finesse with camouflage. We borrowed a bazooka from a nearby company and fired a couple of rounds into the brushy hill. With no discernable results. The dugout was a phantom.

The battalion commanders' eagerness to capture the hillside house pushed Montie to send a platoon after it the moment we resolved the question of the dugout. First Lieutenant Alonzo Frazier, a feisty little mouse, led his platoon through our end of the village, over the remains of a demolished bridge, and toward the top of the high valley wall. Considering the relative carelessness with which headquarters sent them to the house, one assumed the commanders believed the stronghold, like the dugout, was a phantom.

It wasn't. Al Frazier barely made sight of the house when he was dissected by machine gun fire. Several members of his platoon were killed or wounded. The rest of us were emotionally gut shot and instantly furious. Al Frazier was the first officer killed in Charlie Company, and the loss was more disconcerting than we anticipated. Ambushing him in defense of a little farmhouse seemed cowardice.

Even with this lesson, our battalion commanders insisted we keep trying to take the house in daylight. We were pressed for time. The Germans had to be handled before winter, they insisted. From a more practical standpoint, the seriously wounded men in Frazier's platoon couldn't be evacuated until we took out the machine gun nest.

My men and I skirted the back of the village buildings and angled for the remains of the wrecked bridge Frazier had last walked. I stopped the men behind a gray, blockish three-story building standing ten yards from the head of the bridge. Sergeant Belk and Casey Emmett—the famed snorer—went to scout the next hundred yards while the rest of my platoon stuck to the shadows behind the building. Belk returned in moments, a shade shaken.

"And your partner?" I asked, seeing he was alone. He wordlessly motioned for me to follow him and to stay low.

Dodging and weaving, we slipped around the building, dropped down an open-air flight of concrete stairs and came up behind Emmett's narrow frame. He was kneeling by the gate, rifle in hand, and appeared to be eyeing the general area of the stronghold through his gun sight.

"What's the problem?" I asked Sergeant Belk.

"He's dead," Belk replied dryly.

I leaned forward to see Emmett's front. He looked perfectly natural, except for the bullet wound between his still open eyes. It was too unreal to believe. Emmett was all too lifelike. My instinct was to ask him a question, to make a snoring joke, to make sure he was dead. Belk touched my sleeve, and I realized I was directly in the same line of fire.

I spun around, dashed up the steps and back around the building, feeling the sniper's scope on my back. Belk moved as rapidly. We regrouped with the platoon and reconsidered. Making this assault in daylight had seemed foolish before we came this far, and now the dead man at the gate confirmed it. I sent a messenger back to the command post—hoping for a stay. But Montie made it clear that we didn't have a choice. The battalion commanders insisted the house be taken immediately.

How much can one farm house be worth? I wondered, thinking of Al Frazier and his platoon, thinking of my own dead man. Still, there was the issue of seriously wounded survivors we might be able to get out of there.

Platoon in tow, we ran around the other side of the building—avoiding the route our dead comrade had taken—and went pell-mell along a dirt track to the bridge. It was the usual jumble of concrete chunks and twisted steel, the results of the Germans trying to delay or prevent our crossing. Poor as this was, the bridge was the best alternative. The sheer sides of the canal plunged at least twenty feet and offered no purchase for climbing. Besides, if crossing a bridge in daylight was foolish, climbing an exposed rock face was a blazing bull's-eye screaming, "SHOOT HERE."

German snipers opened up from either the hillside or one of the massive stone buildings on the other edge of the canal. Belk and I still made it across the bridge. Then German mortar rounds started singing in. As usual, the mortar tubes had been sighted right on our path, long before we arrived. No German officer had to take a reading or tell his men to fiddle with adjustments. They just dropped mortar shells into their tubes and drilled us. One of the riflemen behind us was hurled from the bridge and into the sorry trickle of water below, the force of the explosion tearing off his left arm and propelling it, end over end, to an unknown location. In the unlikely event he survived all of that, he easily would have bled to death before night allowed us to rescue him. More mortar rounds mashed another one of our men into the rubble in the middle of the bridge. The living scattered back to the village.

"Good God, Belk," I muttered. "Who was it?" indicating the men who had just bought it.

Sergeant Belk shook his head.

"Dunno for certain. Maybe Willie Warren and Brown. Harold Brown."

NINE

It is hard to fight an enemy who has outposts in your head.

—Sally Kempton

October 1944, Seravezza, Italy

Belk and I lay stranded on the German side of the bridge. No way we could go back over the bridge in daylight. We burrowed among the chunks of concrete and adapted to discomfort.

We passed the time by keeping an eye on the general vicinity of the house, in case someone came to pay us a personal visit. Occasionally I looked to our man on the bridge, hoping he would stand, shake himself off, and run for cover. Blood pooled and coagulated around him. He didn't move.

Silence eventually echoed through the street where we lay. The silence inflicted an eerie feeling of impending counterattack, more shelling, the approach of a brave German with grenades. We tried to burrow more deeply into the rubble.

Belk fingered the top pocket of his field jacket without opening it. There was a small bible in there, I knew, from the many times he had pulled it out and read his favorite passage: Matthew 27. I didn't understand this selection—about Jesus being condemned, Pontius Pilate washing his hands, the crucifixion, the ground shaking. Since I didn't want a sermon, I didn't ask. Many soldiers carried a talisman, a touchstone for battle, and I figured this was his.

Aside from religion, Belk reminded me of myself. Under that dandy figure was an angry black man ready to raise his fists at the smallest slight. Luther Hall, the company first sergeant, had joined me in pulling him aside soon after his arrival and counseling him not to follow his fists to a dishonorable discharge.

"Maybe you don't get it," Belk had challenged me. "Maybe a Wyoming nigger don't know what a Chicago nigger knows."

I got it. Maybe my introduction came later in life than his. Perhaps the sources were different. But still I was a veteran of anger and outrage, and the Army had baptized me like nothing else.

I had boarded the train for basic training at Camp Wolters, Texas, via Fort Leavenworth, Kansas, in June 1941. A black draftee from Laramie was the only other Army-bound passenger in my car, and we hooked up because we were both from Wyoming. In our four days as Kansans we received our uniforms and other equipment, swam in the base swimming pool, and marveled at the prospect of someone feeding us three meals a day. Joining the Army was a smart move, I bragged to myself. New clothes and a swimming pool.

We boarded another train after this respite and continued to Camp Wolters. The moment we passed through Junction City, Kansas, the bounty of goodness started to spoil. I was too naive to understand it as it unfolded, and too angry to deal with it after the fact.

A porter came into our car and pointed to the draftee and me.

"Come with me," he ordered.

We shouldered our brand-new duffel bags and walked forward, through passenger car after passenger car, until we reached the compartment nearest the locomotive.

"Y'all find yourselves a seat here," the porter said.

He watched long enough to make sure we complied, spun on the toes of his smooth leather-sole shoes, and disappeared back into the jerking maw of the train. After struggling to get my bag into the overhead rack and settling into my new seat, I began to savvy the composition of the people in our new car. We were all black. I looked at my traveling partner. He silently stared ahead. He hadn't wanted to be in the Army to begin with.

The heat, the grit, and the all-day trip lulled me into an uncomfortable, senseless daze—one I hated being pulled out of. I realized, when a jolt of the train occasionally brought me back to the moment, that I was a sticky glob of flesh in a cooking rail car, not a lucky young man headed for something better than sweeping out barber shops and stacking scrap lumber. Fortunately the countryside between Kansas and Texas was progressively more mind numbing.

Toward the end of that long day, we pulled into Mineral Wells, Texas. I wearily dragged my bag from the overhead rack, negotiated the three metal steps out of the end of the car and dropped onto Texas soil. My draftee friend was close behind. I raised an arm and pointed to a dusty bus idling on the other side of the station, just as the man at Fort Leavenworth had promised.

We traversed the luggage-filled railroad platform and thought about finding friendlier, more hospitable faces. A few quick steps drew me into the bus, which was even hotter and stuffier than the railroad car. A desiccated old black man sat all the way in the back, his disinterested stare glued to the window. He alone comprised the passenger cargo.

I dropped my duffel in the seat directly behind the driver and began to slide in beside it.

"*Hey, Nigger!*" the bus driver roared, pivoting in his seat as he expelled hate through his lungs. "Get up and get to the back of the bus *where you belong!*"

I involuntarily jumped to my feet before my butt touched the cloth of the seat, not because this beluga of a bus driver had so ordered, but more as a reflexive response to the volume and intensity of his voice. My fists bunched and I moved my feet farther apart to give me the best leverage for a set of opening roundhouses to the side of his pallid jowl. My traveling companion froze on the bus steps.

Before I could swing, a hand grabbed my left sleeve and pulled me back a step. My head swiveled that direction, and I was wondering if my move to challenge the bus driver had summoned more trouble. It was the shriveled old black man, his stubbled face stony, but his eyes pleading. He motioned to the back of the bus with a sideways toss of his head.

"Come on," he said, simultaneously motioning to the black draftee.

I pawed for my duffel bag with my right hand, threw a glance over my right shoulder to make sure the bus driver didn't have punches of his own coming via air mail, and followed. It was as if the spirit of my grandfather had materialized at my elbow.

The old man walked to the back, dropped in the seat, and patted the spaces beside him. My companion and I took up residence, one on each side of him.

"You planning to die your first day in Texas," he said in a measured drawl, making a statement, not asking a question. The driver gunned the engine, closed the door, and started the journey for Camp Wolters.

"First day?" I said cockily, not wanting to back down from every challenge.

"You're a black man. You tried to sit up front like's alright for black folks to sit anywhere they pleases. Nobody who lives here would try that on a dare unless he wanna be kilt," he said.

"You better keep those fists in your pockets," he added. "Clenching your fists in the presence of white people's liable to get you assault or 'tempted murder charge. Black man's justice in these here parts is done with a tree and a rope."

He turned, smiled a little, and touched my arm in an attempt to reassure me. "Where you from, son?"

For the next several minutes, he tried to educate us on the rules of Southern living. I shook my head over and over. It only made the old man more intense.

"You in shock, son, you in shock. But you gotta listen. Stuff like this'll get you kilt. You're lucky this here driver's too lazy to tangle with you. Be a point of pride to most any other Southern man to beat you silly. Don't give 'em no opportunity."

Before the lesson was over, I asked why we'd been moved around on the train.

"You never seen that? You are strangers to these here parts," he said, letting out an exclamatory sigh. "South of the Mason-Dixon, son, South of the Mason-Dixon. Porter's supposed to make sure the white people all together in the back and the black people all together in the front of the train. That there's the only place any-body's going to move you to the front. That's 'cause it's the dirtiest place, that car right next to the locomotive."

In any other situation we should go to the back, he warned. Greyhound buses had the bathroom clearly marked, too. Pay careful attention to signs and don't touch the door knob if the door didn't read, "Colored." If we ended up in any town, look for the "colored" drinking fountain, "colored" restroom, "colored" cafes, you name it. If we went on leave, we should go to Dallas-Fort Worth and stick to the colored section of town. A black man found no trouble and no ways of making the type of mistake I had just made. Stay in your place and people will leave you alone, he directed.

I nodded, not fully comprehending all I'd heard, shaken by my encounter with the bus driver; hot, dirty and tired, angry, confused, and thinking I should be grateful to the old man. Selecting one emotion to ponder only led to the explosion of another.

What the hell had I gotten myself into, I wondered. I was angry from that day forward. I didn't trust anyone, especially white people.

The bus driver eventually pulled up to the gate at Camp Wolters, opened the door, and turned far enough in the seat to get our atten-tion. He wordlessly pointed out the door. The old man grabbed my hand. "You're good boys. You keep yourselves alive, hear?"

I thanked him the best I could, stood up, and walked warily past the bus driver, thinking every step about the old man's description of justice by lynching. A "coloreds" bus waited to take us to the far reaches of the post. We were assigned a barracks, individual bunks, and directed to the mess hall.

Hunger joined the day's list of disappointments. Raised to be polite, I waited for my fellow recruits to pass me my share of food when we gathered at the plank tables in the mess hall. The other men gorged every morsel within their reach, guarding, not sharing, the food intended for all of us. The aggressive filled their plates. I ended up with a single baked potato.

Camp Wolters didn't pretty up with the sun. The founder of this camp obviously had dedicated his life to finding the center of absolute nothingness and, to his delight, landed in central Texas. The "coloreds" portion was moored in the remote southwestern portion of this big nothing. Our tight cluster of bare wooden buildings contained everything from our own laundry to our own clubs, everything to ensure we didn't wander out of our corner and mix with white people.

And alkali. Alkali flats with nothing. Nothing grew there, not even a mangy thornbush. We got so coated with the hot, bitter-tasting alkali dust that, after a day of training, we looked like white men. Whatever part of our skin wasn't covered in alkali was lodged full of chiggers. So many chiggers that we jumped in the shower and soaped down with big, thick, mustard-colored slabs of lye soap the minute we were dismissed for the day.

The soap was as mean as the countryside. It rid us of the chiggers and of our skin. One shower with that soap led to two to three days of scratching because there was no way to thoroughly rinse it off. We scratched at alkali burns, scratched at chigger bites, scratched at soap, scratched at scabs.

The Army has two kinds of officers. Commissioned officers run from lieutenant to general and were, back then, primarily white men with at least some college education or grooming at a military institute. The noncommissioned officers—NCOs in military jargon—rise through the ranks of the common soldier and include corporals and all varieties of sergeants.

Camp Wolters had black drill sergeants who were supervised by white training officers. The Army's qualifications for the other sergeants and corporals obviously were measured in brawn and lack of brains. The bigger, nastier, and dumber they were, the more stripes they wore. I managed to stay clear of them. Other soldiers didn't.

One afternoon, I stumbled upon a fight near the latrines. Lured by the sound of a familiar voice, I skirted the building. The dominant combatant indeed was familiar. It was Eli Brooks, the same angry, unhappy Eli Brooks who had tangled with the staff at Father Flanagan's Boys Home in Omaha, Nebraska, where I had spent a couple of years. Here Eli was besting one of the sergeants. Since it was a gambling disagreement, the sergeant couldn't haul him to the brig. All the sergeant could do was fight.

Eli had drifted to Ohio after Boys Home and landed work in the steel mills in Youngstown. He and a bunch of other men from the steel works had been drafted. Eli brought his two best skills to the Army—fist fighting and playing craps. He excelled at both. But he went after a man over a ten- or fifteen-cent dispute. The violence was terrifying. The example helped quiet my temper.

Gambling was strictly against Army policy, so craps was played in the latrines. Men walked out of the buildings counting wads of cash. That appeared a profitable venture to a Wyoming boy like me. I took my first month's pay—thirteen dollars—for a turn at the toilet-side table. As a newcomer to gambling, I didn't expect to win the moon. But doubling my money should be simple, and I was already counting the ways I would spend it. Maybe Leola, the first woman to seriously command my heart, would come to her senses when she learned how easily I prospered.

I kept getting what I thought were the correct numbers when I rolled the dice. The men running the game assured me I was wrong, that I had to roll again, or that I needed a different combination of the dice in order to collect. I spent less than ten minutes with my money.

I never shot craps again. Instead, I gave extra attention to the things the Army intended for me to learn. On the official training field, meanwhile, bulldog-faced drill sergeants taught me infantry tactics and how to shoot mortars and machine guns. Firing mortar rounds cost me part of the hearing in my right ear, something I didn't realize until I was well into combat.

I studied my field manuals, stayed clear of Eli's gang, and stayed out of Mineral Wells all together. Taking the advice of the old man from the bus to heart, I went to Fort Worth's black district when I was looking for entertainment.

In the old man's counsel, I figured my grandfather had spoken. I pondered it often and it saved me many a career-ending brawl. Or an early death.

TEN

The first few times you get nicked you take it for granted that you are naturally immortal. The next few times you begin to wonder. After that you start looking over your shoulder to make sure old Lady Luck is still around.

—Farley Mowat

October 1944, Seravezza, Italy

Blessed darkness descended slowly. Belk and I waited until its inkiest shades settled on the valley floor before dashing back across the bridge.

The command post had the feel of home sweet home. Our arrival was welcomed but wasn't a surprise. Montie had sent scouts back out to see if we appeared alive, and those scouts had predicted we wouldn't try to get back until well after dusk.

We each gulped water from one of a dozen offered canteens and tore into canned meat of some kind. Belk moaned about settling for a less than average supper, so I knew he was dealing with our ordeal fairly well.

Our respite was temporary. Battalion headquarters sent a runner to demand a progress report. Montie grimly told us we'd have to make another try. He and I talked strategy, and I dozed off for a couple of hours.

Somewhere between two o'clock and three o'clock a.m. we returned for an encore. Over the bridge, a short distance down a dirt road, and then onto the path that pursued the steep hillside. Darkness. Silence. No mortars or snipers. I led the way, stalking through the darkness the way my grandfather taught me to stalk elk. Slowly, quietly. Surprise is more valuable than speed. Grandpa reminded me of those words every morning in hunting camp. It always was his final instruction.

As the last twist of the path turned to the left, my men and I saw the house, a compact two-story stone affair with the usual clay tile roof, parked among a grove of olive trees. I grabbed platoon sergeant Jacy Cunigan. He and I would circle the house to the right, I instructed with hand signals. The other men should stay and cover the front and the left side of the house. All nodded. Cunigan and I padded carefully over the face of the hill, willing ourselves invisible.

I'm not certain whether I saw or heard the German sentry first. He shouted something and shot at us. I belly flopped, assumed the classic prone firing position, and let loose. The German shot back, probably figuring my whereabouts from the flash of my muzzle. Something slapped my wrist. I ignored it and kept firing. He eventually quit shooting.

A machine gun had opened up on the opposite side of the house, back near the men we left on the path.

"You OK?" I hoarsely whispered to Cunigan, wondering whether he had dropped as a precaution or was struck down by bullets.

"Fine," he said.

"Let's go for the back," I ordered.

We came to our feet, charged around the house, and threw ourselves against the back door, our guns blazing again when we finally smashed through. Every room received a coat of lead. Five sleepy Germans went to their permanent rest. We knew we were incredibly fortunate the firefight outside hadn't roused them more rapidly.

The rest of the platoon exchanged fire with the machine gunners until they killed the two Germans manning it. Unfortunately, not before two more of my men died.

The machine gun nest was slyly poised to take out anyone approaching the house from the path. It had killed Lieutenant Frazier and at least three of his men. Then it killed my men. Telling my men to stay on that path was my lethal stupidity.

A messenger went to deliver the news of our success to Montie. The rest of us searched for survivors from Frazier's assault but found only three dead men.

I left a handful of our soldiers to keep the house from returning to German hands and plodded back down the hill. A gruesome win, if you could call losing so many soldiers for a lousy house a win.

Montie met us as we neared the canal and told me to head for a stone warehouse, where he wanted the company to regroup. He hadn't really checked the building, he said, but it appeared safe enough.

The city-block-sized warehouse was built of substantial stone walls and, from the outside, appeared a worthy refuge from any unwanted attention our assault had drawn. I walked in and paced along the inside walls, partly out of curiosity, partly to work off stress. As my eyes adjusted, I was mortified. Shells, taller and wider than me, the sort I expected to fit the guns of a battleship, lined the walls of the building and were wired together like sticks of dynamite. This was a giant booby trap for whatever American troops made it to the east edge of Seravezza. The wires leading out of the warehouse soon told us that the detonator was in the house we had just taken, logical since it had the best perspective on the neighborhood. I was both afraid, because of the what ifs, and relieved at our narrow miss.

I walked back out, found Montie, and stammered out, "We've . . . we've got to get out of here. This place is full of big naval shells, all wired to go."

Montie allowed an uncharacteristic flash of fear to cross his face, then nodded, and gestured toward the command post. That was our only alternative.

I sat down in the command post, rolled my head against the wall, closed my eyes, and tried to relax, to work out why I had blundered and told my platoon to stand on that damn path. Cunigan gratingly interrupted.

"You're wounded," he insisted.

"Impossible," I retorted irritably, tired, and not in any pain.

He turned to Montie and said, "Look at him, he's hit."

Montie rose and trotted over to us. "Where?" he demanded, not meaning to sound as concerned as he was.

Cunigan pointed to my right forearm. I looked down. My hand was full of blood. My pants were covered from the waist down.

"Get out of here. Get to the aid station," Montie said abruptly, nearly shouting.

I struggled to my feet, dizzier than I expected to be considering I felt fine until Cunigan told me I wasn't. He helped me walk the two blocks or so to the aid station. Captain Gill, the battalion medical officer, invited me to sit down for a quick examination.

I passed out.

ELEVEN

Great loves too must be endured.

—Coco Chanel

October 1944, Pisa, Italy

I awoke staring into the deep brown eyes of a pretty Italian girl who was asking me if I wanted a cigarette. I wanted to oblige her infectious smile, but even her charm couldn't overcome the lasting effects of Grandfather's smoking cure. Instead, I tried to return her smile and shook my head.

"Don't smoke," I said and attempted to point to myself with my right arm. I realized it was tightly bound in layers of gauze, and I was on a stretcher in a strange building. A line of other stretchers marched both directions along a brightly lit corridor. Bloody bandages clung to the arms, heads, and legs of the men I could see. Official looking people were rushing up and down the noisy corridor, stopping at a stretcher here, calling for action there, or just moving through.

The sweet nurse's aide gestured for me to remain still, using one hand to pull errant wisps of her long dark hair behind her fine-boned head and using the other to nudge my shoulder back to the stretcher. This was the 64th General Hospital, she explained, near Pisa. I probably didn't remember getting here, having lost too much blood and then losing consciousness, she added.

Once assured I was stable, she stood, gave me a polite wave and a warm smile, and moved to another stretcher. I lay there contemplating the infernal brightness of the hospital lights, which both kept me awake and inflicted a headache on top of my existing pain.

Those eyes; that smile. The nurse's aide had Leola's eyes and Helen's smile. My demons were visiting.

Leola Sessler sashayed in front of my periscope that last spring I was in Cheyenne. James Horn and I spotted her in the club her sister Millie ran down on Nineteenth Street for the black soldiers from Fort Warren. We were looking for girls, our primary occupation since we'd first started working as chair-car porters for the Union Pacific. James still worked there. I'd quit within months of Grandpa's death.

"Lookie there," I told James.

"Lookie away," he replied. "That there is C.J.'s girl, and if you plan on keeping all of you in one piece you won't cross him. And, she ain't eighteen yet and you're what, twenty-one?"

"C.J.?"

"Forget it. He'll show soon enough."

Nobody bothered to check for underage drinkers in colored clubs in Cheyenne, Wyoming. Leola languished at the bar, talking to her sister and coquettishly peering around the room to see whose eye she could catch. Our eyes connected several times. I felt wonderful.

C.J.'s appearance on the scene didn't change her behavior much, although she frequently ran the point of a painted fingernail over the top of his ear and down his neckline, as if automatically reassuring him that she was only casting harmlessly, with no intention of hooking anyone else.

"You looking for trouble," James warned.

"I'm looking for a lady," I replied. "I figure I'm as much man as C.J."

James snorted.

I made it my mission to run into Leola often, which wasn't difficult considering I was working odd jobs and could easily be happening by the club most any time. Millie was kind enough to introduce us.

Leola readily accepted my offers to buy her drinks, although she giggled at my reluctance to share her love of alcohol. She was downright scornful of my employment status. Only a man of means would have her heart, she said.

That worked for me. I wanted to be a man of means.

"Try Fort Warren," Leola suggested. "All kinda work out there."

My desperation to get a decent job filled me with illusions of strapping on a carpenter's apron and helping build barracks from concrete floor to peaked roof. The reality was much different. Beginners such as myself went on the night shift—eleven o'clock p.m. to eight o'clock a.m. We'd file through the gate at the fort reserved specifically for construction hands and gathered around a podium where a sawed-off, snarly-faced white guy assigned men to different crews each night. He kept the stub of a cigar rolling around in one corner of his mouth, pulling it out occasionally to spit into the dirt and shavings at his feet and to wipe the tobacco juice from his bottom lip with a broad thumb.

This superintendent always sent the white guys to play carpenter, raising walls here, framing over there. When they were all dispatched, he shifted his papers from one hand to the other, took time for a spit, and cleared his throat.

"All right, now ah . . . all right. Hear this. The men I'm a gonna call will git on over to the nigger barracks and git all ah the lumber pieces laying around," he said. "Ya'all don't forgit to also clean up them sawdust piles, neither."

Invariably all of the blacks on the construction crew went to the "nigger barracks" and spent the next nine hours making stacks of scrap two-by-fours or sweeping up sawdust and dumping it into drums converted into garbage cans. All night long.

After a week of listening to that cigar-chomping superintendent call it the "nigger barracks" I quit. The superintendent was mean and frightening. And by the time I slept and ate and felt ready to go back to work, there was no time for Leola.

Leola, meanwhile, took off for Denver, where her mother lived.

"Oh, this ain't her home," Millie explained. "She's just restless and comes for visits. She hates school."

I dejectedly puttered with odd jobs, unloading trucks for grocers, cleaning a vacant building or two, and the like. I wanted to go to Denver and find Leola. She stirred something in me no woman ever had. It was time to profess my feelings before she was swept away by another man.

James and I had the old Hudson Super Six we'd bought together when I was railroading. I could drive to Denver in a couple of hours but money was a problem. After paying Cass rent and helping with the groceries, I had nothing for gas. In fact, I was behind with Cass because of my intermittent employment.

I ran into Carl Green at Millie's club and hit him up for a loan. He was still working at the fort. I knew he had cash.

"What for?" he inquired.

"Got to go to Denver," I said. "Gotta see a girl."

"Ooo-eee," Carl retorted. "Love saw you comin' and is takin' you for a ride."

I'm sure I blushed.

"Leola's pretty nice," I said. "Gotta go see her."

"Sorry," Carl said. "I'm outa money. Let's ask Overtron. The man's always got somethin'."

Junius Overtron came in response to Carl's wave. He was younger, and since I hadn't gone to school in Cheyenne since grade school wasn't someone I knew. He had no spare cash but did have a typewriter we could pawn. As long as we repaid him. I promised solemnly.

We found Leola was sunning herself and applying new layers of finger polish on her mother's front porch, which was attached to one of downtown Denver's row houses.

"Why, Vernon, Carl, how sweet," she said when we pulled up. "I've been missing Cheyenne."

We went to a diner for lunch, and Carl, according to our prearranged plan, left us shortly after the end of the meal on a concocted shopping mission. His price included making sure I had him back in Cheyenne in time to make it to work that evening.

I poured my heart out to Leola, and she cooed.

"I'm only seventeen," she then explained, "grown-up and all, but my mamma won't let me come back to Cheyenne on my own."

"I'll marry you, Leola," I burst out with the impertinence of youth. "I love you."

I instantly felt foolish, and yet it felt so good, the thought of marrying Leola. There was C.J., to be sure, but I knew if she had the right amount of time with me she would love me more.

"Oh, Vernon. How? You have no job."

I left dejected, although Leola planted a sweet kiss on my lips when we dropped her at her house.

"Don't forget about your favorite Denver girl," she cried as we drove away.

A deputy sheriff's car waited outside Cass's house when I arrived. I leapt out, fearing that Henry, Cass's coarse, unhappy husband, had hurt her.

A deputy stepped out of the car.

"You Vernon Baker?" he asked.

"Yea, what's going on in there?" I said.

"Put your hands up," the deputy ordered.

"But I'm Vernon," I insisted, sure that he was looking for Henry.

"Up," he repeated. "This is about the Gem Coal Company and you."

I was booked into the Laramie County Jail and charged with burglary. A different deputy led me to a closet of a room. I sat in a chair, hands cuffed in front of me, and he paced and pulled on his upper lip. My downfall, he recited, was the typewriter I pawned. Obviously I'd stolen it from Gem Coal Company office on March 7.

My name and Carl Green's name were on the pawn ticket, so there was no question who the burglars were, the deputy continued. All that remained was locating the cash, stolen radios, and stolen tools. Carl, he assured me, already had confessed. I knew that was a lie.

"I didn't burglarize a damn thing," I declared. "I found that typewriter." I didn't want to get Junius in trouble.

"Found? Sure you found it. Where?"

I struggled for a plausible story. The deputy stopped me.

"Typewriter's not commonly found anywhere, boy, except in an office, like the office at the Gem Coal Company. Which is where you found it. Which is where you stole it."

Grandpa had been right. Truth is a whole lot less trouble in the long run. I attempted some recovery.

"I got it from Junius Overtron, but I didn't know it was stolen. I was looking for a loan, and he offered to let me pawn that typewriter if I'd pay him back whatever amount I got."

The deputy shot all of the obvious holes in the story and finally locked me up. I spent the next two weeks in a cell with Carl. Junius was locked up a few doors away.

Carl and I were freed, without explanation. Junius went to court and was sentenced to probation.

A very cross Cass greeted me at home.

"Sit," she ordered, pointing to the kitchen table. "Good thing Grandpa isn't alive, he'd probably take his belt off even if you are twenty-one. What's gotten into you, Vernon? Burglary?"

"I didn't break into anything, Cass," I protested. We argued and I explained. She only backed down when I convinced her I no longer was charged with anything.

"How about the Army, Vernon?" Cass said, pursing her lips between sips of coffee. Her making coffee was a sort of a peace offering.

"You think about joining the Army? I hear the Quartermaster Corps is easy. They keep the Army in supplies. They've got quartermaster here, at Fort Warren. You wouldn't have to go that far."

"What's this quartermaster all about, Cass?" I asked.

"I don't guess I know," she said, shoulders moving in a shrug, hands turning into a "beats me" gesture. "But I guess it's pretty nice as the Army goes."

I cogitated her suggestion as I wrapped my hands around my coffee cup to keep them warm in the blustery April chill.

"How do you sign onto the Army?" I asked.

"I think downtown. They have an office. I think you sign at the office."

At first I disregarded it. Then Leola returned and was seeing me instead of C.J., or so I thought. Our necking had led to the most incredible night on Millie's sofa, upstairs from the club. I had never been happier. The Army was a job, it was money, and it might be the thing to permanently win Leola.

I couldn't jump in alone. I caught James Horn coming off the Omaha-to-Cheyenne run. The Army should appeal to him a great deal more than continuing as a porter.

"You crazy, man? You are crazy. Something done came and stole the last little bit of common sense you had when you still worked the railroad," James said. "Crazy man. Think about the times we had and the times we could have. You and me, we could be finding ourselves another Red Top and Geneva. Quality ladies. None of the Leola shit. Oh, no. You don't want to find no ladies. You want to become a quartermaster so you can marry her. What's this quartermaster?"

I had better luck persuading Carl Green. He was tired of the way "nigger" was every third word from the foreman at the fort. We put on our best clothes and drove the Hudson to the recruiting depot. I was dreamy, thinking about the new car I would buy, my wedding, maybe a new house for Leola—all when I became a quartermaster. Real employment, a uniform, respect, and a family of my own making.

Gold-painted letters announced "United States Army Recruiting Depot" across a glass door in a brick building downtown that also housed attorneys, an insurance agent, and other offices. Carl and I pushed the door open and walked in. There were two desks, perpendicular to each other, in the small office. The walls were covered with recruiting posters that had the stern, imploring face of Uncle Sam declaring, "I Want You." A silver steam radiator belched from the back wall.

A burly man with a brush of closely cropped hair and a neck that bulged and retracted in rhythm to his breathing was camped behind the desk facing the door. He declined to acknowledge us for a few minutes, as if we might realize our mistake and leave.

Finally he looked up. "What do you want?" "You" emerged from his mouth as a long, drawn out "yew," and with enough spite to wilt cactus spines.

"Um, ah, me . . . I mean we, my friend and I, we want to join the United States Army," I said, trying to hold what little bit of temper hadn't disintegrated with the tone of his opening question.

He harrumphed. "We don't got no quotas for you people," he said. The "you" again came out as "yew." The sergeant turned his face back down toward his desk and pretended to have a matter essential to the national defense to finish. Carl and I walked out.

"I'm sorry, Carl. I'm never going back to that damn place," I said after we closed the door.

"I went on my own," Carl said. "You weren't the asshole. But I ain't going back neither."

Cass tried to calm me when I arrived home livid. "People are like that Vernon, people are like that. Maybe give it a little while and try it again."

"Try what? Hanging a sign around my neck, 'Too stupid to hear no'? I'll starve to death first."

"Well, in fact you won't starve, Vernon. Henry and I will take care of you when we can. But we don't have much, and you can't keep saying no. You've about had a go at everything in this town, and you don't like sittin'."

Cass worked on me and worked on me. Unemployment worked on me. Leola worked on me. A month of sitting and the urge for eternal love persuaded me to try again. Neither Carl nor James would have any part of it.

"Told you, you were crazy last time you went in there," James said. "That asshole already told you the Army doesn't want people like us. You've been kicked once and so what are you going to do? Go back for more. I didn't want any of this the first time and I damn sure don't want any now. You could come back to the chair cars."

"I know, James," I said. "But I can't stomach any more of the railroad, I'm not going to shine shoes again, and there's not much else here for me. I'm going crazy. If the Army will take me, I'll have a decent job. People look up to a man in uniform. And Cass says the quartermasters do all right and I can stay right here in Cheyenne."

I swallowed a million times between parking the old Hudson and walking back in the recruiting station. I thought about all of my alternatives, as I had hundreds of times before, and still came up with nothing else. Cass was right. This was the best option.

I gingerly eased open the door at the recruiting office, as if a tidal wave of the sergeant's bitterness might rush out and sweep me away. His desk was empty. The other desk held an older, more relaxed man, who also was a sergeant. He rose and walked toward me.

"Can I help you?" he asked.

I swallowed a few more times. "Ah, sir, I want to join the Army. The ah, United States Army." I relaxed my knees so I could turn quickly and hustle back out the door when he blasted me with "no quotas for you people."

"Fine," he said. "Please sit down here by my desk."

"A . . . pardon?" I said, sure he'd told me "please get the hell out of my office."

"Fine, son. Take this chair here, and we'll see what we can do."

He sat at his desk, pulled open a drawer, fished out a sheaf of forms, and arranged them between us. Name? Age? Address? Parent or guardian? The questions clicked off.

"OK, what duty do you want? What branch were you thinking of?" he asked.

Cass's stories of the Quartermaster Corps sailed to the fore. "Quartermaster, please."

I peered over the desk as he wrote, "Infantry." I didn't protest. I was in.

Leola and I were married June 25, 1941, the day before I left for the Army. Cass and Henry gave us a night at a Cheyenne motel, so we could feel like we'd gone somewhere for a honeymoon.

Leola pulled me in tight, one last time, on the train platform.

"You get me on the wives' allotment, you hear?" Leola said, running a suggestive finger along my neck, the way she had run it along C.J.'s.

I nodded, light-headed with love. We waved as the train pulled out.

I never saw or heard from Leola again.

There was a letter waiting from Cass at Camp Wolters. Leola had moved back in with C.J. the day I'd departed.

TWELVE

What is life but a series of inspired follies?

—George Bernard Shaw

October 1944, Pisa, Italy

One of the German sentry's shots had hit me in the wrist. An American nurse, more severe and businesslike than the Italian aide, delivered this news without emotion. A surgeon would have to inspect the damage, she added.

After an immeasurable amount of time in the corridor, I was moved to an operating table. X-rays, probing, and poking revealed that the bone was broken and needed a pin. A major, who was a bone specialist, did the repair.

I awoke from surgery in a segregated ward, staffed by white American doctors and nurses. All of the nurse's aides were Italian women and all of them lovely.

Our ward had twenty-five beds stuffed into a room at the outside end of a rambling one-story stone building. You had to walk through three whites-only wards to get to ours. My bed was near the entrance. Because there were no doors in the hospital, I passed a fair amount of time watching the white ward next door. I couldn't see much difference in treatment, except that white soldiers dated white nurses and black soldiers couldn't so much as walk down a street where a white nurse lived.

Soldiers in all the wards lay on ooze-discolored sheets, the result of leaving wounds open to drain. The smell wasn't sickly sweet. It wasn't putrid. It wasn't rotting. It was all of those.

My arm hung in a sling, all too close to my nose, for two months. It gave off the same foul odor as the other soldiers' wounds, and my heavy plaster cast was always damp. Nurses came around daily to drain my wound, using the opening in the cast near my wrist. It was simply gagging. Real fortitude is eating your supper in a hospital that smells like a hot summer day in an unventilated mortuary.

I improved steadily despite the olfactory impediments. In time, I learned I was scheduled for physical therapy. I imagined that meant daily instruction from one of the sweet Italian nurse's aides. It was nothing more than a white nurse coming by to help me sit up.

When I could get out of bed, I walked the corridors and watched the flurry in the operating rooms. On one of those outings, I leaned against the doorway for the better part of an hour and watched a bone specialist knit a soldier's thigh bone back together. I considered my wrist and wondered if it was the same specialist who worked on me.

Fate had Lieutenant Hansen and his broken ankle homesteading in the bed next to mine. When I had come to after my surgery and groggily looked around the room, his laughing face was the first thing I saw.

"Hey, Bake," he said with a rueful grin. "You fall off the stairs and break your wrist?"

I had to lie there and take it.

Hansen also was kind and, because I couldn't use my arm to write, took dictation for my letters home. He was a big, handsome man with an identical twin brother who also was an officer in the 92nd Infantry. After I left the hospital, his brother was wounded, and later died on the operating table. Word was Lieutenant Hansen took it hard, that a single bullet essentially killed both of them.

Joe West, the second lieutenant from my battalion who had teased me to no end after telling me the difference between snow-capped peaks and marble quarries, also was recuperating in our ward. He had been badly shredded by shrapnel a few weeks earlier and was nearly mummified in bandages. He recovered steadily, shedding his shroud a limb at a time, but remained in the hospital long after I left.

If we ignored the smells and the boredom, hospital life was passable. The food was good, especially considering what we consumed in the field.

Joe kept us entertained with his guitar as he regained his strength. I marveled at his ability to get the instrument from his last camp to the hospital. He never answered when I raised the question but kept strumming old-time gospel and Mississippi Delta blues, a bandaged leg propped up in front of him. It's the only religious music I ever liked.

When I was well enough to get a day pass, Joe loaned me his Argus C-3—a top-notch 35mm camera for the time—and asked me to get him a picture of the leaning tower of Pisa.

"Don't know if I'll be out of this place before the fool thing falls on over," Joe said melodically, playing his guitar as he told me where to find his camera and how to use it. "Bring me a nice picture, something to show I was here."

I recorded the leaning tower, the basilica, the carved animal heads springing from high on the basilica walls, and the bas-relief artwork in the building's doors. It was the most enjoyable day during my hospital stay and prompted me to liberate a camera, a Leica, from a German *Oberleutnant* we captured on patrol.

After two months in the hospital my wound quit stinking. Doctors inspected me and pronounced me ready for combat. I packed my Purple Heart and gladly departed. I was sick of the boredom, the smell, the atmosphere of the hospital. And the dormitory setting and the bunks reminded me too much of Boys Home.

It had started with Grandma.

"Slap him," she snapped, with her mouth screwed up in a bitter twist. She was speaking to my grandfather and pointing at me.

Other nights, she called "Joe" in her high-pitched voice the moment she heard Grandfather's heavy steps carry him through the front door from work, summoning him to their bedroom for a conference. I knew the discussion had ended when I heard his quiet voice call, "Come here, Vernon."

I always went. More and more often, I rounded the hallway corner to see Grandfather standing by the doorway of his and Grandma's room, pulling off his belt. It wasn't abuse. I deserved every lick.

By age eleven, I had turned unsettled and unruly, as much a pain for my family as Grandmother's arthritis. Chores held no interest for me. I came home later and later at night. The problems compounded from there. Grandma's twenty years of sitting in a wheelchair, around-the-clock agony, and other ailments were catching her like a coyote chasing a newborn lamb. Her patience ebbed as her discomfort grew.

"Damned little hellion," was the best she could say about me. The cursing became more foul as I became more disobedient. But she was too sick to control me.

Her wrath had always repelled me. Adolescence gave me courage to do something about it. Instead of coming home from school to face her mean mouth and my chores, I started running with boys with well-known reputations. One of them scouted out an abandoned garage in the neighborhood on the other side of the railroad tracks and made the deteriorating building into our clubhouse. It was our territory, a refuge for complaining caustically, boasting badly, and poring excitedly over the odd girlie pictures one of the gang managed to swipe from a drunken father.

I was the odd man out, not so much because I was the sole black in the crowd, but because I was the youngest. In retrospect, I think I was nothing more than a rapt, admiring audience for these swaggering braggarts. I mistook their false bravado for confidence, the confidence not to take any grief from people. After years of Grandma's rigid hand and verbal abuse, I was ready for rebellion. But the shine went off hanging out with this crowd when the talk turned from harmless pranks to serious crime.

"Thinkin' 'bout old lady Stanley's house," one of them said as we were sitting around the dirt-floored garage, parking ourselves on old tires, a barrel, and some decrepit piece of iron of no discernable use. "We could get in there so easy when she's off to town, have us some fun. Rich bitch. She won't never figure who jiggered her place."

"She's gone all the time, Saturday night," another boy added. "Some hoity-toity card club or something. Easy. I'm telling you guys, easy."

They laid plans to swipe liquor, or tobacco, or both. Most of these lads smoked and encouraged me to do the same. As willing as I was to defy my family I could not overcome the nausea that touched me at the mere hint of tobacco. Grandfather knew his smoking aversion program.

The talk expanded in the charged atmosphere of teenage hormones to robbing downtown banks, with discussion of details such as who would go for the guard and how we would accomplish the getaway. Filling stations were an easier target yet, they agreed.

"How about you, Baker? You in?" they always asked when their grand plans were worn thin from nonstop talk and from the boys outdoing each other with ever more preposterous proclamations of, "You know what I'd do." They'd crush out burning cigarettes between their thumb and forefinger with macho abandon, showing the toughness I could hope to achieve—if I dared. I didn't answer for as long as I could, hoping their urge to brag would bury my silence unnoticed. Ridicule hissed from their lips if I objected or tried to point out the pitfalls.

My older sisters tried bullying, then counseling, and then bullying to straighten me out. The angrier I made Grandma, the more Grandma cursed my sisters as well as me. I stubbornly refused to change.

Grandpa was tired of drawing his belt. He knew stroking my backside with leather placated Grandmother but didn't dissuade me. I learned to start yelling at a certain point in the whipping to convince my grandparents I had been punished into contrition. I'm sure Grandpa figured out my strategy.

The longer days of summer, after fifth grade finished, broadened the opportunities to get in trouble. My gang started vandalizing homes and loitering downtown without me. They then recounted their grand exploits with taunting dare in their voices. Kids didn't go to jail in those days. The police pulled you into the station, scared the hell out of you, and took you home to your parents. That germinated into serious worry. I figured if a policeman hauled me onto the front steps of the boarding house I would learn a whole new, ugly side of Grandpa.

Grandpa always taught respect, for other people and for their property. His delivery was more by example than by words. The message, however, was infinitely clear. I was conscious of that message when the gang talked of their big outings. It added to the feeling that I was at loggerheads with everyone. I didn't like anyone's company. I was in a panic.

Shep and I went for solitary walks, kicking the lenses of gray shale that lined the gullies. I stalked jack rabbits just to stalk, stared at the blue-mountained horizon as clouds wafted up and down the slopes. These outings helped me arrive at a solution. Run away.

It started as no more than the bravado I apprenticed to with the garage gang and strengthened as Grandma became sicker and the tension at home intensified.

Run away.

By Fourth of July, I had firmly decided it solved all woes. It eased Grandfather's distress, Grandmother's pain, and gave me an escape from the jam of having friends whom I neither wanted to disappoint nor to join. I made for downtown and the annual Fourth of July festivities, thinking the holiday commotion might provide the right cover for my departure.

A band with a big bass drum advertising Father Flanagan's Boys Home marched in the parade. There, in the center of the brass section, was a medium-size black kid playing trumpet. He was the only black in the band. Music captivated me in ways trouble couldn't hope to. I followed the band as it marched to the railroad station. When it broke into relaxed ranks on the station platform, I walked up to the black boy.

"That a trumpet?" I inquired.

"Yes sir, it's a Conn. Not real pearl on the keys, but still pretty to hold, pretty to play," the boy replied. "Smooth as silk."

He demonstrated, with a flick of his fingers, how easily the trio of plungers on the top of the horn could be pushed down, and the vigor with which they sprang back. Then he turned his head and the horn to the side of the platform, opened the spit valves, and blew a long stream out into the dirt, with as professional an air as he could give the disgusting task.

"How'd you get it?" I asked. I wanted to reach out and touch the brassy golden instrument and simultaneously didn't want to leave a fingerprint on the mirror finish.

His shoulders straightened and his eyes took a new shine. "I'm a member of the Boys Home Marching Band. It's theirs but I get to play it," he replied.

"Boys Home?"

"Father Flanagan's Boys Home. In Oh-me-ha, Nebraska. That's where I live."

"What's a Boys Home?" I queried.

"Not a Boys Home, this is *the* Boys Home. Father Flanagan's Boys Home. It's for orphans. Me and my brother, we're from Douglas, Wyoming, up the road. But we're orphans. We don't have any parents."

He stopped, looked at me, wiped a hand on his trousers, and offered it to me. "Albert J. Kercheval," he said. "And you're?"

"Vernon J. Baker," I replied, careful to put extra emphasis on my middle initial so he would catch the similarity.

Albert J. Kercheval talked on. I told him I wanted to learn to be a drummer. He grabbed hold of that as if he was in charge of selling me on Boys Home. It didn't take much. I'd found my ticket to learning to be a musician.

I darn near ran into Grandfather as I rushed off the platform to tell him of my discovery. He was standing watching the crowd, and likely me, out of worry over whatever shenanigan I was on the verge of initiating.

I spoke hurriedly and excitedly about the benefits of Boys Home, repeating Albert's pitch as if I was a veteran of the orphanage. Grandfather listened patiently. What I wasn't saying, and what we both knew, is that I viewed this as the perfect solution to the jam I'd created with my attitude and my friends.

"Can I go? Can I go?" I pleaded.

"We'll talk about it," he said, his face, as usual, showing nothing. He gazed at me for a moment, put a hand on my shoulder, and then ambled off into the crowd. In a moment I noticed him talking to an older man who was mixed in among the members of the band. When he finished the conversation, he shook the man's hand and walked back to me. We walked home together in silence. I didn't nag. I knew Grandpa would speak when he was ready.

A few days later, he lingered with his hand on my shoulder after waking me for my morning chores. His chest drew in deeply, his lips pursed, and, after a moment, he exhaled with sadness and exasperation.

"OK, boy, you'll go," he said. He watched me a moment longer, released my shoulder, and quickly left my bedroom.

Two weeks later, Grandpa walked me to the railroad station, handed me one of the passes he was allowed as a Union Pacific employee, and accompanied me into a passenger car. He sat me in a station-side window seat—I think so he could see me pull out—and reminded me of the details. Uncle Than knew I was coming, would meet me in Omaha, and take me to Boys Home. Grandpa had arranged to pay my expenses, a point of pride for both of us. It meant I wasn't an orphan.

He patted my shoulder—Grandfather never hugged anybody—offered me a handshake and said, "You can come back here anytime, boy."

Grandpa walked slowly out of the car, climbed to the station platform and leaned against one of the pillars. He adjusted his hat and squinted as if inspecting an important part of the train. When we pulled out, he waved briefly.

I watched the summer prairie roll past, drifting in and out of contact with where I was, thinking about the reaction of the gang when they learned where I'd gone. I was relieved. I wouldn't miss their taunts and their dares.

I was sad, however, for lost afternoons on the prairie with Shep and hunting excursions with Grandpa. Cass wouldn't be at Boys Home to give comfort, advice, and encouragement. I tried to take solace in the prospect of playing in a band.

Father Flanagan's Boys Home appeared as a collection of brick buildings and a farm, ten miles west of Omaha, on the highest point in the colossal corn patch known as eastern Nebraska. A dirt track led from Route 6 to a tall gateway where Uncle Than idled for a moment, and I read signs.

Brick pillars held a huge slab of wood announcing the place. A smaller sign, also capping the entryway, said, "Visitors Always Welcome." The left pillar advertised, "Boys of Today, Men of Tomorrow." The right pillar carried a similar wooden plaque that promised, "All Races, All Creeds, All Colors."

An older four-story brick building with neat dormers was the center of the operation. Four dormitory rooms, that each slept one hundred boys on long rows of white iron cots, occupied the top two floors. Each cot was covered with its own handmade quilt.

The classrooms were on the second floor, and the administrative offices—the wheelhouse as I called it—filled the ground floor. The dining hall inhabited the basement.

Five men shared duty as dormitory guards and counselors at night and grounds keepers and handymen during the day. Nuns in flowing black habits taught the classes and lived in a new brick building a short distance up Route 6. I never met more serious teachers or more serious disciplinarians. They grabbed my ear so often that one lobe is longer than the other. They also taught me I could learn, if I tried.

A new gymnasium and swimming pool stood not far from the dormitory in a sprawling three-story brick building. Below the hill there were gardens, cows, a few sheep, a big red barn, and an immense tin-colored silo. Boys who dreamed of being farmers spent their spare minutes there.

Seeing the band play and hearing Albert talk had generated a fantasy the actual place couldn't match. Father Flanagan firmly opposed idleness. There were rules, schedules, chores, and rigid expectations that made my grandmother seem downright derelict. Strangers surrounded me, strange country surrounded me. Instantly, I was miserable. I couldn't gather Shep and walk out my troubles on the prairie, find Cass and ask her advice, or go share in the adventures of the garage gang. I dealt with it the way I'd dealt with most of my conflicts—by turning inward.

I took solitary walks and discovered a good view of the Omaha lights behind the gymnasium. I stood there thinking about Grandpa, about walking the coulees and catching horny toads, about Saturday movies and finding Western magazines in garbage cans. My tears rolled.

A tall man in black, wearing round wire-frame glasses and a clerical collar, materialized at my side. His kindly face was unfamiliar, but it seemed a cinch that I hadn't met all of the staff yet. He put an arm around my shoulder and asked what was wrong.

"Gotta go home," I sniffled. "Gotta go see Grandpa, Cass, and Shep."

The lanky priest let me go on until I worked myself from crying to only chest heaving and the occasional gasp for air. His hand gently rocked my shoulder.

"You know, son, maybe what you need is to make some friends," he said. "Why don't you try that? Why don't you go on and make some friends?"

The priest turned me toward the dorm. I shuffled off, wiping my nose and face with my sleeve, wondering how he knew what I needed. That was my only direct encounter with Father Flanagan. The famed founder of Boys Home knew that spot attracted unhappy boys, and he walked by there every night. Perhaps he had kept his distance the other nights because I hadn't been crying. Perhaps I'd just missed his rounds.

I took his advice about making friends. Albert and I became close companions. As if followed by Lloyd Hammond's spirit, I befriended a group of smaller kids who were the subject of ridicule and torment from bigger boys. Same bullies, just a different place. Lloyd's situation had taught me an important lesson about bullies. I didn't have to whip every one of them to keep them at a distance. Just making them think I was crazy enough to take on all of them at once gave them pause. I also had learned that if I gave them an opportunity to gracefully back away, they generally did.

I joined almost every sport Boys Home offered, because Albert played and because I wanted to stick with him. Grandpa, meanwhile, developed a yen for baseball as the Negro Baseball League and the Kansas City Monarchs built momentum. Knowing there were sports in Boys Home, he sent me a brand-new catcher's mitt—an expensive gift in those days. I didn't care for baseball, and, as intoxicating as the smell of new glove leather was, it didn't overpower my dislike for the game. Yet, I owed Grandpa something. I tried to learn to use the mitt, and still didn't like baseball. After a few days I traded the stiff new mitt for a cigar box of marbles. Deluxe marbles. Smoothies and fish eyes, reds, blues, greens, yellows, stripes, and solids. The box had a Fort-Knox heft to it.

Grandpa met me at the railroad station when I arrived for my Christmas visit, half expecting, I think, to see me step out of the train with a bat slung over my shoulder and my mitt dangling off the end.

"Where's your mitt?" he asked. I imagined, for a moment, that his hands were ready to work the glove, pound it, to show me how his favorite player might field a foul ball or move to nab a low inside curve.

I gulped and considered a lie. Common sense rang in. No, I told myself. Grandpa will know a lie.

"Grandpa, I . . . I traded it. Traded it for a box of marbles. Really great ones. You gotta see 'em."

I held out the brown wooden cigar box I carried from Omaha on my lap. He pulled back the lid and ran a discerning finger through the collection. He shut the box, handed it back to me, and never said another word about baseball or marbles. I knew I had broken his heart.

Music was the magic of that prairie orphanage. I joined the Boys Home band as soon as I could. The band master warmed to me and honored my wish to learn the drums. He rapidly included me in band performances, and I felt a pride that before only Grandpa could instill. And the band master stuck up for me. Once, after the band played in an Omaha parade, we sought out a restaurant for the treat of a nondormitory meal. We filed inside and then left again, at the band master's urging, before we could even sit down or the waitresses could utter a word about the blue-plate specials.

This unfolded in a bewildering whirlwind. Albert explained later, whispering from his steel-frame bunk to mine. The owner of the restaurant had seen us and told the band master he wasn't going to serve "any Negro boys." The band master promptly ordered us out of the restaurant, saying we'd eat only in a cafe where everyone could eat.

This was the first blatant racism I remember. I cast it aside. In Omaha as in Cheyenne, my rule was if they didn't want me in a place, I didn't want to be there.

We all were fascinated by the tall, gangly band master. The band room was in the southeast corner of the same building that held the gymnasium and swimming pool. On a warm day, when the windows were open, we could hear the band master's violin. We snuck to the window and watched him stroke the violin and feverishly pace the room. It was soul stirring.

Not all of the men at Boys Home were so splendid. Especially Pat Norton, the squarish Irishman with a bald pate, sharp nose, thin mouth, and mean looking eyes who was in charge of the dormitory guards.

We boys ate family-style at long wooden tables with wooden chairs, while Norton and the other men were on a platform at the front of the room, strung out along one side of their table as if guests at a banquet. I clowned, made faces, and made noise like many of the other energetic young lads. Norton singled me out as his whipping boy.

Every day of my Boys Home stay Norton leaned forward, cleared his throat, and yelled, "Baker, come here now, lad."

As I neared his chair he grabbed me by the arm, pulled me close, and stuck his mouth to my ear.

"Baker, you black son-of-a-bitchin' nigger, what gets into you?" Norton would snarl. "Why can't you be quiet and sit still." He emphasized "still" by gripping my arm harder. When he was done, he shoved me away. No one else could hear the words and no one else had to. Everyone knew Norton was looking for reasons to make an example of blacks. I was short, and I imagine he mistook the respect Grandpa had taught me as a sign that I feared him. I only hated him.

Norton didn't dare give Eli Brooks the business. Eli, one of the boys from back East that I knew little about, advertised violence with every bit of his demeanor. His arms bulged at the biceps and were wrapped with prominent veins from there to his forearms, as if he lived for lifting barbells. His hands bore more scars than skin and he walked as if he were the living definition of tough, streetwise, and world-weary. He relied solely on his flashing temper for a moral compass, meaning his fists were always swinging. Eli threatened any counselor who rubbed him the wrong way.

Albert had warned me about Eli as soon as I arrived. I responded with a sizeable effort to stay clear of him and for that reason rarely witnessed his pounding fists. One morning, however, a cacophony of clashing furniture, clashing men, and cursing erupted before daylight. Curiosity drew me out of bed and to the door of the next sleeping room. Eli was slugging the newest counselor with intense ferocity and mechanized efficiency. It had started with the counselor dumping Eli out of his cot, we learned later. Nobody bothered to wake Eli after that.

The Boys Home staff decided there were other tasks more worthwhile than reforming Eli. They worked as earnestly to educate me in the ways of the Catholic Church as they did to make me follow curfew rules and grammar rules. I wasn't enthusiastic about their religious approaches. At the same time I knew compliance made a simpler life than fighting these forces. I enrolled in catechism.

After intense religious schooling, they set my confirmation date for Easter Sunday 1933. That Saturday one of the counselors came to find me in the gym where I was playing basketball with Albert. He called me to the sidelines.

"Clean up and get to the offices as soon as possible," he said. I complied, expecting some special discipline from Norton for sins yet-to-be-named. When I arrived, I found Great Uncle Than standing at the doorway of the main offices.

"Vernon, your grandmother's very sick," he said. "I'm taking you home. She wants to see you." I went upstairs for my little suitcase, packed my clothes, and went to Uncle Than's car.

Two weeks later, sitting in the same wheelchair she sat in for twenty-two years, Grandma died at our boarding house on West Eighteenth Street. We buried her near my parents. I returned to Boys Home to finish the eighth grade.

Initially, letters in Grandfather's irregular hand kept me apprised of my family's welfare. Suddenly the handwriting changed to something more cursive and flowing. The new author introduced herself as Susie. Susie announced she was looking after Grandfather, Irma, and Cass, "Now that your grandmother has passed on."

I didn't make much of it at first. Irma and Cass had taken care of my grandmother and hundreds of boarders. I doubted they needed anybody taking care of them.

The tone of the letters slowly shifted, first to tell me Irma, who was fifteen, had run off and gotten married. Susie sounded alarmed, but it didn't resonate with me. Irma could take care of herself. Soon the letters started talking about the trouble between Susie and Cass. Women, I thought, and worried for Cass.

Then the final letter arrived. "When you have completed your studies this term, you will be returning to Cheyenne for good," Susie wrote.

THIRTEEN

Black people are the only segment in American society that is defined by its weakest elements. Every other segment is defined by its highest achievement.

—Jewell Jackson McCabe

December 1944, Near Sommocolonia, Italy

I returned to the front the day after Christmas 1944 as an unwitting witness to one of the most heroic actions by a black officer during the entire war. An intense American artillery barrage was bulldozing the village of Sommocolonia, to the west of me. A German attack was driving our infantry out of the village. From my position, well above the hamlet, I could see our boys greeting the Germans with everything they had. The artillery pounded for hours. The rest of us scrambled to reinforce a defensive line in preparation for the rest of the German attack.

In less than twenty-four hours, we heard about First Lieutenant John Fox.

Fox volunteered to stay at his observation post, the second floor of a house on the edge of Sommocolonia, directing artillery fire to shield the American retreat. As the Germans drew nearer, Fox ordered the blistering barrages closer and closer to his post.

"That will put our shells right on top of you," his commander warned.

"That's just where I want it," Fox replied. "Bring it in sixty yards." His commander protested again.

"Fire it," Fox said emphatically. "There's more of them than there are of us."

The 598th Field Artillery Battalion adjusted their guns and delivered on Fox's coordinates. Fox's radio went silent.

When American troops recaptured the town, a day later, they found Fox's broken body in the remains of the house. And the bodies of the one hundred German soldiers he had taken with him. It took more than forty years for the Army to recognize Fox's courage with the Distinguished Service Cross, and fifty-two years until he received his much-deserved Medal of Honor.

When the hubbub over Fox's heroics quieted, our minds went back to how cold, wet, and snowy it was. Winter in the Italian mountains was hell if you lived in a foxhole, much more tolerable for those lucky enough to stay in a farmhouse. Many of my colleagues slept in wet, muddy foxholes, and, when they were under siege, bathed, brushed their teeth, and went to the bathroom in their helmets. After I returned from the hospital, I often was fortunate enough to be quartered with Italian families who generously moved into a barn or other outbuilding and turned their homes over to us. I always packed as much of my platoon inside as possible. What was good for the officers was good for the riflemen.

Although there were a number of strange faces, I felt lucky to return to any vestige of my old platoon. I wanted to be with the men I had slogged with, supped with, and fought beside. This didn't happen often, one of the mistakes made by the commanders of the 92nd. Taking a man out of the hospital and putting him with a strange platoon was hard on everyone. Camaraderie developed when you proved you would take every risk to keep your mates alive. Nothing is more critical to keeping morale high and men fighting when combat turns from an intellectual exercise of generals to the nasty work of soldiers on the ground.

I took heart in who I found milling around the courtyard of our platoon's stakeout. Dandy Belk was still creased and beaming and cooking up a storm since he'd learned not only to speak Italian but to bargain like an Italian.

"You gotta see what I'm doing with grub," Belk bragged. "You gotta have some of my specialty tonight. I'm cookin' in celebration of your return."

James Thomas, who should have been a weight lifter or a boxer, had gotten himself busted from sergeant back to private during my absence. It had to be the second or third occurrence since I'd known Thomas. We all figured he'd quiet his temper, impress the new company commander, and get his stripes right back—as he always did. Thomas was a hell of a soldier, but a little alcohol and a little anger robbed him of his self-control.

Sergeant Will Boswell was more weary around the eyes, as if they had absorbed all they could bear and more. He attempted a smile when I walked up and gave a solid, "Hey, lieutenant." The half smile faded quickly. I worried. Boswell was psychologically as solid as any soldier I had. If war and winter were getting to him, I feared the rest of the outfit was thoroughly unnerved.

Willie Dickens wasn't.

"Hey, it's Lieutenant Bake," he said, always jovially insolent enough to address an officer by his nickname. "We heard you were in charge of a platoon of nurses and not coming back."

"Well, sergeant, that many women is more trouble than you."

"You just needed a man with know-how," he returned. "Me."

Jacy Cunigan had survived, as had some of the rest of the original gang, including Minor Martin, John Robinson and Marv Finney. John T., as John Johnson was called, and Tom Robinson were the only faces I recognized among the rest of the riflemen. The strangers, the bulk of my company, were replacements. All were older men, many of them late arrivals to Italy, and none of them had tasted combat. Lieutenant Montjoy was gone—no one said where and the matter had a "don't ask" feel to it. I didn't ask.

Montie was replaced by Booker T. Matthews, a giant black man with two silver bars. Matthews was a preacher and one of the few black captains I encountered in Italy. He made me the company's executive officer.

It was an honor, I suppose, but mostly unwelcome. I was a fighter, not an administrator. And since I'd gotten beat up in Arizona early in my Army career, merely for going from private to sergeant, this made me uneasy.

The resentment had started the day I stepped off the train from Camp Wolters. I was made company clerk at Fort Huachuca, Arizona, within an hour because I could read, write, and type. Soon I was promoted to supply sergeant. My pay tripled to sixty dollars a month, and I moved out of the barracks to a room of my own. When the United States declared war on Japan, all NCOs received another promotion. Now I was a staff sergeant.

Men who had spent eighteen or twenty years as privates and corporals watched as younger men with high school educations were rapidly promoted past them. More than sixty percent of those old-time soldiers were illiterate. In their day, a man didn't move up unless somebody died or retired. I understood their resentment.

"So, Baker, you the smart nigger here?" a voice asked from the darkness.

Three burly shapes surrounded me as I walked past the barracks after a night at the Fort Huachuca movie theater. I moved closer to see who the questioner was. His hand shoved me stumbling back into the arms of one of the other men. The man who caught me sent me spinning back into the circle.

"Yeah, here we got us a real smart nigger. You think you smart don't you, Baker? You come in here, get you some stripes, and you shore look smart."

The three older corporals closed the circle, repeating their "smart nigger" chant, first shoving me back, and then throwing punches. One man delivered a blow to my stomach, then an upper-cut to my jaw. As my head whirled back, the man next to him side-swiped my chin with a rounder. Another roundhouse came from the other side. Then I lost track.

They left my bruised, pulpy body in a heap and walked away, laughing and complimenting each other. "Yeah, he look like one smart nigger now. He shore do."

I eventually crawled to the corner of the barracks, pulled myself up, and leaned against the building. Using the wall for support, I staggered, building to building, back to my quarters. The ground kept leaping up to grab me, and my knees and dizzy head tempted me to give in. Only the slowest movement, with several pauses, kept me from pitching onto my face.

Despite the looks I drew, I kept the beating to myself. Not that most people couldn't guess where I had come by my shiners. But reporting the incident amounted to an engraved invitation to another thrashing. Swallowed pride was preferable.

Within a few weeks, the cuts were dried scabs at worst and the bruises were fading. I relaxed a little, believing my run-in had escaped the top echelon—my most fervent hope. Then I received orders to report to Regimental Headquarters, the holy office.

The regimental commander stood eyeing me from behind his desk as I walked apprehensively into his office in the spring of 1942.

"Sergeant Baker?"

"Yes sir."

We traded salutes. He allowed me to stand at ease but didn't direct me to a chair. I braced for questions about my run-in with the corporals. My mind raced for a way to dodge the topic.

"Baker, you are applying for Officer Candidate School," the commander said.

Not the topic I feared, and yet anguish washed through me. OCS? No thanks. I had the best job in the Army. I had the sweet, soft job of a supply sergeant. Why would I trade the good life to wear some bars? And despite the benefits, sergeants' stripes had earned me all of the hatred I could stomach. Second lieutenant? Call for the ambulance.

If my face betrayed my misgivings, the colonel didn't pay any mind. He grabbed a handful of papers from the top of his desk, leaned over, and shoved them squarely into my chest.

"Everything on your application is complete and in order," he said. "All it needs is your signature."

The colonel pushed a pen in my hand. I set the papers on the edge of his desk, signed them, saluted, and bolted from the room. If the gods treated me right, a clerk would lose my application or it would be rejected. Neither stroke of fate intervened. The gods, however, did kindly see to it that the three corporals who jumped me didn't come overseas.

I didn't bother Captain Matthews with such details. He wanted a seasoned soldier of officer's rank to be his company executive, not a biography of my troubles.

We bunked in one of the numerous villages in the area, the name of which is long forgotten, and made our forays from here up into the hills. At least, attempted to. About a week after I returned to the company, Captain Matthews and I staked out a command post just outside the village, in a villa that had a sweeping view of battle lines. We anticipated some German shelling, but the house had solid Mediterranean masonry walls and was fairly safe.

The first sergeant woke me about four o'clock the next morning. "Mortars coming in, sir," he said. Once awake, I heard artillery shells whistling along behind the mortar rounds. They serenaded us until daybreak.

The hill behind the villa was black with German troops by daylight. Enemy soldiers worked their way down the slope behind the villa, by darting from tree to tree. Simultaneously, our platoon attempted to come up the road from the opposite direction.

We found ourselves badly outgunned. The superior view from the villa was our sole advantage. From here, we could at least provide covering fire for the men on the road. Although we exhausted most of our rifle and mortar rounds in the process, the rest of the platoon managed to make it to the command post. Together, we held the Germans off until dark.

When night returned, Captain Matthews ordered me to take a squad back into town and fetch the machine guns. Our platoons had abandoned the guns that morning in their haste to come to our rescue.

I asked Cunigan, Belk, Johnson, and four of the new faces to join me. The rest of the seasoned men needed to stay with the villa in case of another German attack. We ducked outside and ran for the ditch by the road. After a breather there, to listen for any indication we'd alarmed the Germans, we slunk down the ditchline toward the town.

The moonless sky was good luck, I decided, turning my mind from how odd it felt to be back in the thick of the shooting. Too much thinking would unnerve me; I would blunder and get this patrol killed. I focused on how my feet sounded in the brush and weeds and on ways I could take quieter steps.

The stone houses in the village were as silent as the sky was dark. Cunigan moved ahead of me to lead us to the house where they had left the guns. We skittered doorway to doorway, alternating sides of the street as we went. Cunigan finally found the right place and took us to the third floor.

Three machine guns and all of the associated gear is far too much for eight men. Ammunition belts had to be pulled out of their boxes and slung over our shoulders so we had enough hands to carry the guns and tripods. We pushed back to the mansion, moving like sedans loaded until the tires are scraping the wheelwells.

Even with the extra arms, however, we now only counted two dozen rifles, three machine guns, four mortar tubes and a paltry twenty mortar rounds to the Germans rifles, machine guns, grenade launchers, mortars, and artillery. We had a couple of hours of effective defense, at most.

The evening passed without reinforcements or new orders. The next morning, I slipped down to battalion headquarters to explain our dilemma. Pull back, our commanders said. As I returned to the villa with the news, the Germans initiated morning mortar call. Captain Matthews was standing at a window looking at the German position. A mortar round landed on the window sill, cleanly ripping one arm off right at the shoulder. The medics had him bandaged, on a stretcher, and coming out the front door as I pounded up the driveway.

I rushed to the stretcher. "You all right, captain?" I said.

He nodded, his pallid face a sure sign he was in shock. "Yes, I'm OK." He pointed to his bandages and added, "I'm sorry, Lieutenant Baker."

I touched his shoulder gently.

"How can you apologize?" I asked. "This is war."

FOURTEEN

*The Allies made many mistakes. They thought the
most important part of the front was the rest of the
front in Italy. They later realized it was here.*

—Giovanni Cipollini, Italian historian

Early 1945, Querceta, Italy

The front had changed during my hospital stay. We stopped trying to
get at the Germans by going north into the impossible mountains
near Seravezza. Instead, much of the 370th was shifted down to the
flats, around Querceta. From here we made forays into the foothills to
the east, or tried to go northwest—toward the feared Cinquale Canal.

A slender ribbon of water, the Cinquale Canal presented a formidable obstacle. The canal drained the otherwise marshy coastal
plain and connected the Versilia River and other canals to the sea.
For us, it was the reference point, the line of demarcation, the place
where we knew we would encounter Germans.

The north side of the canal sported German foxholes, dugouts,
and machine gun nests among the few remaining bushes and
bombed-out trees. Artillery exchanges had stripped, split, or flattened nearly every growing thing on both sides of the canal. The
remaining trees were scorched skeletons, startling to the eye.

Few buildings were left on this coastal plain. Immediately adjacent to the canal, the Germans had dynamited everything, including

much of the community of Forte dei Marmi, built by the Grand Dukes of Tuscany in the eighteenth century to control the coastal area. Some believe Cinquale drew its name from the five-sided castle built here as the American Revolution dawned. Others trace the origin to the five streams that once fed a nearby lake. In either case, the fortifications provided protection for the ship building community from Saracen pirates and were demolished by the marauding Germans in 1944. The Germans even blew away the buildings of a much newer fascist youth camp to clear the vistas for their gunners—something called "fields of fire" in military terms.

What the Germans didn't demolish with dynamite was razed by the famous guns of Punta Bianca. These 152mm cannons were named for the white rocky promontory that provided their anchorage. Two of the ten guns were pulled from the tower of a German naval cruiser and moved into an impervious tunnel. Four of unknown origin—perhaps salvaged from a battleship or custom crafted for this location—went into equally impenetrable concrete bunkers nearby. The other four sat on a bluff. All were protected by antiaircraft guns, barbed wire, machine gun nests, and mines.

This array of heavy cannons originally protected the port at La Spezia. When the German fleet departed, the giant guns turned south, toward us, and gained a reputation akin to the guns of Navarone.

Punta Bianca rapidly became an expletive. Every imaginable attempt to cripple the guns floundered. Allied bombers consistently failed. The guns of Punta Bianca had better range than our battleships, meaning the Navy could do nothing to help destroy them. Meanwhile, the Germans obliterated all but two or three of the tallest buildings in Viareggio, twenty miles to the south, and much of the territory in between—our territory. The gunners likely allowed the few tall buildings to remain because they needed a reference point.

It was dangerous to walk the coastal flats even at night. Punta Bianca's cannons were famous for "interdictory fire"—random barrages designed to prevent the Allies from using the cover of darkness for any serious effort. When we patrolled the area after dark, we often heard the distant Ba Ba Boom . . . Ba Ba Boom. Five or six seconds later, a shell, sounding like a freight train, roared in.

Even with all of this evidence of the German artillery's prowess, American commanders decided to build an observation bunker in the middle of the coastal flats, to keep a better eye on the Cinquale Canal. Crews stole out to the chosen site after dark over the course of several weeks, bracing themselves for a midnight clock-cleaning from Punta Bianca. The Germans waited silently.

Stones, timbers, and other gear were packed out to the building site by hand whenever possible, ostensibly to keep the Germans from detecting the construction. There was some attempt at camouflage, ridiculous considering there was no accounting for this massive lump of bushes and branches sprouting practically overnight in a farm field

The morning after the bunker was completed, the Germans christened it with a single artillery shell to the middle of the roof. The remainder of the building stood as a monument to stupidity, visible to all who passed within a half mile.

There were other such monuments along the Cinquale Canal. One was the last bridge over the canal just before it met the sea.

The 92nd Division's chief of staff—the man who gathered us at Fort Huachuca and told us it was time for black boys to go get killed—hopped in a jeep and had his driver take him out to survey damage to the bridge after the Germans put the powder to it. Machine guns cut him and his driver to pieces. It took us two days to recover their bodies. Sadly, the chief engineer then repeated that exact scenario and got himself and his driver killed.

In February, one of our night patrols went scouting beyond the bridge and found a sandbar almost at oceanside. It was a way to cross the canal and get at the Germans. Our commanders mounted an offensive.

The first American tank to make it across the sandbar was disabled by mines; the next was stranded when its engine was drowned by the surging tide. Mines crippled the next six tanks. Then the guns of Punta Bianca opened up. German snipers and machine guns did the rest. The situation only worsened as the day wore on. During the afternoon alone, the Germans pumped 325 artillery rounds onto that beach. This nightmare continued for three days, killing and wounding hundreds of our men.

Before wisdom overtook ambition, I was sent out along the canal with a daylight patrol to determine whether the Germans had built a bridge just below the surface of the water. That theory emanated from the fact that German patrols frequently came over to our side of the canal at night to torment us.

As if waltzing along the canal in broad daylight wasn't danger-ous enough, I also had to worry about the unwanted company of a young Italian civilian. Italian kids regularly appeared out of nowhere and attached themselves to our platoons. They wanted to help defeat the "Tedeschi," they explained, always relying heavily on the curse words they picked up from hanging around us to make their point. They were comical in their youthful exuberance for cursing in a foreign tongue, many of them starting every sentence with "goddammit" or a similarly emphatic off-color declaration.

Initially, we looked at these Italians and their eagerness to hang around our men with suspicion. They easily could have been spying for the fascist troops still fighting for Germany. Several battalions of Mussolini's finest supposedly lurked within ten miles of our position.

Trust grew, and soon it was easy enough to allow these kids to pack ammunition or pick up whatever other undesirable chores our men eagerly handed off. Many were even outfitted with American uniforms.

The platoon's current Italian companion was a gangly, good-looking fifteen-year-old with a prominent nose. His parents had named him Emilio Bertolloni, but my platoon called him Mario because no one could remember his name, much less pronounce it. When I was looking for volunteers for that daylight patrol, Mario kept insisting I take him.

"*Io vengo con voi . . . Io vengo con voi,*" he pleaded, "I come with you, I come with you."

"No," I said.

"*Io vengo con voi,*" Emilio repeated dozens of times, tugging on my sleeve.

I fought, begged, and pleaded with him to stay behind. There was a growing list of men on my conscience—Eldridge Banks and his companions, who bought it along the canal; Casey Emmett, Willie Warren, and Hal Brown from the bridge at Seravezza; the men lost on various patrols whose names were lost. I desperately didn't want the deaths of Italian children weighing on my soul.

Soon I was yelling.

"You are too young for war!" I shouted. "Do not beg for it."

Emilio won anyway. He didn't have to take orders from a second lieutenant in the U.S. Army.

John T.—Private Johnson—also volunteered for the patrol. He packed an M-1 and I brought a sniper's rifle—a bolt-action .30-06 Springfield with a scope. Emilio brought trouble.

We started at the bank of a feeder stream, on the brightest, clearest day in recent memory, and followed it to where it joined the Cinquale Canal. To our advantage, the canal channel was bordered by a terraced bank. There was a narrow terrace right next to the water and another earthen wall that rose eight or ten feet to the coastal flats. Unless the Germans had someone sitting on the bank, we could hike along it without being discovered.

As we neared the end of the canal, I could see there was no "underwater bridge," only the remains of the same wrecked structure that had generated other moronic inspections in the past. I suffered my own bout of moronic behavior, as if seized by a curse from the demolished bridge. I decided to peek over the top bank on the German side.

We jumped the narrow stretch of water and climbed the embankment. The view should not have been a surprise. Germans were staked out along the top of the canal, several not more than a hundred yards away. From their relaxed demeanor, it was apparent they weren't anticipating a trio of crazy soldiers popping up.

A rifle cracked. Johnson and I dropped back behind the bank. Emilio lay on top, a pool of blood radiating around his head. He'd caught the bullet.

Johnson and I pressed against the dirt and waited for more German reaction. I mentally struggled for a next move, one that included getting Emilio's body back to camp. The Germans gave me no time to think. A machine gun clattered in our direction. I became angrier and angrier, primarily at myself and at Emilio's death.

In an effort to redeem myself and avenge Emilio, I crawled up, poked my sniper's rifle over the bank, spotted the machine gunner, and shot him with every bullet in the magazine. He jerked with the impact of each round until he toppled backward out of his nest. It was unnervingly satisfying to repay the son-of-a-bitch for killing Emilio, and yet it only intensified my anger.

I lunged over the top of the embankment and reached for Emilio. Hooking a fistful of his shirt, I pulled him to my chest and kicked my legs furiously to propel us backward down the bank. We slid in a cloud of dust to the little bench by the canal. Johnson joined us, keeping his rifle ready for any Germans who might come charging over the embankment.

I began cursing myself for giving in under Emilio's insistence. He stirred. Momentarily he rose to his knees and cocked his bloody face my direction and asked, *"É una brutta ferita?"* Is it a bad wound?

If he could think that clearly, I figured he was less than mortally wounded.

"No," I said. *"Tanto sangue,"* Much blood.

A rifle grenade came whipping over the top of the canal, but went long and landed well away from us before exploding. A succession of grenades followed. We knew it wouldn't take the Germans long to perfect their aim. I handed Emilio my bandanna, he stuffed it against his nose, and the three of us ran back up the canal. Moments later mortar rounds pulverized the ground we had just left.

Adrenaline and exercise pumped plenty of blood into Emilio's handheld bandage, but we couldn't afford to stop even for a breath until we left the canal and made it well along the bank of the feeder stream. We finally sat, panting and sweating, in the scanty shelter of a few bushes. I pried Emilio's hand and the bloody handkerchief from his face and inspected the wound. I was surprised not to find half of his face blown off. Even his ample nose appeared intact.

Once he was cleaned up by a field surgeon, Emilio learned that the bullet barely pierced the skin right under his nostrils, carving a thin scar-tissue mustache. When he checked out of the hospital, Emilio had the guts to come back to the company. But I refused to allow him to go back into combat with us. He wasn't a soldier, and I didn't want to give his possible death a second chance at my conscience.

I was perplexed by the fact that he had been shot instead of me or Private Johnson. It occupied more than a few supper conversations before we were hit with the obvious. Emilio got the bullet because he was the only white face in the patrol. The Germans knew most of our officers were white. It was routine for snipers to try to kill the leaders, thereby sowing confusion and panic among the rest of the troops. That's one reason I never wore my lieutenant's bars into battle.

It was the one and only daylight patrol the Americans sent out along the canal. I received a Bronze Star for that mission. It didn't mean much to me. Officers who never got near the fighting received the Bronze Star so often that we called it the "white officers' good conduct medal."

I disdained the recognition for other reasons. I went to the battalion observation post a few days after that patrol to talk about our foray. I discovered our intelligence officers could see everything from that post that I had been sent to find. In fact they had watched our entire adventure and recounted, in precise detail, our every move. They, too, were amazed by Emilio's resurrection.

I left pissed off. There hadn't been any reason to risk the lives of a foot patrol. The Bronze Star seemed more an admission of my commanders' guilt than a recognition of valor.

FIFTEEN

*Families will not be broken. Curse and expel them,
send their children wandering, drown them in floods
and fires, and old women will make songs out of all
these sorrows and sit in the porches and sing them on
mild evenings.*

—Marilynne Robinson

January 1945, Northern Italy

"You notice there are no train whistles in Italy? I miss a train whistle. Kind of sneaks up on you low and slow, gets louder, overtakes you. But it's regular. It tells you things are regular."

The comment drifted out of the front room of the two-story stone farmhouse where we were quartered. It might have been Dandy Belk, Chicago boy and all, he loved trains. He grew up to the vocal rhythms of the Chicago, Milwaukee, St. Paul & Pacific Railroad.

Or it could have been Paul Dickerson, the Signal Corps photographer, who stopped to visit when he could find the time. Paul and his Lincolnesque stature turned up with a Speed-a-Graphic in the worst places. He was right next to the village where John Fox was calling artillery fire in on himself. Being a photographer, Paul was a detail man, just the sort to notice whether the trains in Italy whistled. Except there were no trains running in our part of Italy, and the voice lamenting the whistle didn't have Dickerson's distinct New York vowels.

I passed on upstairs without finding out who owned the question, or to correct them on the lack of locomotives. I didn't miss a damn thing about the railroads even if Grandpa had been chief brakeman for the Cheyenne division of the Union Pacific. Working for the U.P. had purged me of any romantic notions.

A thread of my unhappiness with "running on the road," as we called it, was woven in my first wage-paying job—shining shoes. It has that trite, stereotypical story-of-the-black-youth ring to it, "My first job was as a shoeshine boy." It's no bootstrap testimonial. People preferred to see us in what now is called service jobs. So that's what was available.

It was a downhill tumble, initiated when I returned from Boys Home. First I discovered that Shep was dead. My furry pal, protector, walking partner, cat killer, warm-muzzled, wet-tongued dog died during my final stay at Boys Home. Then I met Susie, Grandpa's new wife.

Susie was pretentious and unlikable. She stood about even with me, had light skin, and a huge nose that appeared to have been flattened with a Griswold No. 10 cast-iron skillet. Somewhere close to forty, she made sure we knew how pretty she thought she was. I disliked everything about her, especially her excessively solicitous overtures to my grandfather. She fussed over him with false sincerity or talked about how great he was in equally unbelievable tones and turned to us for our approval of this fawning.

"Your grandfather, well he is just the man," Susie said, drawing out "well" to the point it sounded more like "wheel." "Handsome, smart, hardworking, strong. Just the man."

Susie had arrived in Cheyenne as maid and nanny to a traveling white family from Tennessee. When they docked in Cheyenne, the family discovered the "No Negroes" rule at the white hotels and sent Susie to stay at our boarding house. Susie considered this worthy as a permanent home and, by the time I returned, had quit the white family to work full-time on Grandpa. Hard liquor not only appeared in our house for the first time, but Susie consumed it openly and in ample quantity. It didn't fit, considering Grandfather never had allowed anything in the house stronger than the home brew he had fermenting in the storage room by the bathroom.

Susie had extravagant tastes, hence the reason I had to be recalled from Boys Home and put to work. We'd barely scraped by before her lavishness arrived on the scene.

I didn't hide my feelings for Susie. The dislike was mutual. Still, Grandfather enjoyed her attentions. Having a woman run her ruby fingernail along his lips and tell him he was "just the man" was a fair break from carrying the burdens of a woman with rheumatoid arthritis, from caring for a woman painfully confined to a wheelchair for twenty-two years.

And Grandfather was still Grandfather. He was still the quiet, good, gentle man who taught me to keep cool, to respect everyone now matter how they treated me. He had demonstrated, over and over, what love and security were all about. And my coming home gave us more opportunities to hunt together. A confrontation over Susie could ruin, or end, those trips and this relationship. I found work instead of complaining.

My shoeshining station was all the way at the back of one of the half dozen downtown barbershops, just beyond the fourth barber's chair and next to the closet where things such as combs, shaving cream and extra razors were stored.

Mirrors covered most of the walls. Green, blue, and clear glass bottles, smelling of the latest hair tonics, lined the counter behind the barbers' chairs. Clear six-sided glass jars full of black combs were located in easy reach of each barber chair. Well-used razor strops hung near every station, waiting to sing when the barbers put a straight razor to them at a full lick.

Shining shoes paid three dollars and fifty cents a week, plus tips. In a good week, I made twenty-five or thirty dollars. That was big money for a fifteen-year-old during the Depression. The white-haired gent who owned the shop also offered to give me a free barber haircut my first week. I looked forward to something new and snazzy, considering what Grandpa's backyard barbering offered—a wooden stool, a bowl, and the same routine clip.

"Sure," I said. "That'd be fine."

His offer came after closing time, after my polish, brushes, and rags were back in their box and after the other three barbers had gone home for the day. I expected the haircut to happen sometime the following day, or later in the week, when business was slow. Instead, he crossed to the door and threw the dead bolt, hit the switch that controlled the juice for the twisting red, white, and blue barber pole out front, and pulled the shades. He walked to his chair, the one nearest the front door, and tapped the red leather back to indicate I should sit for the haircut right then.

"Don't misunderstand, son," he said, sweeping the cape around me and tying it behind my neck. "I want to give you haircuts. But if somebody walking down the street saw me cutting your hair?" He gestured heavenward with open palms. "I would lose my business. You know this is my livelihood. Only thing I've known for pretty near thirty-five years."

I shrugged, and he gently pushed my head forward and lathered up the back of my neck with shaving cream. I didn't understand. Not in the sense he wanted me to understand. He wanted absolution for going along with the social norms—it's fine for black boys to polish a white man's shoes in a barbershop, but it's not fine to cut a black man's hair in a white man's barbershop. It's fine for customers to ask, "Who's your new nigger boy?" But don't let them think they are going to have to dirty themselves by sitting in the chair where that "new nigger boy" has been sitting.

The barber didn't mean it the way it sounded to me. He was a kind man who was trying to reach out to me in spite of society's rules. The experience stuck anyway. It went in that place in my mind where Pat Norton's taunts were unintentionally filed. I didn't want the baggage. Somehow, it stayed around.

The barber continued to cut my hair for the summer that I polished shoes and swept clumps of hair off the floor. I soon stopped him from shaving my neck as it raised a bed of pimples. After a few months, I stopped working there. I didn't like kneeling in front of big, fat, ugly white men from whom I had to be hidden when I got a haircut.

Where I struggled as a shoeshine boy, Raymond Davis excelled. Raymond worked in the barbershop around the corner from my shop and saved enough to buy himself a brand-new, light-blue Plymouth sedan with cash. He laid down five hundred dollars for that beauty, all of it earned shining shoes.

Raymond had migrated from Kansas City to Cheyenne with the explicit purpose of courting Cass. He was a neighbor of Aunt Lulu and had fallen in love with Cass during one of our family visits to Kansas City. The hot pursuit of love brought him all the way West. She wouldn't have a thing to do with him.

Raymond didn't falter. He found the shoeshining job and started outfitting himself for the kill. He was my size, but a fast talker, full of laughs and full of fun. His standard outfit included a suit with Gambol stripes—a kind of a light gray pinstripe running down a solid gray suit. Ties were rare. The collar of a fine white shirt lay sportingly open at the neck. Every square inch of his clothes was starched and pressed.

His new car brought status to my life. I rode up front as he wheeled around town, proud for the looks we got, proud for the elbow jabs that were traded between the people we passed. I knew folks were saying, "There goes Raymond Davis, the shoeshine boy. Bought that there car with cash. A shoeshine boy with five hundred dollars cash. Go figure."

I imagined the sidewalk gossip included me. "There goes Raymond Davis, the shoeshine boy. And isn't that Vernon Baker with him? How's he rate?"

Raymond drove Cass and me to picnics, sightseeing, and all the way to Sidney, Nebraska, just for fun. With his car, his smile and his clothes, he had all of the girls in Cheyenne dying to catch his eye.

Cass still wouldn't have anything to do with him. Instead she went off and married a crude, illiterate man named Henry Mitchell.

I couldn't see it from her side. But she swears Henry's always been good to her.

Considering Susie's tastes, I couldn't stay idle. Fall found me working for the Union Pacific instead of returning to school. Grandpa helped me get on as a bus boy in the train station cafe. Then I graduated to "red cap"—baggage handler—and a substitute chair car porter, depending upon what was most needed.

The Union Pacific outfitted me in gray pants, with a maroon stripe running down the legs, and a gray jacket. A red cap, of course, topped off the outfit and tipped people off that I would tote their baggage to and from their cars and politely bear their insults.

"Come on, boy; hurry, boy! You're gonna make me miss the train, boy."

As if I had instructed them to arrive at the last minute.

"Come on, boy! I've got places to go, boy. Could have carried it myself if I'd knowed you'd walk as if this were a sight-seeing tour."

Days when I landed train duty—"running on the road"—the red cap was switched for a maroon one. Maroon matched the stripe on the pants and the maroon jacket we donned. Once the train got rolling, we changed into white jackets and served the needs of the people in the chair cars. Many of these haughty white people saw us as their personal servants.

"Here, boy," they summoned, as if we were dogs. "Here, boy, I need a pillow. Here, boy, swing down that valise over yonder and bring it to me. Here, boy, something's spilled and you must clean it up. Here, boy, hurry any time you can."

I seethed after the second day of it and my hatred only intensified.

My unhappiness was eased when I got trips with my big, tall, gangly childhood friend James Horn. We worked the Cheyenne to Omaha run and the Cheyenne to Salt Lake City run. We were fill-in crew, but could work the trains seven days a week. Boys weren't falling all over themselves to take guff from assholes. The side benefits were the rail passes. Rail passes were a bonus when we were chasing women.

The carnival visited Cheyenne that year, complete with a chorus line. Three of the show girls were black and stayed at my family's boarding house. James and I had a car, a Hudson Super Six we paid fifty dollars for, so going out on the town was no problem. We strutted.

A leggy beauty named Geneva fell in love with me. A woman with flaming dyed hair, Red Top, fell for James. No two couples knew deeper rapture. We'd invented the meaning of love. Or thought we did.

When the carnival moved to Salt Lake City, James and I practically moved with it. We used every rail pass we had coming, or could trade for, to visit Geneva and Red Top. When the carnival left Salt Lake City three weeks later, those ladies and our hearts disappeared along with it.

Uncle Will's death intervened after the first year of my railroad career. I didn't even realize we had family in Iowa until Grandpa asked me to accompany him to his brother's funeral.

We took the train to Clarinda, country that seemed flatter than Nebraska but, thankfully, greener. A mass of people seemed to know Grandpa, hugged him, shook his hand, asked after me with a warm, "This here must be Vernon." Family. Aunts, uncles, first cousins through fourth cousins and beyond. And another Vernon Baker. Cousin Vernon Baker to be precise. With two of us, he was dubbed "Big Vernie" and I became "Little Vernie."

Funerals made for sizeable reunions in rural Iowa, and Uncle Will's set the standard. We gathered at the family farm outside Clarinda after the funeral and ate pot roast, chicken, fresh green beans, squash, home-made bread, and all manner of delicious food that inspired contentment all the way down. People talked with one another and talked of more Bakers than a boy could dream existed.

Most of Iowa must be Baker country, I reasoned. Lots of family; warm, wonderful food laid down long tables covered with hand-crocheted tablecloths. Warm summer air, the languid breeze. Why keep this a family secret? I wondered.

"What do you do in Cheyenne?" Cousin Vernon asked, interrupting the after-dinner musing as we stretched out on the farmhouse lawn, watched the sunlight wash out and fireflies flick in and out.

"Work at Grandpa's railroad, the Union Pacific," I said. "Red cap and porter, waitin' on assholes, if you'll excuse my language."

Cousin Vernon pulled a long blade of grass through his front teeth, and laughed. "Farm boys have heard those words before," he said.

"Where do you go to school," he inquired seriously.

"Haven't been since I left the Boys Home," I said, and told him about Pat Norton, Eli Brooks, and my near miss with becoming an honest-to-goodness Catholic. "Even went through catechism," I said, wearing it as a special scar.

I carefully avoided disparaging Susie directly, not wanting to hurt Grandpa's feelings. Vernon, however, must have sensed my discomfort with more than just my railroad job.

"Come here and go to school," he offered.

"What? Where?"

"Here. Clarinda High School," he said, sweeping his arm out over a corn field and back toward town. "They have a real nice school. Best in the county. You could know your family. Our football team wouldn't mind your help."

I grunted and shrugged my shoulders. It wasn't so easy to move away from what I was doing. I had been called home from Boys Town, after all. Cousin Vernon persisted.

I waited until we were back on the train headed home to bring it up. Grandpa listened to the idea with the same nondescript look he'd had when I pitched Boys Home.

He looked out the train windows as we rolled back through Nebraska toward Cheyenne and said little for a considerable time after I had finished. The creases in his face deepened.

"Yes, boy," he finally said with a sigh. "Yes, I think your cousin Vernon is right. Finishing your education in Clarinda is a good idea."

Grandpa looked down in his lap, folded his hands, and pushed his thumbnails together, then looked back toward me.

"Yes. I want you to get an education. I've worked with my hands all of my life. You can do better. You should work with your mind."

Clarinda worked out. I lived with Aunt Elsie, lettered in every sport, made a name for myself in the declamatory club. With persistent prodding from my English teacher, Miss Brown, I graduated with honors. Grandpa bought me a new bell-bottomed suit and came to see me get my diploma. He was prouder than I was.

I hoped this and Grandpa's wish for me to do better than work with my hands meant my railroading days were done. But it was 1939. The Depression had plagued some parts of the West, especially the agriculture industry for more than fifteen years. Our hard times in Cheyenne beat those of the East Coast stock speculators by at least five years. Now, wherever Franklin D. Roosevelt's New Deal was being dealt, its face cards didn't land on our spot at the table.

Grandpa delivered the bad news even before we boarded the train for home.

"You won't have to worry about work, boy," Grandpa said as we ate breakfast the morning of our departure from Clarinda. "There's a place for you back at the railroad. I think you'll be in the chair cars full time."

The wood cookstove—Aunt Elsie was the sole resident of Clarinda not to have electricity or running water—added unbearably to the June heat. We all mopped our brows between bites. Grandpa seemed oblivious to that discomfort and to mine. He scooped eggs onto his fork with a biscuit and enjoyed another mouthful of Aunt Elsie's coffee.

"Wonderful as it's always been," he told her.

Elsie glowed. "Sorry I don't have more opportunity to show you my cookin' Joseph."

I pondered my future. I had returned to Cheyenne every summer during my high school days to work on the railroad. If I had no specific career ambition, I certainly knew what I didn't want—more running on the road. At nineteen, I was ready for something besides being a high-school-educated lackey for the spoiled class. But Grandfather was proud of finding me a job amidst the dregs of the Depression. I could no more tell him how much I hated the railroad than I could tell him I thought Susie was a floozy. When he turned back to me from exchanging pleasantries about breakfast with Aunt Elsie, I thanked him and hoped my face conveyed appreciation instead of revealing my heavy heart.

My porter's job put me back on the Cheyenne to Omaha and Cheyenne to Salt Lake City runs. I had all the work I wanted as a substitute for the full-time porters who were sick, wanted a day with their families, or needed a day away from servitude. The only relief was James Horn, our fun with the ladies, and our cruising in our old Hudson during our time off.

Grandpa retired that year and took sick in the fall. Prostate cancer drew his frame from robust to emaciated.

"Boy," he said, propped up on pillows on the front room sofa, "you'll have to get a deer without me this time."

Charles and Irma needed the meat as bad as our family, so we gave it a try. And failed to give it more than a couple of half-hearted tries. Without Grandpa, it didn't feel like hunting.

Doctors had diagnosed Grandpa's problem and gravely admitted that it fell into the category of "complications beyond our capabilities." Death finally provided the relief they could not. We buried him Christmas Day.

Susie barely finished daubing her eyes before she let the rest of her hair down. And there was some lettin' to do. The boarding house wasn't filled with mourners. It was filled with her girlfriends. And they partied.

I quietly gathered my things and moved in with Cass and Henry.

SIXTEEN

Why is it that you can sometimes feel the reality of
people more keenly through a letter than face to face?

—Anne Morrow Lindbergh

Early February 1945, Northern Italy

Mail call in early February was as disappointing as it had been the entire previous year, discounting the occasional note from Cass. Helen either wasn't receiving my letters or she wasn't responding. The Army, I knew, was still sending her one hundred eighty dollars of my two-hundred-twenty-dollars monthly salary.

I shouldered my M-1, never going anywhere without it, and slogged through the semi-frozen ooze to the command post. Since Captain Matthews left, I was unofficially in charge and could wrangle a jeep for personal use. I needed to find Harry Cox—he knew how women operated. Out of embarrassment, I had avoided seeking his advice. The disappointment of receiving no mail overrode pride. I wasn't going to mull Helen's silence alone any longer.

I found Harry swooning over some chestnut-flour cookies that he had talked an Italian farmer's wife into baking for him. He listened to me for most of the night.

Marrying Helen wasn't exactly an impulse, not in the same spirit as marrying Leola. With Leola I had mistaken lust for love. I thought

I had learned that lesson. Leola did all she could to rub it in, never writing me a single note during our married life. A distorted sense of hope, of thinking she would tire of C.J. and rediscover her love for me, had kept me from divorcing her the minute I read Cass's letter about her reuniting with C.J. If I could only do this or that, I dreamed, she'd beg my forgiveness and come back to me.

As soon as I graduated from Officer Candidate School, I had polished my brass second lieutenant's bars, brushed my new uniform, and took leave for Cheyenne. Cass's letters had kept me up on Leola's exploits—drinking and raising hell at Millie's club and living with C.J. However, my officer's outfit was so stunning that Leola would have to be blind not to come to her senses.

"She won't see you," Millie said when I called at the club for directions to find Leola. "You a fool, Baker. If she loved you, why'd she stay with C.J. all this time?"

"Look at me, Millie?" I protested. "C.J.'s no officer. What's he made of himself? She'll see me and she'll. . . ."

"She won't, Baker."

Millie offered me a drink, and then laughed Leola's scornful laugh when I asked for a cola.

"Army still ain't made a man outa you?"

Millie settled a perspiring glass in front of me.

"She won't see you or anything else. Cass done made it clear you were coming home. Leola hasn't missed three days in here since you left. You see her here waiting for you now? The most thinkin' she does about you is when that monthly Army money comes in."

Millie's words hurt. "The most thinkin' she does about you is when that monthly Army money comes in."

I stomped out in disgust. I'd put up with Georgia and white pricks who claimed to be instructors because I knew being an officer would mean something to my family. Leola was my family or my hope at having one.

Georgia came as close to any place in the United States to making central Texas appear hospitable. Like at every other fort, the black barracks, mess halls, latrines, and supply depots were segregated.

When our white training officers dismissed us at the end of the day, we returned to confinement in an all-black world.

Weekends, buses were available to take the white soldiers to Columbus, the nearest town. Cattle trailers hauled us blacks. If the transportation didn't stoke your temper, being in town did.

We were the invisible people. White people looked through us as if we didn't exist. Black civilians, I noticed, always looked at the ground when they talked to whites. Looking a white man in the eye was uppity, Southern black soldiers patiently explained to me. The penalty? Well, there were still plenty of lynchings to remind people what happened if they got out of line.

A black soldier who came expecting a little respect for his uniform was treated no better. White enlisted men refused to salute black officers, and if the black officer complained, the MPs harassed the black officer for making it an issue. The white civilians just harassed us.

Harry Cox did nothing more serious than step into a telephone booth in one of these Southern towns. A couple of white guys spied him and came after him yelling, "Git outta our phone booth!"

Harry, being in a mood that day, unstrapped his .45-caliber pistol and set it on top of the telephone. He was allowed to finish his call.

All of this replayed in my mind as, flush with anger, I walked around Cheyenne. And walked. I was angry at Millie's stinging words, Leola's snub, and the world overall.

The winter darkness came early and settled me. I found myself on Eighteenth Street, in front of the old boarding house. It wasn't accidental, even if arriving there at that particular moment was chance. I'd decided I had to show off my accomplishment to someone. Why not Susie? Why not deliver the shock of my accomplishment to a woman, step-grandmother though she was, who was certain I wouldn't "amount to nothin'?"

As I drew up the steps a sensation overwhelmed me. I knocked on the door anyway. A heavily perfumed woman in a purple dress and wearing alarming lipstick opened the door.

"Well, we've got ourselves an officer here. A real man," she purred. Or tried to purr. Cigarettes roughened her voice, making her best effort a throaty rasp. She beckoned with a finger and scooted backwards, trying to undulate seductively as she went.

"Come on in, soldier," she said, again trying to purr.

Two or three equally garish women gathered in the entryway. Susie burst into the room in seconds, with a drink in hand and a smile as big as the Milky Way. She recognized me. I recognized her. She tried to hold the smile but couldn't.

I spun, hauled open the door, and flew down the steps. From boarding house to whore house. Even Grandmother's nasty, unhappy reign couldn't beat this.

Cass wasn't home. I went to Irma's.

Irma was calm when I told her what I'd seen, rolling a cigarette around in the ash tray and sculpting the burning tip absentmindedly.

"Just best to forget you went there," she said. "Best to forget all of that."

"Have you been over there? Have you seen what's happened to the place?" I asked.

Irma shook her head, stubbed out her cigarette, and used her hand to prop her weary chin.

"Naw. We hear things. Rumors, she's arrested. Rumors, she's been in jail. We try to ignore them. That isn't who I am, it's not who you are, and it's not who Cass is either."

We sat and sipped coffee in silence. It also wasn't who Grandpa was. I boiled for his memory, for his good name. Whoring. Whoring up Grandfather's good name. A respected man, a black man who had worked when others went on strike, who refused to pilfer from the railroad—taking only what he was owed on payday. A man who wouldn't even allow an orphanage to cover my room and board in days when he was eating prairie dog to make ends meet.

"Treat all people with respect, boy," he said. Maybe we were hunting elk and this was the part of the day when the sun was high and the elk were bedded down in the dark timber. If it was warm enough we'd settle on a log. Grandpa filled his pipe and we sat a spell.

"Women, boy," he continued after dedicated effort to pack the pipe just so and give the exact number of opening puffs to get it burning evenly. "Women especially. Treat women with extra respect. Nobody's life's harder than a woman's."

Irma and I never talked about it again, and I didn't bring it up with Cass. A few years later, Irma sent me a small newspaper clipping saying Susie had died. None of us saw a single stick of furniture, a memento of our grandparents. Nothing.

I pushed off for my new assignment as an airbase security officer at Camp Rucker, Alabama. And soon found Helen.

Remorse justified my plunge into a new relationship. I wasn't in Alabama six weeks before Cass wrote to say Leola had died. Something to do with drinking. I survived it by first ignoring it and later denying it. How could I have ever gotten mixed up with her? I convinced myself that I hated her.

Alabama didn't warm up and hug me in my low moments. No one descriptive term fit. Take one dose of central Texas, and add an amoeba-shaped piece of swamp near Dothan, Alabama. Throw in a lake called Tholocco in case the mosquitoes can't find enough places to reproduce in the surrounding swamps. Bake at 110 percent humidity.

I immediately tried to forget Leola and invited a girl who worked at the PX to be my date at a carnival. Unfortunately I had only a ten-dollar bill where nickels and dimes spent at the booths. I laid my ten spot on the counter at the nearest concession stand and asked the husky, red-faced woman for as much change as she could spare. She waddled over, reached for the bill, and stopped her arm in midair.

"Say ma'am," she instructed.

"Pardon?" I asked.

"Say ma'am. You want change, you say, 'can I have some change please, MA'AM.'"

I snatched my ten-dollar bill and turned to walk away. She started screaming for the MPs. My date fled. I stayed put. Running, I knew, looked like guilt on the lam.

A couple of white soldiers with helmets, pistols, and black arm bands arrived on the run.

"What's the trouble here?" one of them asked between gasps to catch his breath.

The concession stand proprietor's nostrils flared wider as she became more and more agitated thinking about me. She lifted a beefy arm and jabbed a finger my direction, the flab under her arm swinging back and forth.

"This here nigger's the problem. This nigger ain't saying ma'am to me. You hear me? This here nigger ain't saying ma'am."

One of the MPs lifted his hand to call for an intermission in her tirade.

"Ma'am," he said. "That there is a lieutenant."

He nodded at me. We all left, with the dissatisfied woman yelling after us.

Grandpa cautioned against reacting to any kind of provocation, but he had never talked about racism. He didn't give me advice on what to do when people persisted in demeaning me, in making sure I was contrite and crawling and licking their boots before they did for me as they rushed to do for any white person. Was I supposed to lay down like a sidewalk so these people could walk over me?

Grandpa's mantra played and replayed in my mind. I was as angry at him for teaching me not to strike out as I was at the people who treated me like rubbish. I wanted to do something with my anger. Years later, when I woke up and recognized how ugly anger made me, I realized Grandpa had taught me something about dealing with such wrong. Show quiet strength, as he had with the railroad strikers, and continue living honorably and patiently. Time and fate takes care of those who abuse.

Meanwhile, worried about small-town racism, I started ranging farther on weekends. Birmingham became a favorite haunt. It had a Coloreds district, a Coloreds USO Club, and plenty of pretty black women.

Helen Stewart's sparkling eyes caught mine as I walked across the bar room in the Birmingham USO club. She sat at a small table with two other women. I winked, she winked back, but I had unavoidable business and kept my course for the bathroom.

When I came out, she waved and then motioned "come here" with a slender finger. A single strand of pearls, unusual for a black girl in a USO club, ran gently over a soft gray top, which gave Helen's rich face a model's elegance. I was dazzled.

We managed dinner, and nothing more, because I had to work the next morning. I barely finished my food and caught the bus for Camp Rucker. I had a letter from Helen in two days, inviting me back to Birmingham. Finally, a beautiful woman who loved me.

I practically danced back to Birmingham in a week, buying Helen dinner and marveling at my good fortune. She suggested a stroll after the meal, purposefully leading me to a park bench, where she instantly melted into tears.

Helen was a school teacher who found herself pregnant. She'd only been with a man once, she sobbed, at a party where she'd accidentally had too much to drink. Now she stood to lose her job the moment the school district found out she was having a baby.

"Help me, Vernon," she pleaded. "You're the only decent man I know. I don't know what to do . . . hel . . . help me."

A school teacher. She would be a fine mother. I would have a family, the security, something to live and work for, a wife to bring to Cheyenne, a fine, enviable woman to share my world.

We were married. She named her daughter Vernon.

Harry dusted the last of the chestnut cookie crumbs from his fingers and shook his head at this point in the story. "Leola, Susie, Helen. Oh boy, Vernon. You sure get mixed up in it. Where's Helen now?"

"Her address is Chicago," I said. "I guess. Like I told you, she hasn't written for months. No, a year."

"You want a letter from her?"

"Sure. Why do you think I'm here talking to you."

"Fine," Harry said. "Do this. Tell the Army to stop her allotment checks. You'll hear from her."

SEVENTEEN

The Americans were sending their black troops straight into the front of the German lines, instead of around to the side. And there was no reason for it. So the Americans sent these soldiers to die.

—Gino Dinelli, Italian partisan

March 1945, Querceta, Italy

Some say it's the meeting place of ghosts. I have to wonder if the ghosts are ours. Because for the winter of 1944–45 Castle Aghinolfi anchored one leg of what the Italian partisans called the "Triangle of Death." Most of the deaths were ours.

Castle Aghinolfi rules an overgrown knob on the edge of the precipitous dividing line between the mountains and coastal plain at the top of the Italian boot. It was the perfect high-ground fortification to crown the western end of the Gothic Line.

The castle started with an octagonal tower erected in the fifth century, about five hundred years after the locals first started working the area's famous Carrara marble. It eventually became one of a number of forts controlling the only passes through the Apennine Mountains and, therefore, the only routes through northern Italy.

A prince named Aghinulfo added fortifications around the eight-sided tower about 500 A.D., continuing the tradition of ample stone construction. From here, the prince easily kept track of land

and sea trade and charged tariffs to traveling merchants. Five hundred years later, long after the Roman empire disintegrated into a crazy quilt of fiefdoms, a rural noble family took over the castle, bastardized Prince Aghinulfo's name, and christened the place Castle Aghinolfi. The name stuck.

This noble family added another circle of four-foot-thick stone walls and a drawbridge. Inside, they built warehouses, a cistern, a flour mill, decorative stone archways, lofty parapets, and a lighthouse for signaling castles on similar high points along the coast.

Castle Aghinolfi eventually became a troop fort. By the 1500s, another defensive wall was added to the growing ring of walls at the foot of the castle. Cannons and mortars were installed in key turrets and towers. Military minds decided if they had heavy artillery in the castle, they could control the countryside. This philosophy became well-established tradition for those who ruled this territory, including Nazi Germany.

We had a detached relationship with the German-held castle, which we could barely see from the Cinquale flats. We watched from a distance as mosquitoish U.S. Army reconnaissance planes, single-engine Piper Cubs, circled the castle and then skittered away when the Germans became irritated enough to start shooting. The Germans had little to worry about. They had so craftily camouflaged their mortar batteries, bunkers, machine gun nests, and observation posts that our aerial surveillance couldn't distinguish between the weapons emplacements and the hillsides.

We knew German artillery and mortar spotters made fine use of the castle to direct shells and shrapnel at the 92nd during those several months we were precariously spread out across the coastal plain. The Germans could drop a mortar in a man's hip pocket. And often did. To avoid annihilation, we holed up during the day and did most of our work at night. A single soldier visible in daylight elicited mortar fire.

Local farmers refused to stay hidden. They attempted to lead normal lives, treading among the shell craters and battle ruins to tend grapes, olive trees, and figs; visiting neighbors and traveling from Querceta to Pietrasanta or other nearby villages. The Germans didn't tolerate the defiance. Normal lives were bloodied lives for the stubborn Italians.

I understood their restlessness. Small talk, studying maps and aerial photos, cleaning and rechecking gear didn't keep my mind occupied for long. Occasionally I'd grab a sniper's rifle, sneak out in the fields with a box of phosphorus tracer bullets, and shoot at the wrinkle of hills staggering up the skyline. As from fireworks on the Fourth of July, I got a rush of pleasure hearing the crack of the gun and watching how far the glowing streak traveled. Young, dumb, and lucky. After a half dozen rounds, the hornet's nest reacted. Time and again I scooted just before the German artillery observers successfully located me.

Germany instinctively knew these battlefields. Her ancestors, the ancient Goths, were driven back to the exact same Gothic Line in the fifth century by Byzantine troops of the eastern Roman Empire. The war lasted eighteen years. The Goths lost.

When Hitler decided to name this exact same area the Gothic Line, his historians pointed out that Germany's forefathers had been defeated at the same line with the same name 1,500 years before. Hitler unsuccessfully tried to rename it the Green Line.

The Gothic Line follows a natural barrier of rugged terrain, starting where the Cinquale Canal meets the Ligurian Sea. It traces the canal inland to the Versilia River, then follows the river back into the Apuanian Alps. The line loops and weaves along peaks our commanders renamed Ohio 1, Ohio 2, Alaska, Georgia, and Florida, circuitously crossing the width of Italy along the mountains and emerging on the Adriatic coast near Rimini.

The Line was so rugged that in most places a few soldiers with machine guns and mortars easily defended it. It's the logical place to fall back and fight from. Especially if one has months to add weapons and battlements to the natural fortifications. The Germans had the time, and they had tremendous incentive to hold this crenelated boundary. The Gothic Line guarded the route to northern Italy and prevented any advance into Italy's rich Po Valley, an agricultural and manufacturing area important in feeding the German war machine.

Not only did Castle Aghinolfi rule the mountain passes on the western end of the Gothic Line, it was almost atop Highway One, the route we badly needed to travel in order to continue north toward Punta Bianca and Genoa. The 92nd couldn't simply go around the castle and deal with Aghinolfi's occupants later. The series of steep mountains east of the castle, even those not explicitly part of the Gothic Line, were both heavily fortified and difficult to cross.

We attempted to move up the coast on the west side of the castle and were thoroughly thrashed at the Cinquale Canal. All battle plans eventually returned to Aghinolfi. We had to take the castle if we intended to breach the Gothic Line and go farther north.

The British, free Polish, and other troops had some success piercing the east end of the Gothic Line, and yet it was irrelevant to capturing our portion of Italy. It was impossible to punch through along the Adriatic coast and then swing inland in a flanking maneuver. Mountains blocked the way.

By the time we glimpsed our first distant perspective of the castle in September 1944, it was surrounded by barbed wire, mine fields, and trip wires that triggered signal flares. The flares warned the Germans of intruders. At night, the flares also provided enough light for the Germans to unleash every weapon on us. Here as elsewhere, the Gothic Line was as solid as the region's famed Carrara marble.

Field Marshal Albert Kesselring personally designed the Gothic Line defenses, pressing 15,000 Italians into forced labor for nine months. His battlements included 2,376 machine gun nests over a distance of less than two hundred miles. Kesselring even spent a night in the village of Montignoso, just beyond the castle, while we camped on the flats below, and declared himself quite satisfied.

The Allies gave him plenty of reason to continue to feel safe and satisfied. For seven months, we captured little ground and lost many men trying to fracture his defenses. The Triangle of Death was central to our continuing defeat.

The triangle consisted of Castle Aghinolfi and two of the loftier peaks in the mountains behind it—Mount Folgorito and Mount Carchio. The highest of the three, the pyramid-shaped Mount Folgorito, was linked to Montignoso by a crude, open tramway. The tram car, a huge wooden box without a top, brought wounded and dead down to Montignoso and hauled ammunition and supplies back. Mount Folgorito was so well positioned a mere dozen men could hold it.

All three legs of the triangle had communication links to the guns at Punta Bianca and a whole chain of howitzers, mortars, and other artillery. Between the three points, the Germans could see everything we did, from Viareggio to the Cinquale Canal and beyond. A simple telephone call or radio message from one of these vantage points triggered the wrath of artillery, mortars, machine gunners, and snipers. The German soldiers in the surrounding hills didn't have to risk patrolling to find out what we were doing. They waited for their observation posts to report and annihilated us as directed.

Topography and German fortifications made it suicidal to send troops straight across the plain to the castle. Tanks couldn't negotiate the wet, marshy ground, and the only two passable roads were thoroughly mined. Given all of these impossibilities, our strategy was to send our infantry up a trio of small peaks that stair-stepped their way toward the castle from the south.

The Allies named them Hills X, Y, and Z, for ease of battlefield identification. Each hill was terraced for olive groves and grape arbors. Those terraces may have been beautiful to a sightseer, but they were deadly for a soldier. When we crawled up those hills, we never knew what we would face the next terrace up.

The Germans were keenly aware that Hills X, Y, and Z were the logical approach to the castle. In preparation for our arrival, they loaded the area with machine gun nests, snipers, mortar batteries, and high-power observation posts. Some were dug into hillsides and linked to one another by tunnels. Others were built of concrete and steel. All were well camouflaged.

These were the fortifications our aerial observers couldn't find. We couldn't blame them. On the ground, it often was impossible to see the emplacements from more than ten feet away. Infantrymen discovered them by stumbling upon them and were damn fortunate if the discovery didn't kill them. If they got that far. Barbed wire and mine fields on top of the hills forced any attackers to walk directly into the German line of fire.

I missed the first two attempts to take the hills and castle when I was laid up in Pisa with my arm in a cast. In February 1945, about six weeks after I returned from the hospital, I had my first vicarious taste of the challenge. The Second and Third Battalion were thrown against the hills. My battalion stayed in reserve.

When the February assault kicked off, I watched, as ordered, from the observation post from which Harry Cox was directing fire. Harry was the finest of mortar men. I admired him guiding an advancing line of smoke shells up the draws with a jeweler's precision, giving plumes of cover for the men of the 370th to charge the hills.

Our intelligence officers reported the Germans were low on ammunition. It seemed true. Even though our troops followed the exact line of attack that had failed before, we were having a bit of success. Through binoculars I could see our troops taking out bunkers and capturing prisoners in a slow, but steady climb. Hill X and a portion of Hill Y appeared well in hand. The same methodical work should give us control of Hill Z. This meant a foothold to regroup, reinforce, and work away at the castle.

When dusk came, the lion roared. The Germans cut loose with heaps of their supposedly scarce ammunition.

The shelling started with a few enemy guns focused at the center of the top terraces of both Hill X and Hill Y. Additional enemy guns joined the bombardment. The cloudburst of explosives simultaneously expanded to the right and to the left along the top terrace. Once the Germans established a solid wall of fire at the top, they kept every gun firing and marched this wall down the hills, one terrace at a time. Smoke and fire cascaded downslope, a waterfall of gray, black, and white punctuated by flashes of orange and nonstop explosions. When the torrent of shells reached the bottom, the Germans pounded in place for a moment, then reversed course and moved the solid blanket of shelling back up to the top, one terrace at a time.

Once caught in this firestorm, there's not a damn thing a soldier can do but sit and take it. My sense of helplessness slipped in and my self-control snapped. I cried, pounding my fist against the wall of the observation post until the side of my hand was raw and my arm ached. For the first time in my life, I prayed for people. It was reprehensible, horrible, mortifying, mind numbing—more of something than I could ever describe. My stomach ached from taking too-rapid breaths. I sensed shock wave after shock wave of shrapnel zinging over those terraces, and terrified soldiers doing the only thing they could do—cower and wait to die. The most unfortunate were dying slowly, bleeding to death from a dozen wounds.

Many of my comrades didn't come back. Those who straggled down the hill, well after dark, had a single thought: "We will never take those damn hills."

Aside from the obvious shock of the shelling, their pessimism came from the loss of several of our most capable black officers, men like Captain Jesse Jarmon. Infantrymen looked upon Jarmon and those other officers as heroes. It was devastating when those heroes were summarily blown away in twenty minutes of shelling. We already suspected we were being dispatched on suicide missions. The all-out massacre in the February battle proved it.

The disaster took the punch from the entire 370th. We spent the rest of February and much of March doing little but routine patrolling and grousing about what was next. My men huddled in little groups and swapped increasingly jaded versions of the next suicide mission. There had been three major frontal attacks on Hills X, Y, and Z, and the results were progressively worse for our men. Will Boswell, who spoke less and less about anything and became more and more weary around the eyes, summed it up for the rest of us.

"You got to wonder if there's enough sense among these white generals to do anything but throw us straight into the same damn line at the same damn place," he said dully. "Might as well write that last letter home." He tossed aside the remaining contents of his cup and walked off with as much dejection as his voice had demonstrated.

We were certain there would be a fourth frontal attack on Hills X, Y, and Z and knew it was our turn to participate. The Germans must have applauded. They understood that the 92nd had one battle plan and stuck to that battle plan no matter how overwhelming the evidence of its failure.

My company already churned in an uneasy state of flux. We hadn't had a commander for months. Montie disappeared while I was in the hospital. His successor, Captain Matthews, was around less than two weeks. After he was evacuated, I was the senior officer and essentially ran the show. But General Almond and Colonel Sherman weren't tolerating black company commanders. They weren't going to start any new trends by promoting me. And the 92nd was undergoing grand reorganization, the only tactical brilliance Almond and Sherman could muster in the face of their continuing failures.

In late March, three new white men appeared at Company C, a former Continental Baking Co. troubleshooter named Captain John F. Runyon, a Second Lieutenant Botwinik, and another first lieutenant whose name I cannot remember. None of them had much combat experience.

Runyon was self-possessed with his own brilliance. He'd apparently worked wonders for Continental Baking. He was pals with the top brass of the 92nd and had dazzled them by overhauling their equipment maintenance program. His promotion to company commander had come in Louisiana, when his original outfit was on maneuvers and the standing company commander was accidentally shot.

He made sure we knew about his management genius. The story of his rise to company commander didn't get around until after the war. For the moment, we had a boastful white commander who looked fresh off the boat and acted as if we should be thunderstruck by his shrewdness.

Captain Runyon immediately called a meeting of the company officers and bumped me from executive officer back to platoon leader. In a stroke of morale-busting stupidity, however, I wasn't allowed to return to my old rifle platoon. I was given a weapons platoon—two mortar squads and two light machine gun squads.

I wasn't happy. First a de facto demotion, and then I wasn't allowed to return to my old gang. I knew Army tradition required the senior second lieutenant to run the weapons platoon. Army traditions and hidebound tactics were fine in peacetime, but it was our continuing inflexibility in combat that was giving the Germans an easy-to-follow template and an easy-to-follow method for beating us back. Giving me the men I knew, the men who trusted me the most would have made for the most effective fighting team.

One rifle platoon went to Lieutenant Botwinik. The other new first lieutenant became the company executive officer. He also was put in charge of my old rifle platoon. The final platoon didn't have an officer and instead relied on its top noncommissioned officer, an able leader named Sergeant William Bartow.

The old-timers turned morose, whispering among themselves about the new "white commanders." I gritted my teeth, temporarily buried my anger, and tried to quell the growing discontent. "We've got a job to do, let's just do it," I encouraged. "The people who count, your platoon leaders and squad leaders, are still here."

Talking only went so far. My soldiers had no rapport with white officers to begin with. And the newer the officer, the greater their suspicion. I couldn't argue against their fears. If we were going to be moved from the reserve list out on the line, we wanted to know how much we could trust these men.

There was no time to figure it out. In a few days we learned our company would lead the next charge for Castle Aghinolfi. The attack would begin well before dawn on April 5. Fully seventy percent of our ranks now were replacements, strangers to us. Who knew if they were accustomed to combat?

EIGHTEEN

Wars must be fought with weapons, but they are won by men. It is the spirit of the men who follow and of the man who leads that gains the victory.

—General George S. Patton

April 5, 1945, Querceta, Italy

About midnight, soldiers from the 442nd Regimental Combat Team started climbing toward Mount Folgorito and Mount Carchio from the lofty little village of Azzano. The Japanese-American fighters had crept into the village during the two previous days, after an arduous, rainy eight-mile hike in the dark with full combat gear, and stayed hidden in the village houses until now. The other all-Japanese-American outfit, the 100th Infantry Battalion, also used the cover of darkness to start for other German-held peaks, coming at them from the south. Together the 100th and 442nd aimed to rake the Germans out of the high ground overlooking Castle Aghinolfi and the Strettoia Hills.

I watched and listened from the coastal plain far below, pacing outside the two-story farmhouse where my platoon and I lived. I strained to hear any murmur of the advance. Only silence answered.

The return of the 100th and the 442nd from France had been a closely held secret, an attempt to keep the Germans from anticipating a spring offensive. Having the "little men of iron" on our right flank was inspiring. The Nisei were the toughest, most decorated units in the U.S. Army. Many of the men were volunteers from the internment camps in the United States. "Internment" being bureaucratic dressing for locking up 110,000 Japanese—70,000 of whom were born in the United States—because they supposedly posed a security threat to the United States.

The 100th and 442nd bounced from Italy to France to Austria, taking the most dangerous missions and pulling other regiments out of all kinds of predicaments. The men climbing above me included veterans of the 100th and 442nd's recent rescue of the all-white "Lost Battalion" from a hopeless trap in the dense forests of northeastern France. The rescue cost the Nisei eight hundred wounded, missing, and dead. By war's end, the 100th and 442nd would log nearly 9,500 Purple Hearts, fifty-three Distinguished Service Crosses—the second highest honor for valor—but only one Medal of Honor. Racism visited the Japanese-American ranks just as it visited ours.

In one of their most brilliant strokes in months, our commanders decided the 100th and 442nd should go after the two mountains anchoring the other two legs of the Triangle of Death as we went after the third leg, the castle. Through no fault of the Nisei, their gallant assault on Mount Folgorito nearly became a disaster. The German Army learned from its spy network that the Allies planned to attack the peak from the west and prepared an ambush.

Italian partisans—the civilians who fought a guerrilla war against the Germans—caught wind of the ambush and told American commanders. The white commanders, still somewhat suspicious of Italian intelligence reports, were slow to believe the partisans. It reportedly took the partisans four hours to convince the Americans to change the direction of the attack.

I went inside the farmhouse and climbed the stone steps to my second-floor bedroom. My wake-up call came at three o'clock a.m. Or rather a reason to pull myself from my Army-issue mummy bag. I had lain awake listening and thinking for most of the few hours I had been there. Normally I could sleep under any conditions. I trained myself to snooze in snatches, whatever I could coax between making rounds to ensure my sentries were alert and to check on my men. In the rare instance my internal clock failed, my platoon sergeant roused me. Or German artillery thundered me awake.

This morning, despite the lack of sleep, adrenaline masked the inevitable fatigue. There was tension, only tension.

I pulled on my last clean pair of underwear and reached for my dress uniform. A week earlier, I had asked our supply sergeant to fetch my dress greens without any notion of why I wanted them. During my midnight vigil, as I strained for any sound of the Nisei's advance, I knew why I wanted to wear my best uniform the next morning: The day spelled death. I wanted to go up sharp.

I topped off my outfit with my customary cap, a wool helmet liner, and left my helmet near my bed roll. A helmet inhibited my hearing, which had been partially damaged in mortar training. I wanted the best of all my senses. Besides, the so-called steel bucket was worthless at repelling shrapnel.

Two bandoleers of ammunition buckled easily around my waist, and four grenades soon hung from the pockets of my Eisenhower jacket. The Allies had a worldwide shortage of ammunition during these winter months, and Italy was a low priority battle front. I was lucky to have ninety-six rifle rounds to take into battle.

I grabbed my M-1 rifle and instinctively rechecked it thoroughly. The action was smoother than the day it was brand-new. Grandpa would approve.

My platoon cooked coffee in the tiny kitchen downstairs. Or whatever semblance of coffee they had perfected after eight months in combat. I joined them for a quick cup. Some of the men took distracted bites from whatever they could find for breakfast. The usual prebattle banter was quite subdued. Still, Willie Dickens drew a chuckle out of the stoic men by noting that he expected Dandy Belk to always look like he was going on leave, but he hadn't counted on me in dress greens.

"This a one-time thing, lieutenant, or you and Dandy gonna march around dressed like you're dating each other from now on?" Dickens asked.

President Clinton presents Vernon Baker with the Medal of Honor at White House ceremony in the East Room on January 13, 1997. (White House Office of Photography).

Family members of World War II veterans who received Medal of Honor posthumously at White House ceremony in the East Room on January 13, 1997. (White House Office of Photography).

General Colin L. Powell, USA (Ret.) and Vernon Baker share a moment during a reception the evening before the Medal of Honor ceremonies on January 13, 1997. (Craig Buck/The Spokesman-Review).

Vernon Baker wipes away tears while meeting with General Robert Foley at the Pentagon on January 13, 1997, following the Medal of Honor ceremony at the White House. (Craig Buck/The Spokesman-Review).

...on Baker's squad leaders, June, 1944.
...R: Marvin Finney, John Robinson, Jacy Cunigan,
...or Martin, Edward Richardson). (Vernon Baker
...ction).

On leave in Genoa, Italy, after the battle
at Castle Aghinolfi, 1945. (Craig Buck/
Vernon Baker collection).

...h Regimental Headquarters, Chiavari, Italy,
..., 1945. (L-R: Lawrence Spencer,
...on Baker, and soldier Conley). (Vernon
...er collection).

1st Lt. Vernon Baker, 11th Airborne,
Ft. Campbell, Kentucky, 1951.
(Vernon Baker collection).

...on Baker, July 4, 1945, after
...iving Distinguished Service Cross.
...l Dickerson/Harry Cox).

Vernon Baker and Doppo Guerra, 370th Regiment,
Viarregio, Italy, 1945. (Vernon Baker collection).

Training Company, Ft. Ord, California, 1957. (Vernon Baker collection).

Vernon Baker as Senior Drill Instructor, Ft. Ord, California, 1957. (Craig Buck/Vernon Baker collection).

Ft. Ord, California, 1955. (Craig Buck/ Vernon Baker collection).

On duty with American Red Cross in Vietnam, 1969. Also pictured, cousin, Kenneth Griggs. (Craig Buck/Vernon Baker collection).

Grandparents Joseph Samuel Baker and Dora V. Baker with dog, Shep. 1920s, Cheyenne, Wyoming.

The Bakers were responsible for raising Vernon and his sisters after the tragic death of their parents when Vernon was 4 years old. (Vernon Baker collection).

...non Baker's late wife, Fern Baker, and ...r, Cass, Seaside, California, 1953. ...ig Buck/Vernon Baker collection).

Vernon Baker with Mel Prater spearfishing near Cannery Row, Monterey, California, 1956. (Craig Buck/Vernon Baker collection).

Remains of Castle Aghinolfi, April, 1997. (Ken Olsen).

Vernon Baker in his infamous
helmet liner, April, 1997, Italy.
(Ken Olsen).

Vernon and Harry Cox at the Gothic Line, April, 1997.
(Ken Olsen).

Vernon and Emilio, reunited 52 years after
the battle at Castle Aghinolfi, April 5, 1997.
(Ken Olsen).

The American Battle Monument Cemetery, near
Florence, Italy, where many World War II Buffalo
Soldiers are buried, April, 1997.
(Ken Olsen).

Vernon Baker with dignitaries in Montignoso, Italy, April, 1997, where he was honored for helping free the village. (Ken Olsen).

ernon Baker with the President of Italy, scar Luigi Scalfaro (far right) and ournalist, Umberto Venturini, La Spezia, aly, April, 1997. (Ken Olsen).

Vernon Baker greeted by Italian partisans and well wishers, Massa, Italy, April, 1997. (Ken Olsen).

ernon Baker autographs a WWII-era jeep or an Italian history enthusiast, April, 997. (Ken Olsen).

Vernon Baker with 162 lb. mountain lion which stalked him while he was elk hunting, fall, 1995. (Craig Buck/Vernon Baker collection).

On hunting trip in Klamath National Forest, Californ 1970. (Craig Buck/Vernon Baker collection).

Heidy Baker with dog team on her first visit to Idaho, February, 1990. (Vernon Baker collection).

Vernon and granddaughter, Savanna, 1986. (Vernon Baker collection).

Vernon in Idaho with dog, Lucky, fall, 1996. (Craig Buck/The Spokesman-Review).

Explaining myself was far too awkward. I blushed and turned to reinspect my rifle. In the pregnant quiet that followed I wished for the optimism of those early days, when these moments would have been filled with the prediction of marvelous deeds and cowering Germans.

By 3:30 a.m. we headed along the road for the Command Post. Captain Runyon emerged from the tall, narrow stone building a few minutes after we arrived.

Ideally my weapons platoon would have been thirty-six men strong; two nine-man squads with .30-caliber machine guns and two nine-man squads with 60mm mortar tubes and mortar rounds. But casualties had thinned my ranks to twenty-six men, and there were no replacement soldiers available. I was missing yet another man this morning. One of my main sergeants, a man I cannot bear to name, shuffled in the night before, complaining that he was sick and needed permission to go to the dispensary.

"What's the problem?" I inquired.

"A dose," he said.

"A dose?" I demanded. "You've got the clap?"

"Yeah, lieutenant, sorry," he replied, looking around as if he was trying to make sure nobody could hear his private sexual embarrassment; knowing his biggest embarrassment was coming to me the night before a major battle with this crap about the clap.

I tried to figure when he'd contracted this case of gonorrhea. We both knew if he had a dose, he damn sure could have had it taken care of before this night.

"Go on, you son-of-a-bitch," I said. "You'd better hit the dispensary."

He started to speak, maybe to apologize.

"Go on," I repeated, "before I decide to give you something for your sickness."

I was too weary to deal with his fear and too afraid to count on him the next day if he was this desperate not to be in combat. While I understood his feelings, I was fiercely proud of the fact that my platoon always showed up for the fight. We didn't have much incentive.

A great job hadn't earned black soldiers any special notice. Running away, however, earned infamy. And I made sure everyone knew it.

Runyon paced about the company while I agitated over the spareness of our ranks. Not only was my platoon undermanned, Company C was at least seventy men short of the more than two hundred that should have been on hand. Again, casualties and the lack of replacement soldiers worked against us.

Once Runyon was satisfied the company was accounted for, he gave the order to move out. We walked a short distance up the road and then cut through several dew-heavy farm fields. We split into our separate platoons near the junction of two dirt tracks and made for our individual jumping off spots.

Our starting point was another 250 yards from the junction, in the bombed-out trees at the edge of a huge overgrown field. Even the most intrepid Italian wasn't going to cultivate this close to the German lines.

I motioned for my men to stop.

"No talking when we're going up that hill," I warned. "Hand signals only."

Inexplicably, I felt a rush of hope. "Today, we're going to do it," I added. My men nodded.

Doing nothing noisier than breathing, we squatted in the darkness and waited. The spring air was crisp and jaunty, welcome after several sultry days. It was a perfect day for a walk anywhere but into battle.

Italy's northwestern coast was mindful of Wyoming, the coastal plain meeting the Apennines much like the sagebrush prairie that embraces the Rocky Mountains. Italy was altogether different, with oceans, ancient ruins, and fast-talking, impatient natives. Still, spring between the Mediterranean and the mountains carried a sense of life and renewal, as long as you didn't contemplate the rest of the brutal picture.

Time ticked all too rapidly toward 4:45 a.m. My eyes were glued to my watch face. When the hands locked on the appointed time, the Allied artillery began its morning concert. This ritual had begun at exactly the same time, every day for a week, so the Germans would think that this was just another morning of gunnery practice.

Tanks, long-range guns from British battleships, howitzers, and mortars all played parts of the score, rhythmically rolling volleys up the steep Strettoia Hills. Eight months earlier, this kind of barrage would have had us cringing, no matter which side was launching it. Now we were numb to it. And, on this morning, we focused on the hills ahead of us instead of the cataclysmic thundering.

I kept my eyes on my watch. The next cue was far more important. A twenty-minute shelling intermission began at five o'clock a.m. This also was part of the week-long performance, part of making the Germans believe this day was part of the same old routine.

I waited for the echo of the last explosion to ring back through the hills and gave my squad leaders the high sign. We stood and rushed for the bottom of Hill X, a half mile away over the most exposed countryside between ourselves and the Germans. Thank God for darkness.

We crossed railroad tracks, Highway One, and one last small field smelling of alfalfa. The long slope of Hill X pitched 450 feet upward, one terrace at a time, although in this light we could see only a giant black knob. I spotted Captain Runyon as we closed on the trail switchbacking to the top.

It was a good, solid dirt path, the outer edge delineated with rocks. And Captain Runyon, I'll bless him for this, was stepping rock to rock up the outside edge, probing the way with a stick. I admired Runyon's effort. He seemed coolheaded and a quick thinker. This showed he had spent a little bit of time studying the area and was aware of the German's reputation for paving it with mines.

I turned and whispered to the man behind me, "Walk only on the rocks. Pass it on back."

Single file, rock to rock, my men followed with .30-caliber light machine guns, 60mm mortars, and ammunition. I carried nine pounds of M-1 rifle, stretched hand-to-hand in front of my waist. None of this using a sling to carry my weapon. Never. That meant I had to pull my rifle off my back when the bullets started flying—a shortcut to death.

A lighter weight .30-caliber carbine was standard-issue for officers. Experience cured my desire for this convenience. I once watched an American soldier, sitting on one of our tanks, unload five bullets from such a carbine into a German soldier who was charging him with a bazooka. The German never slowed. I immediately traded away my carbine.

My next acquisition, a .45-caliber Thompson submachine gun, was great for throwing a lead shower if you didn't care about accuracy. I traded it away with the same speed it consumed ammunition. I preferred a solid weapon, one I could snap up and fire, like the rifle I had used when hunting deer and elk with my grandfather back in Wyoming. The M-1 rifle, with a custom recoil pad, fulfilled my need. Its heavy butt-to-barrel wooden stock wasn't a hardship to pack up Hill X. It was solid comfort.

With a methodical rhythm of stop, balance, step, stop, balance, step, we moved rapidly, rock to rock, one man after another, up the trail. Sweat, dust, and gun oil blended with the familiar odor of well-worn Army cloth and shot up my nostrils as I labored.

Once we reached the top I signaled for a quick break, so we could catch our breaths. But barely. Our artillery was scheduled to start lobbing shells again after giving us just enough time to cross the fields and get started climbing the hills. Then gunners were supposed to open fire again, with an advancing line of shells, to cover our push forward.

Suddenly the plan was out of whack. Explosions erupted on the slopes we had just climbed. "Damn," I muttered, breaking my rule of silence, "we've outrun our artillery."

We had to keep running or be smashed by friendly fire. With desperate energy, I stood, cranked my arm windmill-fashion, silently exclaiming, "Let's get the hell out of here."

My men pulled away from Captain Runyon, who had other platoons to worry about. We spread out in a line among the olive trees and the stone pines at the crest of Hill X and moved west to skirt

Hills Y and Z. Alpha Company was supposed to be on our left flank, Bravo Company on our right. We busted ahead to set up mortars and machine guns to cover their advance.

After I was satisfied that we were temporarily safe from our own artillery, we paused again and I counted men. Our machine gun crews were intact, but our mortar squads were nowhere to be seen. Running back into the murderous shellfire to look for them was suicide. We must travel without them.

During this respite a handful of men from the third platoon—my old rifle outfit—wandered into our flank. They had somehow gotten separated from the rest of their group. I ordered them to join us and, now a group of twenty-six—equivalent to the platoon I would have had if my mortar squads were there—we hiked.

The higher we moved, the less cover the trees provided. Leaves were almost nonexistent and branches not touched by the constant shelling were rare. The light was just right for attack. It wasn't total darkness, nor the committed gray of dawn. A shade in between outlined the mountains immediately to the east and the two layers of mountains beyond where the 100th and 442nd were fighting.

Sunup later showed this as one of the prettiest places in the world, a macabre contrast to the thrashing ugliness of men killing men for control of old castles, hillsides, and shell-shocked olive groves. At this hour, it was a shadowy maze.

My men placed their steps carefully, yet moved quickly over the level ground of the summit. We soon were stopped by yellow plastic lines snaking through the olive groves about three inches off the ground. My soldiers instinctively turned to me with questioning faces. I couldn't see everyone's expression, but I knew their body language. "What is this?" they silently asked.

Problem was, I had not ever seen this new invention called plastic either. But night patrols taught me to always carry a pair of wire cutters in my pocket to deal with barbed wire. I eased down and pulled them from my pocket. Opening the jaws, I took a bite of the line and exercised the cutter's jaws until it parted with a soft twang. I pocketed the pliers, grabbed the plastic line, and scraped one end of the freshly cut yellow worm with my thumbnail. A solid copper core. German communications wire of some sort. We would foul this yellow spider web.

At my lead, we moved forward again, weaving in and out of the trees. We stayed close enough to see each other, but far enough apart so a single 88mm cannon shell couldn't take out half the platoon. This distance from our fellow soldiers went against every desire. We wanted to be close to someone when we sensed death. The blessing of surviving a couple of battles is that we learned to operate on instinct and reflex while ignoring fear.

The taut yellow lines ran everywhere. I stooped to cut every wire we found. It felt good to inflict any sort of damage on the enemy.

As I rose from each cutting session, I scanned the area, side-to-side, to the rear, and side-to-side again, a habit born of being ambushed on patrols. Well into the web of wires, I imagined movement and froze to study the spot it came from. The movement repeated. It was helmets, two helmets. German helmets.

I silently sidestepped away from my men, raised my rifle, and nestled the recoil pad into the natural slot between my arm and my clavicle. Two quick cracks and the helmets dropped like deer. I crept away from them for forty or fifty yards, and then made a half-circle back, trying to give myself a little edge in case they fired in the direction of my shots. Instead I found two dead German machine gunners. We ditched their gun and replaced it with one of ours—one we had fired thousands of times, one we could resupply with ammunition, one we knew how to tear down, unjam, and reassemble even in the eye of a tornado.

A few hundred yards farther two more German helmets caught my eye. My M-1 came up automatically. Muzzle flashes recorded two more shots. Another pair of Nazi machine gunners crumpled. Fortunately the American artillery working the slopes muffled my fire. Not that there was a choice. It was better to risk a few rifle shots than to risk leaving live Germans.

I grew uneasy about the frequency of German machine gunners. After replacing the latest kill with our own gunner, assistant gunner, and ammo bearers, I moved to the left of my remaining men. If I could reach the edge of the ridge, I could both have a better view of the coming terrain and also keep better track of my troops. Perhaps I could spot our companion companies and figure out where the lagging mortar squads were.

I worked toward a buckle on the outer rim of the hill. Streaks of daylight started to creep up the horizon to my right, lifting our shield. It also lifted a portion of the German camouflage. I could see what appeared to be flared metal tubes poking from a horizontal hillside slit that was approximately two feet long and six inches wide. Flash suppressors for machine guns, I reasoned.

Reflexively, I melted into a crouch, then a crawl, and onto my belly. I inched toward the slit, propelled by my elbows. Once near enough, I came to my knees, raised my rifle above me, and, as I stood up, I put the barrel in the opening and started working the trigger furiously.

The bolt whip-sawed, taking cartridge after cartridge from the clip on the top of my gun. The bunker shouted back the muted echoes of each shot. The empty clip kicked off, telling me my last round was gone. I dropped back, tried to blend into the hillside, fingered a fresh clip from a pocket of the canvas bandoleers, and locked it in place. The solid click of a new clip nestling into the gun always gave me pleasure.

I counted off a minute, maybe less; whatever seemed enough time for the enemy to return fire. If one still lived. Then I moved back to the slit, stuck my rifle back through the opening, and peered inside. One German soldier slumped in a chair. Another was crawling toward a stash of grenades in the corner.

Spinning around the corner of the bunker, I grabbed a grenade from my chest with my left hand. I momentarily slid the rifle to rest on the ground, pulled the pin with my right hand, and tossed the grenade in through the opening serving as a door. The advantages of being ambidextrous. I could throw a grenade with either hand.

I caught my rifle on the fly, feeling as much as seeing the flash and the muffled thump-thump, tasting the bitter smoke and debris roiling out of the bunker as I ran. Fairly confident the wounded man hadn't survived, I returned almost as quickly and ducked into the bunker, rifle at the ready.

The air had barely cleared, but it was enough. A cubbyhole built of rocks, dirt, and logs extended back about six feet. What I had taken for machine gun flash suppressors were the twin barrels of a periscope-style binocular observation scope. I moved to the eye pieces and dared to take the time for a hunter's appreciative glance through the powerful optics. Several American soldiers were clearly visible on the plains below and, if I had been a German, I could have easily called for their snuffing with an artillery round. This observation scope was as lethal as machine guns or mortar rounds.

I glanced around the dugout and spotted two field telephones. Each sprouted a ribbon of the same yellow communications wire I had been cutting. This was part of the yellow web. We had been clipping the telephone wires that made it possible for the bunkers, snipers, machine gun nests, mortars, and artillery to track us. My wire cutters rendered both telephones useless.

Tearing loose another grenade, I went back to the observation scope. I balanced the grenade in the cradle created where the eyepieces turned from the scope and jutted into the room, toward the dead man stitched into the observation chair with lead. After a quick, last look around the room, I jerked the pin.

One thousand one . . . one thousand two . . . one thousand three . . . involuntarily trumpeted through my brain. I sprinted for the door, skidded down the face of the gentle slope and through the olive trees. There was no wasting time checking to see if the second grenade did the necessary work. I took it on faith and sound effects.

I reached my men and automatically scanned their surroundings. My eyes and ears searched for whatever hostility my grenades might elicit. This couldn't go unchallenged all day.

There was no response. Our luck was holding.

I moved to the front of the platoon. From my memory of the aerial photographs and maps I had studied, we needed to cut almost due east in order to connect with the castle. I pulled my rifle up to its preferred position, waist height, and resumed walking through the trees, this time away from the ridge and back toward the castle. In a few hundred yards I had my next jolt.

Not more than fifty feet in front of me a ring of logs and rocks gave away a .50-caliber machine gun, ready to spit. The nest was so well disguised that the only way I could have found it was stumbling upon it.

"Oh, shit," I thought. "Prepare for serious fire."

But the gun was unmanned. Its attendants, two men in Nazi gray uniforms, sat at the back of the nest eating breakfast. Without taking the time to pull my gun above waist height, I swung my rifle barrel forward and started shooting. The Germans staggered, one at a time and yet together, and pitched into their breakfast. Once convinced they were dead, I went back for one of our machine gun squads and ordered it to take their place.

I was high on adrenaline. In a few hours, my platoon had stolen nearly three miles behind enemy lines. Three machine gun nests and an observation post had been eliminated. German communication lines were reduced to a lifeless tangle. We hadn't suffered any casualties.

This might turn out to be the easy stuff, I thought, reviewing the aerial photos in my mind. There was a deep draw between us and the castle. It was time to find Captain Runyon and the other platoons.

NINETEEN

Play for more than you can afford to lose and you will learn the game.

—Winston Churchill

6:30 a.m., April 5, 1945

Three-hundred yards across a deep V-shaped ravine a steep knob rose to hold the German stronghold: Castle Aghinolfi.

The morning sun gathered force over the Apennines and played on the ancient, crumbling fortress, giving it a mystical, white luminescence. Crumbling towers staggered over the boxy summit. Time and neglect had eroded the tower-top parapets to the point that the castle looked more like a flat-topped monastery than a onetime medieval home to sword- and shield-wielding warriors.

The remaining trees on the adjacent slopes had few branches and disfigured tops, casualties of the same artillery shells that also scoured a jarring white scar in a rock outcropping fifty feet below the castle. All of this sat wrapped in morning quiet, eerie and beautiful—a peacefulness we didn't enjoy long.

It was not yet seven o'clock when Runyon and I perched at the edge of the draw to figure how to traverse its steep slopes, scale the knob, and storm the castle. It was as formidable as its reputation. Brush covered all but the last seventy-five yards of ground between us and the castle. That critical seventy-five yards not only was rocky barren ground, but it was ringed with the ancient stone walls that had rigidly defended the castle for 1,500 years. A blind nitwit with any functioning rifle could wipe out half of any invading force brazen enough to try to scale the slope and the walls.

But orders were orders. And this was the only route to taking the castle and punching north.

Runyon and I agreed to move our machine guns to the lip of the draw to provide covering fire for the castle assault. We agonized over the absence of our mortar squads, still somewhere behind us. Our lack of mortars added great disadvantage to our all-out daylight assault. The other ramification went unspoken between us. Our lack of mortars made holding our current ground more difficult in the face of the inevitable German counterattack. We banked on our mortar squads catching up soon. They wouldn't. They had been pinned down by German machine gunners or killed by mines on Hill X more than an hour earlier.

As we contemplated, a German soldier emerged from the brush about twenty-five yards to our left and slightly below us. This was his backyard; it shouldn't have been anything startling, but it was. In sur-real slow-motion, the German started to heave one of the trademark Nazi potato-masher grenades. I started to bring my M-1 around, instinctively trying to kill him before the grenade was airborne.

Runyon simultaneously yelped and scrambled to his feet, not noticing that my rifle barrel was swinging across the front of his midsection in order for me to get the quickest shot off. In his haste to escape, Runyon knocked the barrel wide and nearly knocked the rifle into the ravine. I lunged.

The German soldier's arm reached the end of its windup. He leaned forward and launched the grenade, one leg coming off the ground in the fashion of an Olympic discus thrower. The moment the grenade cleared his fingertips, he pivoted and started to run away.

I clawed the air to recover my rifle, not wanting to shoot him in the back for some reason, but still very much wanting to kill him. The grenade tumbled toward me.

Three things happened. I cannot say in what order or if they were simultaneous. The grenade landed five feet from me, bounced . . . but did not explode. I squeezed off two shots, slamming the German in the back. And Runyon disappeared.

I was livid. First this damn German snuck up on us, then Runyon goes hysterical, as if he'd never seen an enemy soldier with a grenade, and as a result of those hysterics I had to adopt enough cowardice to shoot another soldier in the back. My honor was reparable. A battlefield commander so prone to panic was a more unnerving problem.

Staff Sergeant Willie Dickens, looking much more serious and disturbed than his normal, comical self, came running at the commotion.

"I think I nailed him," I told Dickens as I struggled to my feet, too full of adrenaline to fully realize how close I'd come to becoming a corpse. "But there's liable to be a few more where he came from."

"You want a patrol?" Dickens volunteered.

"No. Keep the guys up top," I said. "Pretty soon the Germans are going to figure out we're stirring around here. I want you guys here to cover each other when the shit gets thick. Trade me guns and I'll go see if this Kraut's got any cousins down in the draw."

I tossed my rifle to Dickens and he tossed me his Thompson submachine gun. "Wait," he said as I started off, and tossed me an extra thirty-round clip.

"Thanks—good idea," I said, glad that he was thinking when I was being hasty.

Despite my strong preference for an M-1, this submachine gun was perfect for close-quartered fighting, especially when I expected to be outnumbered. I dropped into the ravine and scrambled after the grenade thrower. We needed to know where he came from and how many enemy soldiers might be with him. I found him face down, and dead, almost at the entrance of a dugout. I stuck the submachine gun into the entrance and let loose with a dozen rounds and darted to the side to await a reply. Nothing happened. I moved inside. The small cavern was empty except for a few hand grenades strewn about the floor.

I stepped out in the daylight, crouched down by the dead soldier, and studied the area. The dugout was on a path that continued around the hill. The path led away from the castle, as if going to overlook the coastal plain and the Cinquale Canal. I followed it, sweeping the submachine gun to and fro, ready to spray the enemy soldiers I expected to come pounding along this path to find their dead buddy or investigate the rifle shots. In about a quarter mile, the narrow, chalky trail veered toward the face of the ravine and a partially-concealed Volkswagen door, strangely hanging on the side of the draw. Or not so strange. Another dugout, I reasoned.

I heaved on the door, ready to unleash the Tommy gun the moment I cracked it open. It didn't budge.

Not knowing what I was up against, or when I could resupply myself, I retraced my steps to the first dugout, dashed inside and grabbed two of the German grenades. I returned to the Volkswagen door, nudged one of the grenades under the bottom edge, pulled the pin and ducked into the cover of bushes that still afforded a view of the entrance. The grenade ripped the door off the hillside with the shriek of tormented metal. My gun came up in anticipation. Moments later, a dazed, half dressed German soldier poked his head out the entrance. I split his skull with a single burst, charged the entrance, pulled the pin from the second grenade, and tossed it in. A roar of dirt and rocks kicked out of the opening as I dove to the side. Without waiting for the entrance to clear completely, I rolled back to my feet. I wheeled into the doorway, emptied the submachine gun's magazine into the darkness, and ducked to the side in case of a hostile reply.

Nothing.

Jamming a new magazine on the gun, I stepped over the dead soldier, through the entrance and moved to one side, out of the light, while my eyes adjusted.

Nothing.

No Germans came bursting from whatever catacomb lay at the back of the dugout; none appeared from the outside to investigate.

Other than the clack and clatter of rocks settling inside the dugout, all was quiet.

I inched ahead to see the rest of the cool, dark room. Three dead German soldiers had been heaped into opposite corners by the grenade blast. A table, overturned in the middle of the eight foot by eight foot room, was surrounded by tin plates. Breakfast was plastered against the walls and spewed over the soldiers' faces. My second breakfast kill of the day, I noted, forcing myself to think mechanically, not emotionally. This luck wouldn't last. I bolted.

I retraced the path, moving past the first dugout, and kept going until it led me to the top of the draw, almost right where Runyon and I had dangled our feet and studied the castle. Had we seen the path, hidden by the thick brush, we might have anticipated company.

As I emerged at the top, rifle fire signaled that the Germans had discovered us. Then came mortar barrages. Then came chaos.

Our forward artillery observer, Second Lieutenant Walker, grabbed the handset from his radioman and barked coordinates. He repeated the instructions over and over. Shaking his head, he pulled the telephone-style handset away from his ear and looked at me.

"Goddamn, they . . . goddamn, they don't believe we're here. They don't believe we're this far . . . behind enemy lines. Goddamnit."

Walker looked as if he wanted to break the handset on the nearest rock. We desperately needed artillery fire on the German mortar positions. Our medics couldn't get to our wounded because of the airborne shrapnel saturation.

A moment of uneasy quiet punctuated the melee. I scanned the edge of the ridge, expecting attacking Germans.

"Hey, what's that?" one of my riflemen yelled. "Look at that flock of birds." He pointed to a cloud of black specks flying toward us.

"Cover!" I yelled and dived for the dirt. Those weren't birds, they were mortar rounds. Explosions rumbled in rapid succession around us. Men screamed. This round of shells carved the life out of three of my soldiers and left three others bleeding. I swore at the Germans and swore at the American intelligence officers who doubted our location.

The Germans continued warming up. Castle-side machine guns opened at full throttle. I crawled back toward Walker as he grabbed the radio handset again, this time screaming with all possible intensity, "Get me some goddamned artillery up here now!"

He paused, obviously listening.

"No, the castle!" Walker shouted in response to some question. "Hit castle and Hill R-7, to the northeast."

Intense haggling followed. Walker repeated the coordinates. It finally worked. Low-trajectory 90mm antiaircraft shells screeched from the far side of Hill X, skimmed in low over our heads, and smashed into the castle and the draw. We ducked with every round. The castle was barely higher than the ridge top where we were huddled. The margin of error between our position and the German position was negligible, as long-range artillery goes. But once we convinced our guys, they delivered on target. The antiaircraft shells temporarily quieted the German mortars.

In the next moment of calm, some of my men started going for the cover of the trees and digging in. Mortar rounds started winging in again; whish, whish, whish, KABOOM; whish, whish, whish, KABOOM. I woke to our folly and darted into the trees, shouting and grabbing people. Trees were bursting. Those that weren't a hurricane of giant, jagged slivers toppled over to crush men.

"Move. Move. *Move!*" I yelled. *"Keep moving!"*

Disintegrating trees were more dangerous than a wide open space. The Germans knew it.

Men scattered. I grabbed, snagged, yelled, and prodded, trying to get control of them. In the distance I heard the bark of a German accent.

"Feuer!"

Fire! It was the German mortar battery commander giving the order to fire. I pulled at the man nearest to me and shouted *"Move! Move or die!"*

For the next several rounds, we played this game of chicken. When I heard the German command to fire, we jumped and ran to a different place. For a time, it worked. The mortar rounds always landed where we'd just left. The Germans stepped up their effort and added artillery. The howls of shells, mortars, and wounded men intensified. The air was more burned explosives and bitter cordite, than oxygen. A foggy kaleidoscope of dust, debris, and blood boiled around us.

Men dropped. A few pitched forward, others went bulleting backward, as if struck by a freight train. I ran to them, saying, "Please God, let him be alive." When I got to each man, I saw an arm or a leg or half of the man's face blown off. An hour before, charged with adrenaline, I'd felt born to do combat. I'd known I was an invincible giant. This slaughter jarred my immortality.

The mortars paused again. I checked for wounded and living. It was gruesome. Walker's radioman was dead, and the shell that killed him also demolished the artillery radio. Walker was alive and moving, though blood oozed from dozens of gashes.

I pointed to the radio questioningly.

"They promised reinforcements," he told me of his final conversation with headquarters.

"When?" I asked.

"They said right away."

"Ah huh," I replied. "Well, we gotta have them today."

I yelled for Dandy Belk.

"Where the hell's Runyon?" I asked.

Belk shook his head. Then I realized he had no reason to know the name of a white officer who had been around but a week or two. "The captain, company commander," I said.

Belk pointed behind me.

"Over there, in the little stone house, the shed," he said. "He headed there the minute that Jerry pitched a masher at you two."

Using the meager brush for cover, I ran for the squat building. Runyon was sitting on the dirt floor, knees pulled up to his chest, his arms wrapped around his legs. His face was translucent, the color of bleached parchment.

"Baker," he said with a note of disgust, "can't you get these men together?"

"I'm doing the best goddamned job I can, captain," I snapped, boiling angry that he had the audacity to cower in here and still criticize those of us out in the fray.

"*Feuer!*" echoed in the distance. Seconds later, the whish, whish, whish of mortar rounds returned. I followed Runyon's gaze out the door. Lieutenant Botwinik was crouched behind a low stone wall. A mortar cascaded into the top of the wall, right above Botwinik's head. Bricks spewed from a cloud of disintegrating wall.

Runyon gasped. I muttered a kind thought for Botwinik's soul. And Botwinik stood up.

He staggered toward the shed. Runyon and I grabbed Botwinik, sat him inside the door, and checked for physical damage. The flash of the explosion had blinded him, and he was a bit dumb from shock.

Runyon cleared his throat. "Are we going to stay here?" he asked raspily.

I couldn't believe the question. We had accomplished something four other attempts hadn't matched. And we were within conquering distance of the castle.

"We're staying," I replied. "We can do this."

Runyon blinked rapidly and looked at me as if I was crazy. "Look, Baker, I'm going for reinforcements," he said, fighting to make his shaking voice sound flat and controlled.

Reinforcements? A captain going for reinforcements? Wasn't this the task of a sergeant and a couple of privates? I kept my thoughts to myself. His face said it all. He hadn't stopped running since that grenade had come flying toward us.

"All right, captain. We'll be here when you get back," I said, hoping my stare told him what my mouth hadn't.

Runyon waved a palm in front of Botwinik's face. Botwinik grabbed Runyon's arm and looked at him.

"My eyes are coming back, captain."

Runyon helped Botwinik to his feet and signaled his personal radioman to take Botwinik's other arm. The trio eased out of the shed and walked toward my men.

"We're going for reinforcements, taking what wounded we can," Runyon announced.

A murmur rose from the remainder of the enlisted men.

"*Mother fucker!*" a disheartened voice called.

"I'll be back," he declared.

I waved for silence.

"Right, captain," I repeated. "We'll be here when you get back."

Runyon, his radioman, and Botwinik trudged off into the late morning haze. Much later, I realized Runyon was taking the only remaining radioman because he didn't believe we could survive. That realization stirred my anger, my outrage. The bastard had simply walked away. Here was a commander whose only thought was for himself, not for his men.

The moment of battle, however, did not allow time for the luxury of anger. And Dandy Belk needed me.

"Lieutenant, do you want a perimeter?" he asked.

"Right. Yes. Up here," I said.

We turned, and I pointed out what seemed the most protected spot—a depression shielded by a slight rise, almost at the outer edge of the ridge. Belk gave orders. The men gathered rifles and spare ammunition from the mortally wounded and the dead. I followed them. When I reached a dead man, I pulled his helmet off, gingerly lifted his head with one hand and slipped his dog tags off with the other. I tried not to look into the faces. Their eyes were not quite vacant, still holding a small hint of life, even as the rest of their bodies were contorted in death. Some faces shouted terror, others shouted pain, but these men had battled to their last pulse anyway.

Gathering the dog tags maybe required fifteen minutes. It took the energy of fifteen hours. Dirty, smudged with the blood of others, but imbued with anger and determination, I rejoined my men, and we built our perimeter using whatever logs and rocks we could scrounge. I sent a man back for our machine gunners and their weapons. They were out of ammunition, scuttled their guns so the enemy couldn't use them, and came forward to join us. Each drew one of the recovered M-1's.

The last spare rifle was barely checked when the Germans renewed our acquaintance with their mortars. And so began the pattern.

Mortar rounds came first, followed by heavy machine gun cross fire. Then German soldiers attacked from out of nowhere. Dirt, exploding trees, and dust roiled so thickly that the first thing we saw were shapes, not men. We distinguished between friend and foe based upon motion. We lay still. The Germans moved. When we saw movement, we shot, albeit methodically, so as not to waste precious ammunition. The M-1 rifle saved our butts.

A third wave of mortars cascaded in. By now, the fine dust of exploding everything made a boiling cloud six or seven feet tall. We stayed burrowed into our little depression and strained to see what was next. An uncomfortably long silence.

My soldiers reached into their pouches or the dead men's bandoleers, pulled out extra clips, and stacked them by their sides. It made for faster reloading. It made their ammunition more accessible to a fellow soldier if they were killed. We gripped our rifles more tightly and scrutinized the smoke.

A flag with a red cross came trotting out of the haze and slowly connected itself to a flag bearer. He was followed by a platoon of Germans, most carrying stretchers. All of the men had red crosses on their helmets.

"We've got to fire . . . we've *got* to fire." The panicked whispers ran down our ranks toward me, and my men's eyes pleaded. I held my hand up, signaling for calm, and kept my eye on the advancing stretcher bearers.

"You don't want them shooting your medics," I replied sharply. "We're not going to shoot theirs."

The gray shapes grew closer, a hundred yards, seventy-five yards, then fifty. The German entourage stopped.

The stretchers dropped to the ground and the blankets were stripped off—revealing machine guns. One stretcher bearer reached for the gun while the other reached for the tripod and a third man readied an ammunition belt.

"Hit the bastards!" I yelled.

Will Boswell was up on one knee firing well before I finished my sentence. He shot the three men closest to having their machine gun operational. Our other riflemen cut loose with a vengeance. Phony medics staggered under the impact of our lead. The enemy platoon dissolved. Surviving Germans evaporated, leaving their dead and wounded on the slope below our little hummock.

Again and again, I checked behind us. No messenger darted forward to tell me we had reinforcements. No reinforcing platoon moved through the trees toward our position.

The intensity of combat must have dulled my senses. It finally came to me. Our commanders hadn't believed we made it three miles behind enemy lines. If artillery support was difficult, reinforcements were impossible. We held this ridge for nothing.

I didn't have any fear of dying myself. Grandfather was long gone, Helen wasn't in love with me. I would leave no great hole in the world.

But I was more and more afraid for my remaining eight men and our chances of doing anything meaningful. They crouched along our perimeter and stared at me. I can still see their faces—I see them every day, in my mind. Dandy Belk was no longer crisp; his creases sagged, his cheeks sagged. His normally ebullient face was pancaked with dirt and dried blood. Twigs and bark hung from the netting on his helmet, plastered there by the mortar explosions.

The other men radiated hopelessness and exhaustion. Even with our scavenged ammunition we were down to one or two clips apiece, too little to do anything—attack, stay put, or depart. I reluctantly called for our withdrawal.

My men moved out ahead of me. I lingered for a few moments to catch any Germans who might be waiting for this opportunity to renew the attack. I was not disappointed. Four enemy soldiers immediately appeared on the edge of the draw. I shot one in the chest, and the other three disappeared. They didn't reappear.

Mortars started again as we hit the olive groves running. Another one of my men went down. I jerked the dog tags from his neck. We pushed on. Sniper rounds pinged around our heads.

"Keep moving!" I shouted.

Thomas went crazy. He rolled behind a tree, brought his BAR around, and started shooting in the direction of the sniper. A German rifle clattered downslope to us. Thomas had killed him in the time it took me to free my medic's dog tags.

I kept my men hustling back to Hill X. Until we heard the machine gun fire. Unbelievable as it seemed, we had missed a pair of machine gun nests on the trek up. Now they spit five hundred rounds a minute, making sure no one moved up or down the hill. For the moment, fortunately, they were focused toward Hill X and not in our direction. Still, we couldn't get around them. Without deliberation, Thomas shouldered his BAR as lightly as I would have lifted a balsa-wood replica and set it chattering. I hit the ground, cradled my M-1 in my elbows, and started wiggling like a snake toward the backside of the machine gun nest. Thomas's bullets barely whistled over my head, and I began wondering about the possibilities of him accidentally running a round up my rump. The crowning end to a disastrous day.

I made it to the waist-high hole at the back of the nest, likely the access port for the gunners. The rest of the bunker was logs, dirt, and branches, save for the slot on the other side, from which the gun hammered the slopes below. I ripped a grenade from my jacket, yanked out the pin, and lobbed the grenade inside without ever rising off of the ground. Then I sucked the M-1 to my chest and rolled away from the machine gun nest. A geyser of dirt spit through the timbers and branches on the top of the bunker. A dull "uh" followed, perhaps the last reaction of a surprised soldier.

Thomas moved to where he could cover my journey to the other machine gun nest. I kept up my crawl, came in close, and repeated the grenade toss. It was all reflex. Serious contemplation would have been paralyzing. When the WHUMP sounded the end of the second nest, I lay for a few seconds to catch my breath. A very few.

I stayed at the rear of our column to continue the watch for a German attack. When we reached the last tip of Hill X, I heard the WHUMP of two more grenades. I ran to catch my men and found another German surprise we had missed: a tank dug into the hillside to the point that only the turret poked out, like a huge mosquito stinger. Before I reached it, my men had pulled open the hatch and popped grenades inside. We kept running.

From the tank, we plunged straight down the face of Hill X instead of dealing with the switchbacks of the path. Brush crackled under our charge for hundreds of yards, until we emerged amid our own chaos. Highway One was dizzy with tanks, jeeps, and wounded men hobbling along with the help of others.

"You men who are hurt, go find an aid station," I ordered the moment we reached the road. "The rest of you hit the command post and report in."

I turned, lowered myself to the side of the road, hung my head between my knees, and heaved my guts out.

TWENTY

I was a child during the war but I don't go to war movies now. The noise gets to me somewhere.

—Sandra Bonsanti, editor, *Il Tireno*

Early evening, April 5, 1945—Near Hill X

Oblivious to the world around me, I shuddered and heaved, shuddered and heaved. Seeing the men you live with, eat with, and fight beside blown to pieces, hour after hour, seizes your soul and finds the place where anguish lives, no matter how artfully you hide it. Here, I was no match for my emotions. It was unnerving, after so many months of combat, to be so affected, to lose control. Violent death wasn't new to me. Something about this day was beyond overwhelming.

Too preoccupied to notice my misery, the men and machines of war moved along on the highway beside me. I wasn't the first soldier to lose it after a battle, so I hardly was a spectacle. I was grateful for this anonymity.

I was too exhausted to get up after my stomach settled. I sat in the boiling sun, even though the smell between my boots was vile. Once I thought to finally check my watch again, the first time since Runyon and I had sat on the edge of the ravine, I discovered it was well past five o'clock p.m. I regained my feet and started for the command post to report my return.

185

A sergeant, just transferred to the company, saluted me and reached for the telephone to report my presence. He hung up and turned to me with bad news.

"Sir, Colonel Murphy at Battalion wants to see you right away. Jeep and a driver?"

I nodded, gathered my rifle, and asked for a drink of water to rinse the taste of bile from my tongue. The sergeant proffered a canteen cup full, and I tossed it down. It didn't much relieve the bad taste, but it cut a little of the dust in my throat.

Lieutenant Colonel Murphy had been in charge of First Battalion for six months, and I'd had only three or four conversations with him. I didn't give much thought to his wanting to see me. I just rode along, thankful to be sitting down, wishing the din of the day's shelling would leave my ears.

We pulled up to Murphy's headquarters within minutes. Inside, Murphy's aide pointed upstairs.

"Go to the first door, straight across from the top step, knock, and announce yourself," he instructed. "The colonel knows you're coming."

Fatigue tore at my legs as I climbed the steps. I made the top slowly, crossed the hallway, and rapped on a massive door.

"Lieutenant Baker?" the voice inside shouted.

"Aye, sir," I said.

"Let yourself in."

Murphy was covered in soapsuds and parked in a tin wash tub in the center of the room. I brought myself to attention and started to throw a weary salute.

"Sit down, Bake, forget the formalities," Murphy said. He was the only white officer who had the warmth to use my nickname. And it was a credit to Murphy he bothered to learn it.

"Hear you had a pretty rough day up there," Murphy said. He pointed in the general direction of Castle Aghinolfi with the bar of soap clutched in his left hand. "Runyon was here," he added.

This was a kindness—to forewarn me that my company commander had already delivered an assessment. What Murphy didn't share was more significant: Runyon had told him not to worry about the men left behind, that we were wasted. I didn't learn this until the war was over. Another reason why there hadn't been reinforcements.

I nodded. "Rough. Yes sir. But we did it. We got within a few hundred yards of the castle. With more men we'd have taken it."

"Tell me about it," Murphy said.

I recounted the basics, including all of the information but choosing not to explicitly detail my feelings about Runyon, the lack of reinforcements, or our trouble getting artillery support.

Murphy scrubbed, soaked, listened, and said little. "How many came back with you?" he asked.

"Six besides myself, sir," I answered. "Lost my last medic to a sniper as we pulled back."

Murphy grunted sympathetically. "Tough. Damn tough."

He asked a dozen more questions: How many enemy mortar batteries did I estimate? Were the Germans firing 88mm cannons at us or something bigger? How many enemy soldiers did I think held the castle? He covered every significant strategic angle.

"OK, Bake. Appreciate you coming over," Murphy finally said. "You've got to be damn tired. Better go back to your company and see if you can get a little rest."

I pulled myself up and walked to the door.

"Bake?"

"Sir?"

"Damn fine work today with those machine gun nests and the bunkers," Murphy said. "And snagging those telephone wires was smart soldiering. Tell your boys I appreciate it."

"Yes sir. Thanks."

He waved good-bye with his bar of soap.

I slipped my hand in the pocket of my Eisenhower jacket as I descended the stairs. My hand encountered the rounded metal corners of dog tags. Damn. Another chore. I wanted to get rid of the dead men's tags before I tried to sleep. I asked the driver to take me to Regimental Headquarters.

I fingered the dog tags as we drove to a three-story villa that was perfect for regimental commanders because it had both the comfort they believed they should be afforded and because it was connected to an underground tunnel they could escape to during shellings. The dog tags felt oddly warm, as if they breathed the life their owners had lost. I started to pull the handful of metal out with the purpose of inspecting the lettering in the fading twilight, to memorize each name, to remember who among the new recruits and members of my old rifle platoon had died, and to make peace with those nineteen faces.

My arm refused to move, my hand similarly paralyzed in a half grip around the pile of metal in my pocket. In my mind I heard a sniper's rifle crack, and my medic pitched forward. A succession of mortar rounds exploded, and the chest of one of my riflemen, who hadn't heard my scream to move or was too stunned by earlier poundings to react, erupted in a pinkish fog.

"Sir," the driver interrupted, his hand gently shaking the arm buried in my jacket pocket.

"Huh?" I asked.

"Sir, this is Regimental, just as you requested. You wanna go in or go back to the Command Post? You look sick."

"Huh. Oh, in. I've got to go in," I said.

I got myself out of the jeep without taking my hand out of my pocket and walked up the gravel and dirt drive toward the villa. My mind churned. I thought about examining the dog tags here, between the jeep and the door. I paused and pulled, but my arm would not comply. I could not do this. I could not read the names. Putting names with those faces made the day too real, the price too high.

I walked the rest of the distance to the door and went inside. Coming to Regimental HQ was a monumental mistake. Instead of being able to turn the dog tags over to the intelligence officer and leave, I was forced to face Colonel Raymond Sherman, the regimental commander. Here I knew what to anticipate and preferred returning to the battle to listening to his drivel.

Sherman offered no solace, no opportunity to sit down, no appreciation. "You just out of the field?" Sherman asked.

"Yes sir, with stops at the Command Post and Battalion HQ," I answered.

"Where's your helmet, lieutenant?" he asked.

"At my quarters, sir."

He looked me over and launched one of the better ass chewings I ever received in the Army. Overall, I was a disgrace to the universe, God, country, and the standard list of other vaunted symbolism Sherman reached for, all for not wearing a helmet into battle. My stupidity as well as my irreverence for authority were an abomination beyond words, he continued.

So stop trying, I wordlessly countered.

"Worse, lieutenant, you have a reputation . . . *a reputation* for never wearing a helmet," Sherman said, working himself further into a lather. "What kind of goddamn example do you think you are to your men? How about that, lieutenant, how about if none of your men wore their helmets into battle? 'I don't have to if Lieutenant Baker doesn't?' Huh? What about that?"

Sherman wasn't seeking answers to those questions, and I didn't offer any.

"This will not stand, Baker, this will not stand," Sherman continued. "You hear me?"

"Yes sir."

His intelligence officer handed me a helmet, and I jammed it on my head.

"Now that you're in uniform, lieutenant, I've got other news for you," Sherman said, pacing back and forth in front of me. "The 473rd's taking over the advance to the castle tomorrow. They need somebody who knows the terrain. You're volunteering to lead them."

"Yes sir," I said.

"Report to their Regimental Commander at 0430 hours tomorrow. Now get the hell out of here and wear your goddamned helmet tomorrow or I'll bust you to buck private."

"Yes sir," I said.

"Dismissed!" Sherman shouted.

And damn glad to be, I added silently.

I walked past one of the clerks on my way out and wordlessly slammed fistfuls of dog tags down on his desk. In my anger, I completely forgot my dilemma, my paralysis. The burial had begun. The names were soon safely beyond recall. I anticipated that the memory of the day and the faces of those men could be as easily shunted, not out of disrespect, but for self-preservation.

I collapsed on my bed. I did not sleep but mentally drifted in and out of scenes from the day's battle. "*Feuer!*" echoed and reechoed.

Before dawn I returned to the Command Post to find a company commander from the 473rd Infantry Regiment and three dozen men. A few all-white groups such as this one were added to the 92nd Division during the recent reorganization.

After a brief conversation with their captain, we started hiking. We crossed the same fields my men and I had run through the previous morning. Once at the base of Hill X, we avoided the switchback path and climbed nearly straight up the slope, using the shortcut I had discovered coming down the evening before. From there, it seemed best to follow the same route my men and I had so optimistically taken to the castle.

I led the 473rd silently, keeping vigil for mines and machine gun nests. The only sign of Germans were the yellow communication wires I had clipped, lying useless here, partially buried by debris there. Not a single enemy bullet whistled by.

When daylight arrived, we saw smoke spiraling from the ghostly trees shredded by the previous day's mortars, part grave markers, part funeral pyre. I half expected to hear explosions begin anew. I heard the echoes of mortar rounds that day, and still hear them to this day.

A month or so after this hike I found a piece of shrapnel lodged in the metal case of the compass I customarily carried. On April 5, as every other day, the compass dangled from the right side of my webbing belt. If not for the compass deflecting it, the chunk of shrapnel would have burrowed into my groin, torn an artery, and bled me to death. For days after the battle, however, I was too pre-occupied to make the careful inspection of my equipment that would have revealed this near death.

As my expedition with the 473rd drew closer to the final ridge, I began to see the bodies of my comrades. There was nothing on those hills but American dead. All of them barefoot. The Germans had robbed them of their boots and socks before withdrawing. Otherwise my soldiers lay undisturbed. I counted sixteen men but did not have the energy to search for the other three.

Once we reached the ridge, I could not go on. The taste of cordite again coated my tongue and the roof of my mouth. Shouts of agony reverberated in my mind. I began to sense the intensity of what had passed, not only for my men, but for the people we had killed or maimed. The same unseen hands that squeezed my soul at the side of the road the previous day squeezed again; anguish returned. I did not want to relive this, did not want to see men falling around me, did not want to lose control again. I told the captain we had arrived, pointed out the trail into the draw that led to the castle, turned, and hiked homeward.

We proved we could go up and fight and die. We had cleared the way for this all-white company to go all the way to the castle without hearing a shot. We had made an ass out of everyone who said we couldn't do it. This was some success. Yet, I still wanted respect and the acknowledgment that we were good. Our thanks was an ass chewing and an assignment to scout for white soldiers. It was a way of life for my men. It made me furious. I wanted to find Runyon and Sherman and . . . .

At the lip of Hill X, I clamored to the top of the buried German tank and levered open the top hatch. Curiosity instantly turned to regret. The disfigured bodies of two young German boys, too young to grow whiskers, lay inside. Dark pools of blood had coagulated by each lifeless form. Germany was so desperate at this point in the war that she was using anyone to prolong her hopeless conquest. The day before, I was lobbing grenades like all of the rest of my men. Now I was chiding myself, thinking that if I hadn't been dragging along at the rear the night before, if I had arrived sixty seconds sooner, I could have prevented this. We could have captured these lads instead of killing them.

These two days had impressed me more with the futility of war than the previous eight months of combat.

I involuntarily dropped the hatch cover, suddenly exhausted, and sat on the tank. Images of my barefoot men marched from my subconscious. Their dead faces stared as I removed their dog tags. My medic pitched forward and died. Futility, hatred, and helplessness called. I fought back. This is what makes men crazy, I knew. Warriors didn't contemplate, they moved on.

I struggled to my feet and walked to the switchbacks where my men and I had followed Runyon rock to rock. And descended into more horror. Mine craters pocked the path. Beside each crater lay another dead American. Revelation fused me with fear. The previous day, after we'd reached the top of Hill X, I heard a series of explosions and judged that we had outrun our artillery. It was nothing of the sort. It was the sound of our men walking into mines. I counted at least six men I knew. The rest of us escaped only because we had followed Runyon up the rocks.

Why did he save us only to desert us? Why did I coldly kill Germans one day and mourn the lads in the tank and the people we had killed and maimed the next? This was a new enemy, this mind game. I had to ignore it.

I studied the pattern of mine craters and bodies, dropped to my knees and gingerly lifted a rock from the middle of the path. At first glance the rock appeared well ensconced in the dirt, one of those semi-boulders too deeply embedded to remove. In reality, the rock was barely balanced over a mine, so the first brush of a soldier's boot triggered the explosives. I gingerly removed the rock, and flicked back the dirt with the blade of my knife until I found the fuse. The remainder of the day I dug as many of the mines as I could find. The engineers who came behind me a few days later found many more.

After the war, the Allies trained 2,500 Italian men to defuse the mines sown throughout their country by both sides. The task required three years and killed 1,000 men. It took fifteen months to clear the mines from Hills X, Y, and Z alone.

TWENTY-ONE

I confess without shame that I am tired and sick of the war. Its glory is all moonshine.

—William Tecumseh Sherman, Civil War General

Mid-April 1945, Northern Italy

My shooting war ended the day my platoon helped chase the Germans from Castle Aghinolfi. The Nisei dislodged the enemy from the heights above the castle. During the following days, the Japanese-Americans fought their way, peak to peak, to Montignoso, Massa, Carrara, and other villages north of the castle.

Our artillery moved forward to take on the guns of Punta Bianca. Three dozen 76mm guns focused on one of the cannons. When Punta Bianca fired, our gunners fired back. Then our gunners focused all thirty-six guns on one of the other German cannons. Nearly 12,000 rounds went special delivery to the notorious cannon battery using this technique, but it silenced only a portion of the menace. The Germans scuttled the remainder and fled. The impenetrable western flank of the Gothic Line was breached. My platoon never heard another hostile gunshot.

The remainder of Company C, under the command of yet another nameless, forgotten captain, slowly regrouped after those brutal days in early April and slogged north for the remainder of the war. The Germans ran. The remaining Italian fascist troops disintegrated. We never met any of Mussolini's forces in combat, but I did get a close look at Mussolini.

As a developing fan of Italian architecture, I wanted to see the famous *Il Duomo,* the largest Gothic cathedral in Italy, located in the center of Milan, with a golden Madonna capping its three-hundred-fifty-foot spire. I took a few days when we neared the area, secured a driver and a jeep, and went exploring. The streets of Milan were awash with people. After several minutes of cursing and only creeping forward, it was obvious motorized transport wasn't going to get me anywhere. I hopped out of the jeep and told the driver to wait for me.

I elbowed my way into the crowd and moved toward the nucleus of noise. Italian partisans with guns lorded over a pile of bodies at the center of the throng. The crowd cheered as the central figure, a sinewy man with a handsome mustache and kinky hair, shouted and raised his fist. I worked my way as close to the bodies as possible. Mussolini's pained face was piled among the dead. I snapped a quick photograph.

As the cheering intensified, the partisans took each body and hoisted it feet first to a long concrete beam exposed along the front of a bombed-out building. Mussolini, his mistress Claretta Petacci, and a half dozen other fascist officials soon dangled from the beam by their feet, arms draped lifelessly below them, shirts slipping down to reveal their wounds. An enterprising young partisan painted the dead fascists' names above their feet. A Who's Who of Hatred, a piece of history, I told myself, snapping more photographs and beating a hasty retreat before the crowd dispersed and further clogged the streets.

Outside of that spectacle, our move north was dull work. I never walked so much in my life. Day after day, we tramped from mountain village to mountain village along narrow, twisting tracks, looking for remnants of the German Army. We slept wherever night found us. If a village was nearby, we picked out a group of houses and asked the owners for permission to stay. None turned us down. They were too afraid. They had been through a much ruder version of this routine when German soldiers beat on their doors with rifle butts and demanded hospitality. We understood the villagers' anxiety.

The saddest sample of their apprehension surfaced in one of the tinier mountain villages east of Genoa. We received orders to stay in the village until our supply line caught up, which now took four or five days. Our quarters of choice was the usual two-story, gray stone-and-adobe house with enough backyard to accommodate our mortar tubes. We slept in the simple front room on the ground floor. The couple who owned the place, a man and woman in their forties with gray-streaked dark hair and worry-etched faces, were compliant but reserved. We initially met two teenage daughters who immediately disappeared.

Three mornings after we arrived, I was sitting in a chair by the fireplace, sipping coffee from a cup the woman of the house had generously provided. She handed it to me gingerly, as if afraid I might snatch her arm. Anything but the lip-burning metal canteen cup was a treat. I thanked her profusely but her terrified expression remained. As we talked, a young, dark-haired girl, whom I had not seen before, came timidly down the stairs. The woman blanched in fear but kept silent.

The child, four years at the oldest, shuffled to the hearth, sat down, and cried with abandon. I leaned forward and asked her what was wrong.

"My mama said buf-a-lo soldiers are going to kill us and eat us," she said, hiccuping out the words between sobs. "Will you kill us and eat us?"

I nearly whirled to her mother and demanded to know who was passing such bullshit. But anger signaled aggression and could worsen the little girl's fear. I stifled it.

"Oh, no. We're not going to hurt you," I replied in my best imitation of Italian. "We're just like you, except we have darker skin. We have feelings, just like you, and sleep and think just like you do. We don't eat other people. We eat the same food you do. Those stories you hear about the Buffalo Soldiers aren't true."

Her mother stood nervously by and translated the parts of my explanation that her daughter didn't understand. As we talked, two other slightly older girls, whom I also had not seen before, came down the stairs, one biting on the sleeve of her blouse, the other nervously twirling her hair. Their parents judged it safe to let us know they had teenagers—or found it unavoidable—but kept the younger girls hidden. They didn't even take food upstairs to the girls, for fear it might alert us to their presence. The girls had become so desperately hungry that they crawled out of hiding and nearly into my lap. Eat people. No wonder their mother had been mortified when the first child came down.

I talked to each of the girls and then went outside and hollered for Sergeant Dickens. He offered the kindest face we could show the children.

"Do we have any rations . . . chocolate . . . anything?" I asked. "This family's got three kids they've been hiding upstairs, not even feeding, because they've been hearing *the rumors* about us bad old Buffalo Soldiers. I'd like to offer them a sample of what we eat when we're not eating people."

Dickens agreed. "See what I can round up, sir."

My platoon delivered everything they found. We spent the remainder of our free time in that community trying to show our hosts that we weren't the threat the Germans and the fascists made us out to be. Before we left, I heard laughter from the little girl who first came down those stairs to ask if I was a cannibal. It was more satisfying than our most resounding combat victory.

The march north continued at a more considerable pace. Somewhere in the dizzying stupor of this exhaustion, in early May, the Germans surrendered Italy. The village folk were electrified, as if born to dance. We tried to share their enthusiasm but only managed to nod wearily at one another and mutter, "Thank God!"

A few weeks later we pulled back to near Viareggio, not far from where we lived before the last push on Castle Aghinolfi. The word was regroup, resupply, and ship out for the South Pacific. We were joining the invasion of Japan. I had enough combat time to avoid it, but I wanted to go. I rationalized it by telling myself I was born to be a warrior.

Lieutenant Colonel Murphy appeared unannounced at our command post soon after our return. In one hand he held a set of orders. In the other he had a set of single silver bars—first lieutenant's bars.

"First Lieutenant Baker, step forward," Murphy said. "You've been promoted."

Among the white commanders, only Murphy would have troubled himself to arrange a warm, impromptu little ceremony for a black man who had been a second lieutenant so long that a promotion seemed out of the question. And Murphy made the unusual move of buying me my first set of bars. I proudly watched him pin the new rank on my collar.

My unit decided I should take a celebratory trip with another brand-new first lieutenant. They found a jeep and a driver and sent us to a little resort town along the Swiss border called Stresa.

Stresa is docked on the north side of a huge lake called Lago Maggiore. Rental rowboats invited people to paddle over to Switzerland or to drift in lazy circles and admire the stunning mountains from the peacefulness of the still lake. I had the Leica camera I liberated from a German officer and snapped frame after frame of the town and the peaks.

One day, during this respite, my fellow new first lieutenant and I walked to a nearby village. Italian mountain valleys are like this, one cluster of houses, a short break, and then another group of houses. Each is a separate town. This place was no different, except that it was more remote than any village we had encountered during the fighting. As we entered the town square, bewildered people started cracking their doors, peeking, and then slowly coming out of their homes. An Amazonian woman in her late thirties boldly walked right up to me. Her long dark hair was pulled back with barrettes. She wore a sleeveless blouse, a long skirt, and dusty sandals.

She was a typical Italian country woman except for her imposing height, which put her about five inches over me. I looked up. She pointed and, best as I could understand, asked to see my teeth. I reasoned this out and decided she wanted me to smile. I smiled.

The woman reached to my face, stuck her fingers in my mouth, and pried my jaw open. She ran the tip of her index finger along my teeth, simultaneously forcing my head back so she could get the best view.

"Bella ... bella ... bella," she said, "bella ... bella ... bella."

She repeated this over and over. Beautiful. Beautiful. I finally understood. Beautiful teeth.

Her attention turned to my skin. She rubbed my cheek and inspected her fingers to see if my color came off. Then she gently pinched my face. Two dozen women and children watched from a respectable distance.

My fellow lieutenant stood to one side, laughing.

"You're a freak, Bake, you're a freak," he said. "Look at you, the village freak show. This act is up when your color rubs off."

We laughed together. I pulled out my camera.

"Picture? Foto?" I asked. The people—nine women of all ages and ten young boys—swarmed for a spot in front of the camera. I was touched. People in these high mountain villages were born, lived, and died without traveling more than five or ten miles their entire lives. Undoubtedly they had never seen a black man. They didn't look at us as if we were from outer space. They handled our differences with curiosity instead of contempt. Here people talked to us, studied us, acted as if they were interested in us. Some people, like the farming couple with the young daughters, were frightened at first. But once they came to know us, they rapidly dropped their prejudices. I loved Italy and vowed to stay.

Life back near Viareggio settled into a pleasant routine. I liked waking up in the morning without hearing artillery rounds, mortar rounds, or bullets snapping overhead. When the Germans occupied the hills and mountains, the most we could risk was crawling to the window, edging up from one corner of the casing, and letting one eye peek over. I liked being able to stand and look squarely out the window when the sun came pouring through in the morning.

There also was relief in not marching off to a new village every day and a great deal of relief in not being housebound during the day for fear of a shrapnel shower.

No good news came from home. Helen had written one letter months earlier, demanding to know why I had stopped her monthly allotment check. "You must help me, Vernon," she wrote. "I've had to leave little Vernon with her grandmother in Birmingham and move to Chicago to find work. Now I'm living with my brother. This is absolutely miserable, and I have no one to help."

Harry Cox wasn't surprised.

"Well, Vernon, what did you expect? Say, do you have any life insurance?"

"Ten-thousand-dollars worth."

"She's the beneficiary, isn't she?"

"Well, of course. I married the woman."

"Vernon, Vernon. This woman's been waiting to cash in on you as a war widow and, with those monthly checks, cashing in while she waits," Harry said. "Oh, Vernon, you've been a fool. Quit. Don't send that woman anything but divorce papers. Not a letter, not a post card, and damn sure not a check."

I started to plead. Give the woman time. She might come around.

"That's F-O-O-L, fool, Vernon. Forget it. Check a calendar. She's had plenty of time."

May eased into June. The men around me counted and recounted their combat points—calculated from the number of months they had seen action—to figure if they could go home instead of going to the South Pacific or Japan. We joked about all of the possible ways a man could tally his points if he served with white outfits. A plethora of white officers from headquarters units, engineering units, and other noncombat jobs made a habit, during the war, of showing up at an observation post, taking a quick look, turning around and heading right back to their desks. For their trouble, they received the Combat Infantry Badge and a boost in pay. We infantrymen had to get shot at to earn ours.

A third of the way into June, I was hanging out in the company command post when a battalion training officer dropped by.

"Hey, Bake, when do you head up to Division?" he asked, referring to the 92nd Infantry Division Headquarters, which had moved from its safe haven south of Viareggio to more plush quarters in Genoa. I only vaguely recognized him but he seemed to know me.

"Division. Why would I be going to Division?" I asked.

I couldn't think of any recent incident I might be chastised for, unless I had again been spotted without my lousy helmet. That was possible since I still didn't wear it.

"Division for the DSC. You're getting the DSC. For the hill," he replied, the jerk of his head indicating Hill X, off to the east. He was showing off, proud that he had new gossip. Getting new gossip is no small feat in a circle of bored GIs.

The DSC. The Distinguished Service Cross.

"I don't know a thing about any DSC," I assured him.

He gave me a "trust-me" shrug and walked out. Within a day, orders came down from Division: report to Major General Edward M. Almond, commander of the 92nd Infantry Division, by ten o'clock the following morning.

I didn't welcome the summons. It invoked fear. And I didn't know the training officer well enough to trust this was about a Distinguished Service Cross.

I'd never met Almond before, but I knew he made it a policy that top decorations weren't going to any black soldiers for what he considered failed missions. Almond never met a Buffalo Soldier mission he couldn't call a failure.

Oh, there were Purple Hearts. They kept a generous supply in dispensaries and hospitals and passed them out like pancakes. Even Lieutenant Hansen received one for the ankle he broke on those marble stairs. At least we were under fire when he was injured. The only way to avoid a Purple Heart was a self-inflicted wound. Any white officer with a pulse and two legs could claim a Bronze Star and the Combat Infantry Badge. But a Distinguished Service Cross for a black lieutenant? Never.

A white general wasn't calling a black first lieutenant in order to throw a surprise birthday party. And my birthday was months away. What trouble could I be in? I again asked myself. I brought my helmet with me to Genoa, just in case.

A jeep and driver carried me the eighty miles up Highway One early enough that we had a little time to inspect the cluttered cobblestone streets of Genoa before my date with Almond. His headquarters were easy to find, a huge villa with an enviable view of the Mediterranean coast in the swankiest part of the city. A sparkling jeep with general's stars sat ready in the sweeping circular driveway. I reluctantly climbed the steps to the villa doors, making sure I entered a few minutes early.

The inside of the villa overwhelmed the outside. High ceilings stretched heavenward. Ornate trim carried the high, horizontal line where wall met ceiling, and the ceilings were embossed with cathedral-style murals. Each door was as large as a 500-year-old tree. The swirls carved in the doors were intricate and extraordinary. Gold-plated door handles gracefully curved back to grant passage to those bold enough to enter.

My visit was anticipated. But Almond's nervous aides were not going to allow me to see the general immediately. Following an obligatory fifteen-minute wait, I was led up the wide marble staircase, down a foyer, to another massive door. My guide knocked, listened for an invitation, and pushed open the door. I was announced and directed inside. The door closed heavily behind me.

There was no hint of June's Mediterranean warmth as I crossed the threshold. I waited stiffly, the minimum number of steps inside the room, for the general to turn from the second-floor window of his palatial office. Almond finally spun around. He more waved me off than returned my salute. He didn't offer a salutary good morning, didn't offer me the opportunity to sit down. Under no circumstance would he offer me refreshment from the neat cart of heavy glass decanters positioned in one corner of that grand suite. It wasn't that he knew I didn't drink, based upon reports that I customarily gave my monthly ration of hard liquor to my men. My lips simply weren't going to touch his crystal-thick glasses.

"I want you to write me a report about what happened up on that hill," Almond hammered out in pure Virginian tones. "I want it day after tomorrow," he added, drilling his desk with his right index finger to emphasize each word, and simultaneously drilling me with his intense eyes.

"Any questions?"

"No, si . . ."

"Dismissed," Almond snapped.

I saluted. He glared and turned away.

I was mystified by his request but was not about to inquire. A lieutenant doesn't debate with a general. He takes orders. It wasn't that unusual for Army brass to generate reports. Summoning me to Genoa for a three-sentence conversation, however, seemed odd. Especially for a general who didn't mix with the field hands but meticulously relied upon the chain of command to keep himself aloof.

I turned and walked to the door, attempting to appear brisk, professional, unshaken. There was little relief in pulling the door closed and only a hint of the pressure easing after I settled into the jeep. We headed down the cobblestone drive and began threading our way through the narrow streets, toward Highway One and Viareggio.

Germany had surrendered more than a month before, but bastards like Almond still wanted a fight. He didn't have a single conciliatory word about the hell we had endured up on that hill. He didn't seem to care about the men we lost. He didn't seem to care about the strategic success of April 5 and 6. Didn't seem to care about the welfare of the battle's survivors.

The gossip about a Distinguished Service Cross obviously was wrong, and I didn't care. It would have been nice, however, if Almond had acknowledged our effort, made a one-sentence statement about how we had accomplished the difficult—knowing there was no way he would admit we had done the impossible. Considering the number of casualties our platoon had taken "up on that hill"—almost half of the forty-seven men killed in the entire battalion were mine—an utterance of sympathy or understanding would have been rewarding. Much more rewarding than any medal.

I stewed. I could no more raise my fists to my oppressors than I could change official Army colors from olive drab to fuchsia. Not that I was given to fist fighting. But circumstances frequently gave rise to the urge.

Almond was the rule, not the exception, among the 92nd Infantry's majors, colonels, and generals. His reaction was the best we could expect, considering that it was deliberate Army policy to put white Southerners like him in charge of our all-black units. These white heirs of the plantation era commanded black men whom they were raised to disdain and distrust. At the same time, blacks who had been persecuted, whipped, and spit upon, as soldiers had to defend these commanders and their culture to the death. An unpalatable, unworkable mandate.

Historians finally call mixing white Southerners with segregated black units "A Recipe for Failure." But it was tradition. A similar Army strategy had clearly failed more than two decades earlier, when all-black infantry units went to France during World War I under the direction of white Southern commanders. The American Army mostly ignored its black combat troops along the Western Front while the French hailed their valor and awarded the *Croix de Guerre*, the Cross of War, to every member of three all-black regiments. Mainstream American history books fail to record any of this, and the Army certainly didn't bring it up.

Almond's credentials were impeccable, considering the same false qualifications for commanding black combat troops persisted during World War II. He was part of the Virginia aristocracy, a graduate of Virginia Military Institute, and married to the sister of General George C. Marshall. That was no small connection considering Marshall was top general in the Army and still climbing.

Almond commanded a battalion of all-native troops in the Philippines for three years during the 1930s, perhaps adding to his supposed talents for handling non-white people. Whatever these particulars, I sensed something more banal was the top qualification for handling us: hatred, disregard, and a total lack of faith in the black man's fighting ability.

This was all subconscious—not part of a lengthy intellectual diatribe with myself—as we soaked up the Mediterranean breeze and wheeled down the narrow Italian highway. I simply figured my encounter with Almond as another of the expected skirmishes with the white bosses.

When we got back to the command post that afternoon I went straight for a typewriter, found a sheaf of legal-size paper, and tapped out a three-page statement. I skipped the emotion, my resentment of Captain Runyon, and other problems. I already was in trouble with Almond. I wanted to drop back out of sight. My ticket to anonymity was a simple, bare-bones discussion of that April day. More details were more truthful, but more truth meant more trouble.

I finished the report and set it aside for a night's contemplation. The next morning, satisfied with my effort, I drove to Regimental Headquarters and gave an aide the papers. He could send them to Almond.

Nothing more was said. Three weeks later, however, the training officer's gossip proved true. A ceremony was set for the Fourth of July in Viareggio. I was to receive the Distinguished Service Cross, supposedly making me the most highly-decorated black soldier in the Mediterranean Theater. I thought little about it. I'd had a job; I'd done it. I didn't want a medal for it. I wanted one of the commanders to verbally acknowledge we had far exceeded their expectations, that they were sorry for the scurrilous lies they had told about the performance of black soldiers in combat, and that they regretted the loss of my men at the castle. A sentence or two of contrition for failing to provide reinforcements also would be welcome.

The ceremony was my last encounter with either General Almond or Captain Runyon in Italy. Both were up for honors of their own. Almond was receiving oak leaf clusters on his Silver Star, Runyon the Silver Star.

Because I was receiving the highest decoration, tradition dictated that I was supposed to have the place of honor, at the far right end of the line of men getting medals. Almond knew it and took the position of top honor anyway. My anger boiled. General Lucian K. Truscott Jr., commander of the U.S. Fifth Army, pinned on my decoration, shook my hand, and murmured a few words. None of them included, "Sorry this asshole next to you took the top spot of honor. Pardon me while I put him in his place."

I left the minute the official ceremony was over in order to avoid Runyon and Almond. Later, I read the orders from Almond's superiors regarding my Distinguished Service Cross. They were signed June 10, 1945—the same day Almond had demanded I write that report. He must have known what was coming and was looking for ammunition to fight it.

The good news was my pay increased two dollars and fifty cents a month for my Distinguished Service Cross. The down side was that the ten dollars a month extra I received for the Combat Infantry Badge, earned by anyone who held binoculars, went away when Germany surrendered. The irony over being paid so much less for the Distinguished Service Cross than the Combat Infantry Badge might have lingered for years if I had given a damn about medals. At least American medals.

Well before 1945 was over, the Italian government presented me with the *Croce di Guerra al Valore,* the Cross of Valor in War. The free Polish government, whose forces fought on the Adriatic end of the Gothic Line, followed with the Polish Cross of Valor. Those honors meant more to me than the Distinguished Service Cross, because I knew the Italians and Poles genuinely recognized our efforts and appreciated our hell.

The war in Italy, meanwhile, kept on killing well after the armistice. In mid-July I took a bit of leave, went down to Viareggio, and got a third-floor room at the Hotel Excelsior, which was reserved for black officers. There was a Hotel Excelsior in Genoa, also set aside expressly for blacks, and perhaps one in Florence. It seemed every hotel approved for us was named Excelsior.

Viareggio's Hotel Excelsior was less than a block from one of Italy's most perfect beaches, its white sand ebbing into the Ligurian Sea, the sea becoming a deeper blue-green the farther it stretched from shore. The Excelsior, Hotel Piedmont, and Hotel Astor were about the only tall buildings that survived Viareggio's near total demolition by the guns at Punta Bianca. These were the buildings we figured were purposely left to give the artillery spotters reference points.

I came out of the bathtub one morning and was standing at the window toweling myself off, thinking about walking the eight or so blocks to the USO Club for breakfast. They had great pancakes with maple syrup. As I daydreamed and dried myself, there was a harrowing rumble, and the sky to the south suddenly darkened. It came from the direction of the USO Club, which shared quarters with the American Red Cross.

My next memory is being fully dressed and running down the street, toward the explosion, as if I expected to find the second German invasion. It was as bad. The USO Club was in ruins, as was the building behind it. Bodies and pieces of bodies were blasted in every direction. Men furiously pulled and dug people out of the rubble, on the off chance any lived. I joined in the effort.

Seventy soldiers, nurses, and Italian workers had been in the building. It wasn't difficult to figure out what had happened. The building next door to the USO Club had once been the villa of a rich, powerful fascist family. As post-war revenge, the villa became warehouse for all the mines being dug up on the beach, supposedly defused, and stored until future safe disposal. I figured someone missed removing a fuse, the live mine was jolted, and the whole mess blew skyward taking the USO Club with it. The mystery is why we so thoughtlessly allowed a villa located inside a city—and next door to a USO Club—to be used to store something so dangerous.

As we pulled the bodies onto stretchers and carried them to a building across the street, I found First Sergeant Luther Hall, who had gone all the way with Company C. Hall was identifying bodies. Several from our company were killed, including three of the six men who had survived the horror of Castle Aghinolfi. I couldn't make sense of it. They survived one of the bloodiest hills in northern Italy only to die by a dance floor.

TWENTY-TWO

*The girls don't love us anymore because we wear the
black shirts.*

—Italian fascist marching song

September 1945, Genoa, Italy

Her name was Signorina Sanna Giovanna—Miss Giovanna Sanna.
Thick, lovely dark hair swept back from her face in a kind of a halo.
She had pencil-thin eyebrows arching over dark, dancing eyes and a
demure smile that always began at the left side of her mouth. She
was smaller than I was, bowlegged, and a fiery little beauty.

As in most of my best times in Italy, I was on R and R, this time
in Genoa. It was September, as fine a fall as I had had since hunting
with my grandfather. I hitched up with another black officer who
managed to secure a jeep all to himself. I didn't know him well, but
he had wheels, and the women all loved to go for a ride in an
American jeep.

We bumped down the cobbles of Genoa, enjoyed the afternoon
sunshine, relished the coming week of fun. I was looking at a beauty
pirouetting along in a red dress when my new officer friend pulled
to the curb. He elbowed me and pointed at two women.

"Hey, Baker, zero in at three o'clock. Incoming beauties." I
looked and immediately engaged my rough Italian.

"*Cosa fai?*"—"What are you doing?" I asked the two women.

"*Passeggiamo*"—"Just walking," they replied, looking at one another a bit shyly and looking back at us. We introduced ourselves. They were Giovanna and Marisa. Marisa had the sweetest voice I'd ever heard.

"Would you like to go for a ride in our jeep?" I said, not wanting to be quite that abrupt but not wanting the pair to walk on by. Both nodded rapidly and smiled.

I climbed from the front seat to the back and offered my hand to help one of them in back. Marisa moved forward. Giovanna blocked her.

"No, I will sit in back," Giovanna announced and leapt to the back before it could become an issue. We drove off into the sunshine. I don't remember another thing about Marisa or the officer with the jeep. I remember only Giovanna.

I spent the next seven days wooing her. Somewhere early on, I asked her how old she was. "Sac-a-steen," she replied, her face screwed up with intensity as she labored to put it into English.

"Sixteen?" I said with alarm.

She nodded vigorously and smiled.

"Sixteen? Too young," I said. "I'm twenty-five."

"No. Not too young," Giovanna replied. "In Italy, sac-a-steen old enough."

We didn't even kiss during those seven days. Giovanna had run away from home and was living with a woman whose house was about two blocks from my hotel—the Hotel Excelsior, of course. Her father apparently was dead. She was the oldest of several children. I didn't ask why she had run away, and she didn't tell me.

Giovanna wasn't allowed upstairs in the hotel. It was for officers only. So I took her home each night by her ten o'clock curfew. Mornings I went around and fetched her for breakfast at the hotel or in one of the many tiny mom and pop *ristorantes*. She was reserved and kind, with both a strength and a softness that appealed to me in ways I can't articulate. The other Italian women I dated drank and smoked. Not Giovanna.

She filled me with this overwhelming feeling of euphoria. And all we did was sit and talk, stroll the streets, and watch the ocean waltz to the beaches below the city. Or wordlessly watch each other.

Giovanna couldn't pronounce Vernon, although she tried many times, fidgeting with the ever present cross hanging around her neck and trying to force vowels that her Italian accent didn't allow. She finally settled on Fernando. I had never met anyone I liked better. Sadly, I was stationed at Viareggio and, at the end of our week together, had to return to duty.

The night before I left, we paused in front of her house. I looked down into her dark eyes as she stood patiently studying my face.

"Giovanna, I'm leaving tomorrow, in the morning," I explained. "I probably won't see you again. Please know what a wonderful week I've had. You are . . . you are beautiful."

I couldn't stammer out anything else that made sense, although a myriad of feelings rushed through my mind. I wrung my hat anxiously.

She looked down at her own hands, folded together above her waist, and then looked back up into my eyes.

"Where are you going?"

"Viareggio, back to the Army camp. I must return to work," I replied. "My leave is over."

Giovanna stood on tiptoe, kissed me, whispered *Ciao,* and walked into her house without so much as a wave. A stunningly sudden goodbye, but what else could I expect? Even if I were stationed in Genoa, what would be the use of really getting to know a woman? My attempts at serious love were failures. And who knew how long I would be in Italy?

I was trying to stay. I transferred to the 3373rd Quartermaster Corps when, after Japan surrendered in August 1945, the 92nd Infantry Division was deactivated and sent home. The Quartermaster cleaned up after the infantry and artillery and helped Italy patch herself back together. I was stationed at the camp at Viareggio, but my job was overseeing a refinery at nearby Lucca. The Italians provided the labor. The Army supervised and made sure none of the gasoline was stolen.

A week after I returned to Viareggio, I was walking out of the camp gate when Giovanna reappeared in my life. She was standing not twenty yards away, smiling her shy smile, one hand running her cross back and forth on her necklace chain. I shook my head at the certain mirage. But she walked over, slipped her arm in my arm, looked at me and said, "Hi, Fernando."

Giovanna didn't even give me a chance to stammer. She put a silencing finger to my lips and ordered me to walk her to Viareggio, about a half hour away. She had something to show me. The something was a two-room apartment, one of a half dozen carved from a tidy three-story house. A stone charcoal-burning stove was built into one wall of the kitchen-dining area. The other room was the bedroom.

"I'm here to stay," Giovanna announced. "We live here."

There was no explanation of how she had managed to find the money to rent us an apartment. I didn't ask.

Her arms swung up around my neck, she tugged me close to her and kissed me warmly.

"Finally," she whispered in my ear. Her teeth playfully tugged at my ear lobe followed by the wet tip of her tongue. Followed by deep, luxuriant kisses. Hands and clothing flew a dozen directions.

"Fernando," Giovanna eventually sighed. "Fernando, my little piece of coal."

Every night as I left the camp, she was waiting by the gate. I loved most everything about Giovanna except that habit. I didn't want her classed with the ladies who hung around the gate soliciting business. Giovanna was forcing me to learn a lot more Italian, but I couldn't make her understand why I didn't want her waiting there for me. Finally she agreed to honor my request, although she didn't trust me.

If I got stuck on duty and came home late, she inspected me like a bloodhound, sniffing for strange perfume, eyeing my collar for lipstick. I finally learned to make an extra effort and let her know I was delayed at work. Sometimes things backfired on both ends.

I showed up late for a dress formation one morning and was restricted to my camp quarters for a week as punishment. I knew Giovanna would conclude I had found another woman and left her.

Harry Cox, now a captain, also had transferred to the 3373rd. He agreed to go to town and sneak Giovanna back into camp so I could talk to her. Unfortunately, the battalion executive officer heard her voice through the wall of my tent and burst in.

"I'll have to report you, lieutenant," he said grimly.

"You can see there's nothing going on here," I replied. "Go get Captain Cox. He'll take care of this. He'll take her home."

"Absolutely not. I'm the executive officer," he snapped. "I'm reporting you. It's my duty."

The only advantage I had was fear. White officers like him, who had not been overseas long, were afraid of blacks when they had to deal with us one-on-one. If there were witnesses around and they were giving me the business, I automatically complied. In situations like this, I didn't take any bullshit. I flashed him the meanest black-son-of-a-bitch look I could muster. He blinked, backed off, and found Harry. The executive officer didn't raise the issue again.

Giovanna and I lived as husband and wife in that tiny apartment, which was always filled with the wonderful aromas of her all-day cooking projects. Despite her flair for cooking, she loved it most when we went to the officer's club or found a restaurant.

"Fernando, we go dancing?" she asked. Or, "Fernando, you take me to the club?"

Giovanna brooked no guff from anybody, especially about dating a black soldier. If we went in a restaurant and someone came by and said something about my color, she invariably jumped from her chair, followed them through the restaurant, grabbed them, and chewed them out in the finest Italian fashion. Arms waving, voice climbing higher and higher, she would have made any regimental commander proud.

Then she marched back to our table, sat defiantly, wiped her mouth with a handful of the tablecloth, and we resumed our evening as if it had gone uninterrupted.

Giovanna wore no makeup, save red lipstick. She walked out of our bedroom, ready for our first night on Viareggio, with it smeared over half of her face.

"Jesus, Gianna, you look like hell," I said. "You look like a *puttana*."

Her eyes went to tears.

"*Puttana?* Fernando, why you call me a whore?"

"I'm not saying you're a whore, Gianna, I'm saying you look like one. Look at yourself, with that red lipstick everywhere. That's what the *puttanas* at the camp gate look like."

"No, no *puttana*," she said.

"Look," I offered, "I've seen my sisters and my grandmother put on lipstick a hundred times. I'll help you."

The verbal jabs went back and forth for a half hour. She finally stalked off to the mirror to find reason to prove me wrong and then returned with her face wiped clean.

"All right, Fernando," she said sulkily, "if you are so smart, you show me how."

Giovanna handed me her gold lipstick case. I pulled off the top, set it on our little eating table, and motioned for her to come to me. I smeared a bit of lipstick on my finger, then spread it along her lower lip.

"OK," I instructed, "now put your lips together like this."

I showed her how to purse her lips, with a smack, to evenly spread the lipstick. Giovanna followed my example slowly and deliberately.

"Now that's beautiful," I said. "Go look for yourself."

She let out the Italian equivalent of "wow" when she saw herself.

Giovanna taught me an important lesson about making a woman mad and then walking away before coming to an understanding. It first happened when I came home with a couple of other lieutenants. They wanted me to join them at the officers' club and leave Giovanna home. I stopped by to tell her where we were going and turned to walk out the door. In seconds a sharp pain shot through my scalp. My hand found blood.

I whirled about to see Giovanna with her arm cocked and her hand holding the high-heeled shoe she had clobbered me with.

There were a few more performances before I quit giving her a clean shot at the back of my head when her Italian temper rose. Her temper percolated and manifested itself in more than just a high heel sunk into my scalp. There were nights I couldn't stay up and argue because I had to be at work early the next morning. Convinced of the futility of the situation, I went to bed. Giovanna waited until my eyes closed, then came over and punched me in the nose. I grabbed her and held her until she settled down. Eventually she softened, nuzzled into my neck, and fell asleep.

Giovanna wasn't demanding of material goods. And as much as she admired clothes, as much as she repeated the commonly held myth, *Tutti gli Americani sono ricchi*—all Americans are rich—she never said a word to me about buying her this or that. I still gave her money and told her to buy herself clothes. Few new clothes appeared and the money disappeared. She sent it to her mother.

When we visited the officers' club, I noticed all the other officers' wives and girlfriends had fur coats. Giovanna had a worn serge cloth affair that likely was someone else's castoff. Giving her money for a new coat was pointless. Instead, I found a new mid-length silver-fox coat for a hundred and fifty dollars. She unwrapped it, draped it elegantly over her shoulders, and twirled about our apartment. Then she ran to me and kissed me until the side of my face was one red splotch of lipstick.

"Now, Fernando is *puttana*, she said, laughing at her handiwork.

About three months after she moved to Viareggio, Giovanna made her one request—money for a train ticket so she could visit her mother. I happily obliged, although I wondered if, like Leola and Helen, she would make this her disappearing act. A week later she returned, with her mother. When I walked in and found Senora Sanna sitting at our table, I braced for a stern lecture or serious inquisition. At a minimum, I was an older man and a foreigner. The other complications were more obvious.

Senora Sanna rose, walked across the room, threw her arms around me, and hugged me like a son. I didn't understand all she said to Giovanna in her rapid Italian, but it seemed from her gestures as if she approved of me.

The Quartermaster Corps kept me busy. There was a long strip of fields around Viareggio filled with pallets of blankets, pup tents, entrenching tools, stacks and stacks of C-Rations, gas cans, jeeps, tanks, rifles—everything needed to run an Army, even typewriters. We called it the "Black Market Expressway." Keeping out civilians, who had endured five years of war and depravation, was nearly impossible. Keeping our own men from feeding the black market was more difficult.

Gasoline was in especially short supply, and enterprising soldiers could make all kinds of spending money helping a truckload disappear here and there. This only gave the Criminal Investigation Division, the FBI of the Army, a new reason to live.

One of my new lieutenants at the refinery near Viareggio approached me soon after his arrival.

"You know, we could make a lot of money diverting a few trucks," he said. "Nobody but you and me will know. And both of us could use a little extra. Lord knows the Army isn't that generous."

Greed didn't tempt me. Grandpa had taught me that the fast track to anything was the bad track.

"If I catch you taking a truck out of here, I'll shoot you in the ass," I replied. "Get out of my office. Stay away from the gasoline trucks."

He was transferred a few weeks later, heightening my suspicions. A little checking finally revealed that he was an undercover agent for the Criminal Investigation Division.

Not all of my men were as prudent. One of the sergeants I put in charge of a small refinery down near Livorno couldn't resist temptation. Not two weeks after I assigned him to the operation, I started hearing about gasoline discrepancies. I sent the MPs to arrest him. I wasn't going to have my ranks spoiled with even the hint of something rotten.

The Quartermaster Corps also kept me moving. From Viareggio, I went to Florence as commander of the guard detachment at a prisoner-of-war camp. Giovanna beat me there and had a home set up for us by the time I arrived.

Life in Florence was wonderful and terrible. I made friends with one of the Germans at the camp. He spotted my Leica and offered to teach me about all of its buttons and levers. Photography became my second love. I was sorry to see him shipped back to his homeland.

I also loved wandering the streets, taking pictures of Michelangelo's statues and of all the wonderful buildings hugging the valley of the Arno River. It was one continuous cathedral. Giovanna and I strolled the streets above the Arno at night, never running out of wonder at the splendor.

But because of the white military police, I was never so happy to leave a city. Lieutenant Nathan Alexander, one of my counterparts at the prisoner-of-war camp, struck a chord with me that led to our run in with the MPs. He approached me in the camp guard office as I sorted through the end-of-the-day paperwork.

"Bake, you as tired of these drivers as I am?" he asked after coming in and closing the door behind him.

"Oh, yea," I answered. "Days that they aren't hungover and late, they show up drunk. Some days they are both late and drunk."

"So, what do you say that you and I go into Florence this weekend and find ourselves a couple of motorcycles?" he asked. "Your girlfriend will love it, you and I can ride together, and we won't have to rely on these drunk slouches to get to camp and back."

We found a couple of used Italian machines with enough horsepower to both deafen us and take us to frightening speeds. They were great. But they were a magnet for trouble. Two weeks after we mounted up, a pair of white MPs came calling.

"We are going to be forced to confiscate your machines," the senior MP said.

"Because . . . ."

"We have reason to suspect these motorcycles were procured with black market profits," he said. "The keys?"

I knew MPs had used the "black market" line on other soldiers. It was a cover to confiscate the things they wanted for themselves.

"Black market, my ass. My money comes from Uncle Sam," I said. "This is bullshit."

The senior MP bristled, stepped forward, and put his right hand on his holster.

"Lieutenant, I'll be taking that motorcycle. Care to give me the keys? Or maybe I'll wrap a chain around the damn thing and drag it out of here."

I fished the keys out of my pocket and handed them to him.

Six weeks later, a gruff voice identifying itself as belonging to a military police property clerk called to say our motorcycles were being released. I drove mine to Florence and traded it for a camera within an hour of repossessing it.

The MPs had nastier habits. If a black soldier was seen walking down the street with an Italian girl, the MPs had the *carabinieri*—the Italian police—pick up the girl and have her checked for venereal diseases. It was a none too subtle way of telling an Italian woman if she was in the company of a black man, she must be a whore. When it happened to me, it was the closest I came to punching a white officer.

I stormed into the Military Police Headquarters, found the captain, and demanded to know why he had Giovanna picked up. Nate Alexander came close on my heels, trying to dissuade me every step of the way.

The captain was fit to kill.

"Get out of here," he barked.

I pressed him anyway.

"What the hell are you doing? That's no whore. That's my girlfriend!"

"Get out of here or I'll put you in the stockade," the white captain said, with more emphasis.

"I'll give you a reason to put me in the stockade." I started rolling up my sleeves. "Maybe several reasons."

Lieutenant Alexander wrestled me out the door and saved me from working myself into a bigger fury as well as prison time and a dishonorable discharge. I contemplated finding that captain alone and evening out the score. After thinking about it I realized that the MPs who had taken on Giovanna received fairly thorough punishment by virtue of her temper. Her smirk and unconcerned air when she was released, confirmed that.

From Florence I was sent to a refinery at Foggia and then to another refinery at Bari. Giovanna always left before me and found us a place to live. In late 1946, however, I received word I was making a move she couldn't.

For the previous eighteen months, I had made every transfer and taken every posting I could in order to stay in Italy. I had no desire to go back to the United States. I loved Giovanna like no other. The complication was that the Army was out of jobs for me and was sending me home. I didn't feel I had the skills to land a job in a foreign country. My orders were to sail February 7.

Giovanna dreamed of going home with me. *Tutti gli Americani sono ricchi,* she would say and then describe how American streets were paved in gold, everyone had a big house and a nice car.

"Fernando, you love me, yes? Then take me there."

"No, Giovanna, that's the America of the movies you watch," I told her. "My family didn't even own a car. There are no streets of gold, only difficult roads. And the issue isn't money," I added, holding her face, swollen and puffy from the tears now pouring into my hands. "I'm black, you're white. My country won't ever accept us."

She cried more, kicking, screaming, flailing at me with her fists, and eventually collapsing into my arms. I cried with her, stroking her hair, struggling for reassuring words.

"Fernando, you love me? Fernando, we do good in America. You take me, Fernando. You take me."

I held her until she could cry no more. We repeated this scene over and over again. Finally we knew we had to write each other, to find a way to reunite. For the moment, I had to sail, and she could not accompany me on a troop ship.

Two mornings before I sailed from Livorno she kissed me, ran her hand over my face, said, "Good-bye, my Fernando . . . my little piece of coal," and walked out of our apartment. She went home to her mother.

That last morning, a Sunday, I walked around our apartment, trying to impress every detail, every smell, every thought of her indelibly into my mind. Pieces of her personality were everywhere— the way the dishes were arranged in the cupboard, the neat order of things on our simple wooden table. For a moment, I saw her standing by the sink, looking at me, absentmindedly fingering the cross at her neck. I heard her "wow" when she discovered herself in minimal lipstick.

Shouldering my duffel bag, I trudged to the dock with tears in my eyes. I thought my country had done it all to me before. I was wrong. I didn't know they could so effectively break two hearts.

TWENTY-THREE

A broken bone can heal, but the wound a word opens can last forever.

—Jessamyn West

February 1947, The Atlantic Ocean

The *USS Henry P. Stevens* rolled to port side, the waves kissing the last precious inches of freeboard while the sea contemplated whether to swallow us or just shake us. We grabbed wildly at anything to stop our headlong pitch into whatever god-awful stretch of ocean we were upchucking our way across.

The troop ship settled upright once more, and the man in the wheelhouse fought the *Stevens* back into the waves.

"Now hear this, now hear this," loudspeakers blared. "Clear the decks. No personnel, repeat, no personnel on deck."

I had been topside trying to record these moments for people who would not believe the size of the waves washing over the deck. All that was visible was a tunnel of foam and water. I stuffed my camera into my coat and, hand-over-hand on the guardrail, staggered to my bunkroom.

Once in the refuge of my cabin, I pulled off my rain gear and wet clothes. I would have been better off without rain gear. The wind, rain, waves, and whatever else was coming down from the sky, sideways off the ocean surface, and upward from the sea had found their way through the opening in my hood, the legs of my rain over-alls, and the openings in the sleeves of my coat. I was as wringing wet as if I had gone swimming in my uniform.

The pounding intensified during the next four days. The *Stevens* was like a possessed windup toy, plunging down the trough of one wave, struggling up the face of the next. At the crest, when the pro-peller came out of the water, the *Stevens* shook side-to-side with rivet-splitting intensity. Then the ocean dropped suddenly out from under us, jamming us down the next trough to repeat the cycle. Twenty-four, forty-eight, seventy-two, ninety-six hours. Plunge down, slam up, shake, shake, shake.

I lay on my bunk, feeling every twist of the ship's frame as if it were a part of my skeleton. "I survived combat," I thought to myself, "only to drown two years after the war ended in a miserable stretch of the Atlantic Ocean."

When my mind wasn't focused on my mortality, I missed Giovanna, her nuzzling my neck, the way she called me "Fernando." I wanted to pen her my thoughts, to reassure her. The tossing ship made it impossible to write letters.

Peace came when we put into port somewhere in England. For the first several hours on land, I walked with stilted anticipation, as if the sidewalk might roll up to meet my face and just as rapidly pitch me head over heels. I unconsciously reached for guardrails that weren't there.

As a few days passed, solid ground seemed solid, and I managed to quell the sound of pounding waves and moaning hull. I regained my camera and my curiosity for sightseeing.

Through the happenstance of inquisitiveness, I met a fair-haired English maiden while strolling about an art museum. We struck up a conversation. I loved the rhythm of her accent. Five minutes led to fifteen minutes and led to dinner.

She suggested a hotel several blocks from the wharf, where nar-row wooden booths packed everyone into one intimate package. We ate slowly, me savoring the most American-like beef dish I'd had in years. And we talked the gamut from music to drawing. The crowd around us came, quaffed their pints and kidney pie, lit their cigarettes, and left. The place was pretty well ours about an hour after we arrived.

The woman leaned over the table, looked both directions, and looked at me. "I wonder, soldier, if you'd be willing to show me your tail?"

I damn near spit my mouthful of food.

"Where did you get the idea I might have a tail?" I asked, after taking considerable pause to recheck my temper into a safer, more controlled corner of my mind.

"Oh, come now, mate, it's a well-known story," she said. "All of me girlfriends talk about it. And the Yankee soldiers told us about ya. 'Our country's got its own band of soldiers, black as the heart of night, all with tails,' they said."

"You're taking a hell of a chance having dinner with me then, aren't you?" I asked. We both knew that with the tail story came the story of cannibalism.

"Aye, and we were warned to be very careful of ya. But you appeared quite nice to me. So I thought it fine to come and see what you was all about," she said.

I laid down my fork, wiped my mouth with my napkin, and leaned back in my chair. Are these the people I risked my backside for? I wondered. Are we good enough to fight for their freedom, and yet not worthy of comparison to something better than a flesh-eating ape?

I shook my head and looked at her. "What do you think? Do I look that different to you? Do you think dark skin is the key ingredient for humans to grow tails? I have no tail."

The woman blushed and bit her bottom lip. She realigned the silverware and stared into the table cloth.

"Sorry. I was curious, that's all."

I didn't reply.

"Did I insult you then, mate?" she finally asked.

It wasn't that she insulted me, per se. The insult came from the men who had filled her full of lies, the girlfriends who had repeated them, and the culture and education that persuaded her to so easily trust such an incredible story. The insult came from the ease with which she was willing to believe the absurd.

Her questions sent my mind spinning. Late in the war I had wandered into Pisa and spotted a sign at a Red Cross outpost asking for blood. I walked into the converted stone house, went up the stairs and to a long wooden table in the upper foyer. Five women sat behind the table. They looked at me but said nothing.

Finally a spinsterish woman with her hair wrapped around her head in a braid, stood up, wrung her hands, and coughed.

"Can I help you?" she asked.

"Yes, the sign says you need blood. I'm here to give blood."

Her head swung back and forth, and she held up her trembling right hand like a frightened crossing guard trying to stop oncoming traffic.

"Oh, no, no. You can't. Not here. You see, we're not taking any Negro blood."

My fellow soldiers had warned me the Red Cross considered black blood contaminated. My Wyoming naivete dismissed it as an ugly rumor. Now here it was. "We're not taking any Negro blood."

"Did I insult you?" My dinner date reached over the table and tugged at my sleeve.

"Ma'am?"

"Did I insult you? With, you know, the tail question."

I shrugged. The *Henry P. Stevens* and I were here only long enough for the Atlantic to exhaust its tantrum. What good did it do to go on and on about all the silly, demeaning crap.

"I don't know," I said. "It's a little hard, after all this time, to still hear those rumors. Anyway, I need to get back to the ship. Might be sailing tomorrow."

Within seven days of leaving England, our ship steamed past the Statute of Liberty into New York Harbor. No bands struck up a rousing John Philip Sousa march; no flakes of confetti poured from windows. We walked down ramps, climbed into trucks, and went to

Camp Kilmer, New Jersey, with less fanfare than when we'd docked in Naples three years earlier.

Army doctors gave me a once over, the paperwork processors gave me thirty days off, and I caught a train for Cheyenne. My sisters awaited me with a warm welcome. When I got all visited out, I bought an old brown Chevy sedan and returned to Camp Kilmer to figure out my future.

The Army had nothing for me, which was expected two years after the war in a military with too many first lieutenants. I was scheduled for discharge in two months, when my officer's commission expired.

Before leaving Italy, I had made a stab at keeping officer status. A pile of paperwork led to a hearing before an Army board in Naples. They found me qualified in all areas but one: education. "Lacks a college degree," the return paperwork explained.

With sixty days of terminal leave—the precursor to my discharge—I loaded up my Chevy and headed back west, aimless, restless, without a home here or in Italy. I crossed the upper Midwest, half conscious of the road, totally focused on Giovanna, her tearful face, her pleas of *Tutti gli Americani sono ricchi.*

The roads led to Lincoln, where I spent a few hours wandering the campus at the University of Nebraska. I sat on a sidewalk bench with a sweating bottle of cola, admired the fine women who walked by, and compared all of them to Giovanna. At first it was diversion. Then it was a decision. I motored over to Aunt Cordelia Walker's home, confident of my destiny.

"Well, Vernon, what are you going to do next?" Aunt Cordelia asked as we finished wiping the last roast beef gravy off our plates with her spongy homemade bread.

"College. My officer's category expires the end of next month," I said. "I'll take the GI Bill people are talking about and enroll over at the University of Nebraska."

"And take what?"

"Mmm. Well, I haven't come to that decision. Stopped at the university on my way here, though. The campus is full of pretty women, and I'm smart enough, I think. Besides, Grandpa wanted me to use my head, not my hands." Grandpa's point, I figured, sewed it up.

My aunt smiled and nodded. "Well, Vernon" she started again, patting her well-maintained swoops of white hair. "I think you'd better reconsider. How long have you been in the Army?"

"Oh, six years. Or will have when my commission's up. But I'll lose my officer status. Board in Italy said I'd have to have a college education."

"It doesn't mean you quit the Army," she said. "Six years is a long time. Can't you re-enlist? Look, this is what you know. You must do fairly well at it. Look at all those ribbons you have."

Oh, Christ, I thought. I make a decision and now my family wants to confuse me. I listened without giving Aunt Cordelia's suggestion serious consideration.

Her daughter, Mary—the same girl who'd put me in Irma's clothes and turned me out on the front porch for a sissifying before the whole world—wasn't nearly as polite.

"Why aren't you listening, Vernon? That's good advice. How much money do you have?"

In truth, I had little. The Chevrolet consumed dollar bills and quarts of oil in equal quantity. College? Well, the ladies seemed nice. Still, I had no idea how far the GI Bill would carry me or what I wanted to do with a degree. Mary unearthed every possible doubt and hung them on me like millstones.

Mary won. The day after my commission expired, I donned my uniform, was warmly greeted at the recruiting station, and embarked on my new career as an Army photographer and as a master sergeant. Briefly, anyway.

"NEGRO SOLDIERS WANTED." My bored, traveling eyes couldn't miss that "Negro" and "Wanted" hanging on a bulletin board. The Army was pulling together an all-Negro airborne division. Qualified recruits could expect an additional fifty dollars a month in pay. Jumping out of airplanes didn't thrill me, and I wasn't enamored with the arrogance of the white paratroopers I'd known.

They were fraternity brothers with shoulder patches and attitude. An extra fifty dollars a month eased a lot of misgivings.

If I had thought the move through I might not have done it for one reason: Fort Bragg and nearby Fayetteville, North Carolina. It was perhaps the only major hate-ville I hadn't toured in the South. It didn't strike me any more favorably than the other places.

Things clicked at the fort. I finished jump school and graduated from NCO school at the top of my class. The rest of life was more unsettled. Giovanna's torrent of love letters had turned to a trickle and then faded.

"I think you will never come for me, Fernando," she wrote several times. I had tried to be realistic and reassuring. I told her I was saving my money for us, but I hadn't found a town that would accept us.

Fayetteville was as segregated then as it had been since slavery. I was strolling down a Fayetteville street when a bulbous nose, dropping below the black brim of an officer's hat, rammed itself into the last three inches of space in front of my face. A fine little scar creased the bulb.

"Sergeant, git that DSC ribbon off a yer uniform," the owner of the nose growled, a mist of spit spewing from his rubbery face.

I checked around the officer—a colonel—and looked quickly over my shoulder. We were alone. That was as much to my benefit as his.

"Ah you a hearing me, nigger? Look here at me. Get that goddamn ribbon off a yer uniform. Ain't no nigger I ever saw deserved no Distinguished Service Cross."

I edged back, kept ramrod straight, and fought the urge to wipe his spittle off my face.

"First Sergeant Vernon J. Baker, 82nd Airborne Division, 3rd Battalion, 505th Infantry Regiment, Company K," I said. "Check my record."

"What?" he roared, moving in closer for maximum intimidation. "Check yer record? You uppity nigger, you take that goddamn ribbon off now."

His shoulder patch and his uniform testified about his insecurities. He was a ground pounder, an infantryman. He wasn't airborne qualified and probably hated anybody with guts to do what he couldn't. His chest was festooned with ribbons he could have received in a deep slumber anywhere in the peacetime Army. I clenched and unclenched my fists, and debated if he was worth a five-knuckle imprint right on the jaw line.

"No sir," I replied. "The ribbon stays. First Sergeant Vernon J. Baker, Company K, 505th Infantry. Check my record."

"Ah yew refusin' a de-rect order?" he sputtered, pointing to the bird on his collar that showed he was a colonel.

"Yes sir, I am. Check the record. This is mine," I said, tapping my ribbon.

The colonel rocked back an inch at most, but a discernable distance. The surprise in his eyes told me he had expected to bully me into this one. He was alone, however, and like many good old boys and other variety of bullies, his courage was directly proportional to his numerical advantage. Alone, he was just another guy and not sure if he could take a black man who was tough enough to bail out of airplanes and tough enough to tell him to go to hell. I braced myself and watched for his move.

He raised an arm, hesitated, then formed his hand into a pointing finger and brought it level with my face.

"Yew shall hear from me!" he shouted and stomped off with the determined gait of a disciple who had just accepted an important mission from Jesus. No doubt he'd gone to check my record and to discuss my court martial for insubordination and disobeying a direct order with the judge advocate general's office.

I heard nothing from the bulbous-faced colonel again, at least not directly. But he stayed with me. When I awoke angry in the morning, the image of his ugly face and the sound of his uglier words replayed in my mind. "Ain't no nigger I ever saw deserved no Distinguished Service Cross."

Giovanna quit responding. My letters weren't returned, but neither were they answered. I wildly searched for ways to forget the hurt.

Betty Alexander and I crossed paths in a club, and with rebound remorse I dove in. We weren't together a week when she came pleading to me with her own wounds. She was pregnant, the father was long gone, and her family had no money. In a dizzy moment of misjudgment, I vowed to save her honor and told the Army she was my wife.

Marriage? Betty pleaded.

There I balked. It wasn't my strong suit. Outside of Giovanna, I'd been a loser at picking women for long-term relationships. I had other, more immediate worries once the Korean War broke out in 1950.

A tall, rugged black captain named Morgan, who had been an artillery officer in Italy with the 92nd, was an officer I could neither talk back to nor ignore. And my troubles with him went full tilt soon after America started sending troops to the newest conflict.

"Baker!" he yelled. "Come in here." This had become part of my Fort Bragg routine.

"Baker," he said after I was seated, "you change your mind yet?"

My mind was supposed to be agreeing to apply for active duty as an officer again. The war meant they needed platoon leaders—more expendable lieutenants.

"I've got my reservations, sir," I started. "I like it here. I've got a good job. Why would I want more of the bullshit I had in Italy?"

"Baker, you're a smart man. The Army needs a few more smart men. You know that. But you're acting stupid. Here's one place you are always acting stupid. Here you could be back in the ranks as first lieutenant. But no, you want to play Airborne sergeant. Lord knows you've a reputation as a hell of a combat soldier. And as a reluctant garrison soldier. Well, here's your chance to swap the petty boot-polishing rules of peacetime for combat."

Morgan was as rough as any man I knew when his momentum and his mouth were in sync and running at top speed. The topic always was the same. I had been a fine officer in Italy. I could be a fine officer in Korea.

Combat appealed to me. The politics of dealing with people like

General Almond and Colonel Sherman, however, still gouged me. But after six or eight of Morgan's verbal bruisings I surrendered. It got me out of Fort Bragg and Fayetteville.

It also gave me a ticket away from Betty. My hesitation about marrying her was prophetic. She was a drinker. I'd come home to our Fayetteville apartment to find her stupid drunk by five o'clock in the afternoon. Her baby had been farmed out to her family the week it was born.

After delivering Betty to her parents, I took off for Fort Campbell, Kentucky. Within days of joining the 11th Airborne Division, I volunteered for Korea. I was a soldier and if there was a fight, it was my job to go. The Army refused.

"Lieutenant Baker, we're not sending any DSC, Medal of Honor recipients, any of those kind of men over there," the chief of staff explained. "We don't have so many of you highly decorated guys. We want to keep you around. That's part of good morale and all."

I didn't know what to believe. I knew there were few black Distinguished Service Cross recipients. But white Distinguished Service Cross recipients had gone to Korea. Was this about color in the sense that the Army wanted a few decorated black soldiers around to prove it had a broad, inclusive outlook?

The 11th wouldn't take me to Southeast Asia, but it took me places like Alaska to practice winter paratrooping and 101 ways to freeze my ass off, Army style, so as to be adequately prepared to freeze it off in time of critical need. As the Alaska operation wrapped up in the winter of 1951, top Army brass came by for one of their officious inspections. My company commander pulled me aside after the official review.

"Hey, Bake, didn't you serve with Ned Almond?"

"The general?"

He nodded.

"I didn't serve with him, I served under him. In Italy. He honchoed the 92nd. Why?"

"Almond's here. He's the three star. Don't you recognize him?"

I looked. A balding man strutted across the room, closely covered by a gaggle of aides.

"Nope. Don't say as I recognize the face. No reason to. Only saw him twice up close."

"You want to meet him again?" my commander offered.

It came without malice, and I tried to make my response even. "No, I didn't enjoy the last two encounters."

TWENTY-FOUR

It was argued that through integration we would get into all kinds of difficulty in staging soldiers' dances and other social events.

—General Dwight D. Eisenhower

Fall 1951, Fort Campbell, Kentucky

Sweet revenge of a sort materialized on September 10, 1951. At midnight the order to desegregate the Army finally hit the 11th Airborne. I rose from platoon leader to company commander by daybreak.

I opened the door to the commander's office at Company K the morning of September 11 without knocking. A white second lieutenant sat with his feet propped up on the desk and, when he saw me, he scowled. He dropped his feet to the floor, sat up, and looked at me.

"What can I do for you, Lieutenant?"

"Climb up out of that seat," I replied. "It's mine."

I tossed my orders on his desk. He unfolded them, read them, his jaw dropping as his eyes traveled back and forth over the page. He turned pale; his eyes showed fear and anger. He stood anyway, saluted, and went to get a box to carry his belongings out of my office. He didn't say "welcome" or "congratulations." And I didn't expect it.

The company was glacially gracious about the change. Their eyes flicked coldly over me and then at each other whenever I walked into the room. The silent tension, lack of small talk, lack of joking when I was around also made their disapproval clear.

Three years earlier—1948—President Harry Truman decreed, by executive order, that the military desegregate. Instead it became the year the Army began ignoring Truman's desegregation order. Nothing monumental happened, beyond the same old debate about how the black man was too uneducated to compete against white soldiers. And the debate about how blacks would never be good enough to compete against whites for promotions if they were part of integrated units.

But the issue wasn't going away, no matter how many studies concluded a black man and a white man couldn't fight together. Of course, those studies relied on the wisdom of high-ranking officers who had no more combat time with black soldiers than I had serving in a presidential cabinet. And are part of the reason some National Guard units were still segregated in the 1960s.

Those first three years of debate over Truman's desegregation order convinced everyone that some minimal change was inevitable. They probably imagined a handful of black privates, and perhaps a few corporals, joining their ranks. They planned on black units taking the worst of their fellow white soldiers—the irascible losers who didn't respond to any amount of time in the brig or on their hands and knees scrubbing mess-hall floors. If segregation had to be, this was the acceptable package.

The concept of a black officer in charge of an all-white unit hadn't come up on their radar screens. Now, they not only faced a black commander every day, they faced the prospect of many more coming behind me. The all-black units were loaded with officers because, for so long, there had been no place for us to go.

There also was an oversupply of black NCOs—corporals and all variety of sergeants. So when integration finally was forced on the 11th Airborne, top commanders also transferred blacks into white companies as the first sergeants, the top enlisted men in the company. I expanded on that. I examined the records of my company and found several white NCOs not qualified to hold their ranks and responsibilities. Wherever possible, I replaced them with a solidly qualified black soldier.

I tried not to let my already ample anger agitate the situation. A few of the soldiers defied me, simply ignoring whatever order I gave as if I was no more than a dog whose bark was lost in a howling wind. I wrapped them up in a typewriter. Defy an order, expect discipline, I told them as I sat them down and wrote them up with the keys of whatever standard black Underwood or Royal typewriter sat at my desk. I didn't yell it. I said it and backed it with action.

Being in an Airborne unit eased the transition considerably. Paratroopers tend to be more gung ho than the most eager infantry. The expected grumbling rapidly turned to grudging compliance and then relative harmony. Most of the bigger problems came from men who would have been trouble under any circumstances.

I made sure the worst of the problem men woke up staring through bars. Eventually the Army got smart and started getting rid of them. Society's losers were our losers. A uniform and basic training didn't smarten them up or make them agreeable human beings.

The 11th Airborne ended up liking me much better than I liked it. My battalion commanders spent countless hours trying to persuade me to re-enlist at the end of 1952. I didn't. I'd had all of the overzealous "Go Airborne" stuff I could stand. I didn't like the politics of being an officer in the peacetime Army any better. The problem surfaced on my otherwise spotless efficiency reports.

"Baker is not sociable," it read time after time. Or, "This officer does not desire to mingle with his fellow officers." Or, "While otherwise rating well in all categories, Baker is reluctant to make after-hours contact with upper echelon."

My friends and I called it "Uncle Tommin'." In order to get ahead, we needed to go to the bar, buy drinks with abandon, and bullshit the colonel all night. Or we were supposed to drag our wives and girlfriends to cocktail party after cocktail party so they could lobby our commanders for our promotions. We, meanwhile, were expected to make inane conversation with the other people in the room who could advance our careers.

I didn't drink, smoke, or cotton to stroking the brass. It was one reason I didn't go to the officers' club. I couldn't see myself standing around with a cocktail glass pretending I was any part of it.

When the Korean conflict ended, I left the Airborne and went back to the Signal Corps and photography. Without a college degree, I also relinquished my lieutenant's status and returned to the NCO ranks. In the blink of a flash bulb I was back at Fort Huachuca, running a photo laboratory, working as a regimental photographer, and finding a social life in Tucson.

And she was there.

Shy, smiling, attractive in her bashfulness—a slice of Giovanna. As tall as me, her hair waved along her brow in neat bangs, then waved darkly to her shoulders and beyond. Add agate-eyes in a narrow face with a dainty pinpoint nose and a perfectly proportioned chin. Fern V. Brown.

One of my ever present Army buddies started it all. He was dating her older sister, Ruth. Ruth insisted on the double date, said her little sister was perfectly nice and downright beautiful, yet a bit of a wallflower. When I got to know Ruth, I realized she was like that—pushy in her kindest moments.

My buddy finally agreed. I doubt he wanted a double date and yet Ruth's persistence convinced him, like it did most people. Acquiescence cost less with Ruth.

"Hey, Baker. Got a date for you," he said.

"OK," I said. "When and where?"

Ruth both glowed and glowered as she looked me over. Overall, she appeared only too happy for me to take her sister dancing.

Red flags flew up instantly. Fern had twin daughters—Lilli and Lore. She was in the midst of a divorce. Part of this story was all too familiar.

Fern was patient and persistent. She didn't plead, like Helen and Betty had. A swimming instructor, she was proudly self-sufficient.

She loved her four-year-old daughters with an exuberance neither Helen nor Betty had for any child, their own or someone else's.

Then there was Fern's former husband. She offered little explanation and I asked for little. I had my own failures. I wasn't going to criticize hers. When I met him, I understood completely.

He stopped by her house in Tucson one sweltering Saturday afternoon, demanding to see her. He burst in the front door, exploded when he saw me, and went after Fern. A revolver came out of his pocket amid words of how he was going to kill her.

I dove across the room, caught his midriff with my shoulder, and jammed him into a small lamp table. The gun clattered away. I started swinging. Some inexplicable moments later Fern was pulling me off him. He lay in the ruins of the table and the lamp, his hands over his bloody face. He struggled to his feet and stumbled out. We never saw him again.

Fern and I were married the following summer—June 1953. Daughter LaVerne joined us four days after Christmas 1954.

The nightmares returned when Fern was packing us to move to Fort Ord, California. She found my Distinguished Service Cross certificate in a box she was sorting. She showed it to me when I came home from work.

"Honey, what's this all about? You've not talked about this."

I hadn't seen the certificate in four or five years. She passed it to my hands and I reread it.

"Oh, this," I said, not wanting to begin. "Our last big push in Italy. This is from the last big push in Italy."

Fern laughed. "OK. There must be something to tell about 'our last big push'?"

"Not really. There was a battle. Lots of men got killed. I killed some of the Germans that day and received this."

I tapped the certificate with the back of my fingers. "I was doing what they paid me to do. I didn't expect anything else, especially this."

The faces of my nineteen men flashed through my mind. The sound of mortar rounds drummed in my ears. Trees exploded. I could see, hear, smell, and taste the battle. The questioning began anew. Was I responsible for their deaths? Was the ground we gained worth their lives, especially considering their sacrifice had been totally disregarded. I saw Almond's face, his finger drilling his desk. I hated it, hated it all.

"Vernon? Are you going to finish? Vernon?" Fern tapped my arm, bringing me back from my mental journey to Castle Aghinolfi. She studied my face. I must have looked unhappy. Her hand touched mine affectionately.

"No reason you have to say more," Fern said. She gently lifted the certificate out of my hand. "I'll put this back in the box."

It took weeks to shake the memory, the instant replay—the German hurling the grenade at Runyon and me, my medic going down to sniper fire, the taste of burned cordite. Events conspired to take me back to Italy, no matter how much I tried to bury the memories. Three years earlier, a call from *Ebony* magazine had stirred this.

"Mr. Baker, we'd like you to send us a portrait of yourself," the woman explained. "We are researching an article on your Distinguished Service Cross. There are so few such as yourself."

So few. So few black men honored. There were no Medals of Honor bestowed on black soldiers in World War II. Distinguished Service Crosses were barely more common.

I reluctantly agreed to *Ebony's* request, leery of dealing with the story. It was all too raw; the sight of the dead men's faces as I removed their dog tags, the shrieks of agony.

Nineteen men, however, deserved better. Their memories deserved to be honored. I wanted someone to say, "These soldiers did the impossible. They proved the worst of the white commanders wrong."

I posed for their photos. Nothing happened. I never heard another word. Rest in peace, fellows, I silently told my men. We will have to be satisfied knowing we did it.

Fort Ord led back to the infantry and that led to a tour in Korea. It was the only route to a promotion. Considering it was only for a year, I went alone.

It was memorable in all kinds of forgettable ways. The women came on to the men in incredible numbers. Prostitution was rampant; alcoholism was epidemic. Soldier after soldier came, spent most of his time toasted, and was busted back in rank often enough to where he left the country with nothing. Calling it debauchery dresses up the disaster, gives it too much romance.

The partying and the free-for-all with women hardly started the year I stepped off the airplane. The country was full of orphans, and a fair share of those orphans were the work of these GIs. My American doctor at Camp Kaiser made it a personal project to find homes for the orphans. He started working on me to adopt the moment he found out I had daughters.

"A girl isn't so highly valued in this society," he explained. "A boy, a son, can expect more respect no matter what. This country is full of orphans, thousands of orphans. You're a good and decent man. How about taking another daughter home?"

I wrote Fern and she talked it over with our three daughters. The youngest, LaVerne, petitioned the hardest. If we adopted someone the right age, she would no longer be the baby of the family and would no longer be goalie for all the older sibling torment. Fern conducted a family poll. The vote was unanimous in favor.

I contacted the doctor and made the appropriate applications. He sent me to the orphanage to meet my new daughter almost immediately, although it would take months to complete the paperwork.

She was nine years old, half black, half Korean, and lived among hundreds of other children in a grubby, rundown building on the outskirts of Seoul. She rested a finger on her teeth, as if such was necessary to keep her chin off her chest. Occasionally she looked at the running, screaming horde of other children. Her eyes seemed to be saying, "Being with them is safer. I want to join them, however lonely the company of so many strangers is."

I crouched down, smiled, and held out my hand. She refused it and continued looking at me suspiciously.

"I'm Sergeant Baker," I told her, and pointed to my name patch on my uniform. "Baker. B-A-K-E-R."

She said nothing. I stood, held out my hand for her, and offered to take her for something to eat. We went to a USO Club, I loaded her up on food, talked to her, and studied her.

And so our acquaintance began. I went to find her on the weekends. We went to a restaurant, and I told her about her life-to-be in America. She shoveled food into her emaciated cheeks and watched me carry on. The only word she could muster was her Korean name.

I returned to Fort Ord before she arrived. My daughters and my wife hadn't said hello before announcing that our newest family member was going to be named Larise. We collected her at the San Francisco airport a few months later, after passing serious inspection by American adoption authorities. Fern and the other girls instantly took to Larise.

Within a few years, Larise was part of all their rituals. My favorite was coming home late in the evening and finding the girls in a semicircle around Fern on the living room floor. As if born to raise girls, Fern quietly talked about life, about what happened if they ended up with boys. We had no problems with any of our daughters.

Sometimes I stood back and listened to these living room chats, amazed at how lucky we were, amazed at how lucky I was. Fern taught swimming classes, often pulling in more money a month than I did. She saved enough for us to make a sizeable down payment on a house and overcame the hurdles to finding a house we could buy.

Although she was black, Fern looked Spanish and so she fit right in when she started shopping for a place around Monterey Bay. In no time she found a brand-new house well within the budget she made us live by. She called me at Fort Ord.

"It's all we've wanted Vernon, but I don't think it will last. Can you come to the real estate office after you leave the Fort?"

I agreed. But things turned sour the minute I walked into the real estate office. Fern pulled me up to the real estate agent's desk and said, "This is my husband, Vernon. He's here to sign the papers."

The agent looked at me with terrible shock and looked at Fern. He made no effort to get up from his desk and shake my hand.

"Oh, uh oh," he said. "Yes, well, Mrs. Baker, I'm sorry. The house is sold."

My anger soared. I wanted to reach across the desk, grab him by his lapels, and jerk him into next Sunday. I stared hard, right into his eyes, to give him a sense of what my fists were too well behaved to tell him.

Fern also became angry, but it spurred her to work harder. In no time she found another house under construction, in Seaside, and she plotted to outwit the agent who had refused us.

"Don't you know somebody in that real estate office?" she asked. "A retired colonel or something."

I pondered. "Retired colonel . . . maybe a lieutenant colonel . . . you mean the guy who came around to each of our units before he got out and delivered that 'if you ever need anything' speech?"

Fern nodded. "That's him."

"And?" I asked.

"Maybe you can talk to him before we go in to sign the papers this time. Maybe he can handle our business."

"He's in that same real estate office," I protested.

"Maybe you can talk to him," she replied.

I agreed to give it a try. I called him and asked him to meet me for coffee some place other than his office. I told him about Fern's dream house and how my presence killed the last deal.

"OK, I'll help," he said. "Have Fern call me and let me know where the place is. We will make sure your financing is in order. I can make sure the house is available and you can afford it."

A few days later we returned to the same real estate office. The man who refused us before never looked up from his desk. Our friendly lieutenant colonel accommodated us immediately. He wrapped up the transaction by announcing to the rest of the office that he was selling us the house.

Fern beamed.

Many of our battles didn't go so easily. Larise's early school days required all the resolve Fern could muster. Larise rode to the Fort Ord school with me every day and then rode home with me whenever possible. One day she came to the car, in tears.

"Daddy, one of the teachers says I'm stupid," she said.

Fern exploded when I told her and grabbed the telephone. Before the hour was out we were meeting with the teacher.

"Your daughter doesn't respond, Mr. and Mrs. Baker," he opened defensively. "I'll ask a question of her, and she knows I'm talking to her because I address her by name. All she does is smile."

Fern didn't have a chance to speak. I was already in the fray.

"She's from Korea. She's new here. Can't you see? She doesn't speak English yet. How can you say she's stupid . . . she doesn't understand you."

I'm sure I went on, heated well beyond what a thermometer could register.

"Mr. Baker, Mr. Baker. This is hard for you, I'm sure. The blunt truth is, I think your daughter might be retarded."

Fern tugged my arm and jumped in.

"She's not retarded, stupid, or anything else. I'll tell you what. I'll be coming to school with our girl and we'll see if, when she understands, she's not quite a bit smarter than you think."

For the next six months, Fern went to school with Larise every day, sitting in the back of the classroom while the lessons went on. Larise not only passed third grade with flying colors, she graduated from high school as a straight-A student.

Her academic ability led her one place I didn't like—to Italy. Most of us were at home on that weekend day. She was working on a project for school, pouring over a pile of books as she sat on the floor of her room.

"Daddy," she yelled, running through the house to find me. "Daddy, you're in this book."

A volume flapped from her hand. I took it and began to read as she held a hand to her chest and worked to catch her breath. It was a small mention of my receiving the Distinguished Service Cross for the battle in Italy. Two of my four daughters had gone all the way through high school without ever stumbling across this, and I had been relieved that it was undiscovered.

"That's you, isn't it, Daddy? That's you?" Larise asked excitedly.

"Yes, that's me."

"What's a Distinguished Service Cross?" she asked.

"Oh, it's a decoration, for soldiers," I said. "It's something given for stuff on the battlefield."

"Stuff?"

"Larise, it was a situation where we had a big battle against the Germans. They were our enemy then. I killed a lot of people, and that's about it."

I held up my hand to stop the conversation. I didn't want to discourage her. She was a bright, earnest child. Simultaneously, I hated the feeling that started in the center of my stomach and radiated outward when the questions about the Distinguished Service Cross, about the battle, started closing in.

When Larise's son, Brandon, was born several years later, he got wind of my Distinguished Service Cross. He pestered me for more details. I tried to avoid his questions.

"Grandpa, tell about when you were a hero," he'd implore.

"Grandpa, tell me about all of those bad guys you got."

My brush-offs did nothing to discourage him. Finally, one winter afternoon, I sat Brandon on the couch and handed him the small velvet-lined box with my Distinguished Service Cross.

"Brandon, the simplest way I can say it is this: One day in Italy, many years ago, there was a big battle," I said. "I ended up killing a lot of people. There's nothing more to be made of it."

He opened the box with the Distinguished Service Cross.

"Wow, Grandpa, this is pretty cool."

"Keep it," I said, hoping I was giving away the memories as well as the medal.

TWENTY-FIVE

A life spent in making mistakes is not only more honorable, but more useful, than a life spent doing nothing.

—George Bernard Shaw

Fall 1967, Germany

Combat, racism, and beatings couldn't chase me from the Army. Drugs and desertion did.

I dreamed of finishing the last three years of a thirty-year career in Germany. Fern and my daughters relished a European adventure. We sold our home and moved to Mainz.

It was a little crazy from the start. I was forty-seven years old and jumping out of airplanes again. Riding on the jump planes often was more frightening than jumping out of them. During one training mission, the back door fell off. No one was hurt on the plane or on the ground. Unless we drew the best planes—the C-141 transports—we were riding aboard flying sieves. Cold air or cold rain or whatever else we encountered at jump altitude whipped at us through the numerous cracks, crevices, and holes. Coolant invariably leaked from some inexhaustible supply. If this didn't get your attention, the noise and vibration threatened to leave you deaf and shaky for hours to come. Free-falling was much less intimidating.

Fern found us a place fifteen miles outside of Mainz that was close to our normal landing spot. She and the girls loved to gather and watch me parachute.

For the Army, these years were a mess. Good Morning, Vietnam. Some 6,000 American soldiers had been killed in the war by the time I went to Germany in 1967. Those weren't overwhelming casualties. But they were significant enough to stir considerable opposition because, among other things, so many of the soldiers were draftees.

Two years earlier—1965—the military doubled the number of people it drafted. That galvanized the opposition. College students back home, already agitating for the civil rights movement and the campus free-speech movement, easily joined the antiwar movement. Key public figures, like the famous baby doctor, Benjamin Spock, joined the public outcry.

The antiwar fever easily infected the barracks in Germany. Men deserted by handfuls, even those with families. Most often they struck out for Switzerland, either on a weekend pass or in the middle of the night. The dishonor of desertion, in their minds, was far better than doing their duty in Southeast Asia. It reflected poorly on all of us. It made me angry to tally yet another missing soldier or, more often, missing sets of soldiers. Other tasks were worse because rampant LSD, marijuana, and heroin use also blossomed in the Army of the sixties.

As company first sergeant, I woke the soldiers in the morning. Waking a soldier who is strung out on heroin came with all the elements of an Alfred Hitchcock movie. Some of them lunged at me, some of them lay there, stinking, filthy, too screwed up to take care of themselves. Some passed out in the bathroom stalls, tourniquet still half tied around an arm or a foot, a spoon and a syringe nearby. I did regular business with the MPs.

Stories circulated of men robbing their best friends or intimidating the weakest soldiers to get the cash for another fix. Many mornings I walked in the barracks to find a zoned-out soldier lurking in the shadows, mute, vacant, appearing as if he had nothing to lose. I started strapping on my .45-caliber pistol when I left the office for my rounds.

Having the gun didn't comfort me. Fighting in Italy, it was clear who the enemy was—the other guys with the strange uniforms. It also was plain that anytime I went on a night patrol or toward the German lines, I could expect an ambush, mines, artillery shells, machine gun fire, or grenades. The odds were bad, but the threat was well defined.

Racism is somewhat the same. The enemy is pretty well defined, and I could prepare to defend myself from what likely was coming. At least I kept myself alive and employed.

Walking into a barracks full of strung-out American soldiers, I felt out of control. I couldn't tell who might try to jump me. I didn't know who would recoil, in a drug-induced haze, and pull a knife or a gun.

It started as a small feeling that I might be mugged by my own soldiers. And grew. Fern watched the tension build. Those mornings when she awoke to find me fidgeting before dawn, she offered gentle words of encouragement. I finally snapped.

"Fern, I'm going to kill somebody or be killed. I can't stand it. I'm not the first sergeant of the headquarters company, I'm the warden for a bunch of drug lunatics. I'm getting out."

My commander was understanding.

"I don't care to lose you, Sergeant Baker," he said. "As you well know, I also cannot refuse your request to retire. You've got your time in."

The window of his office looked across the green lawns, past the red brick barracks, and off into the trees hiding their branches in low, gray clouds.

"I know what it's like," he added. "It's a crazy time in the Army. I wouldn't want to go out there and wrestle those soldiers in the mornings either. I don't know what's happened to the Army I joined."

I jumped out of my last airplane at age forty-eight and checked out of the Army in Fort Hamilton, New York, a week later. It was in August 1968. I declined the standard retirement parade. The Army dealt me the hardest lessons of my life and had given me some of my greatest satisfaction. Not finishing thirty years was disconcerting.

Ending my career in an era where my own men were the greatest threat to me was agonizing. I was a warrior, a soldier, an officer, an honorable man. I couldn't believe, in the end, what undid my pursuit of these things.

I could not slip gently into the good life. My pension gave me less than three hundred dollars a month to support my wife and my two children still at home. Fern went back to teaching swimming. I went to work for the Red Cross.

The Red Cross dispatched me to Vietnam in early 1969. It came with a sad side trip to Cheyenne. My oldest sister, Irma, died of emphysema. Her only daughter lived only three more years before losing to cancer.

Fern stayed in California with our two youngest daughters as I made my way to Pleiku to work as a counselor to military families. That's a fancy title for delivering death notices and making loans to soldiers who needed tiding over until payday. I lived in the military compound at Pleiku, in the center of South Vietnam. The nights forced me to think of Italy. The North Vietnamese regularly shelled us with mortar rounds. The days of not being able to look safely out of a window, of having trees explode into shrapnel, of men disintegrating, crept back into my dreams. I worked to shake it, to bury the memories of the nineteen men. Control meant forgetting; control meant diversion.

I spent hour after hour in a helicopter, flying to the Army artillery bases strategically located on top of the old volcanos, to tell men of trouble back home. A parent was dead, a brother was gravely ill, a girl friend was pregnant.

Six months later, I shifted to the coast, to Da Nang, and repeated the same work for the Air Force. After a year in Vietnam, I went back to the states and Fort Ord.

Stateside, my "assistant field director" job mostly consisted of loaning money to GIs. They went out early in the month, spent all of their bucks on booze, and then, when rent or their car payment came due, didn't have enough to cover their bills. So they came to the Red Cross.

Most of them were a bad risk. They were no better at repaying the Red Cross than they were at taking care of their main obligations. I balked. I didn't care to make another bad loan to a guy I was hounding to repay a string of prior bad loans. And I got into trouble for my reluctance.

"Mr. Baker, our mission is SERVICE to military families," my field director crossly informed me. "We make loans. If we're not making loans, we're not in business."

Translation: Mr. Baker, keep making the bad loans because it helps us continue to show our need for money. We cannot go on raising money if we're not showing people we're spending it. It was like cops arresting speeders merely to keep their performance statistics high.

The work covered our bills and kept me in contact with a few of my Army buddies. It also provided enough time off that I could go back to what I liked to do best: hunt.

I read everything I could find on the best places for elk after learning California had none we were allowed to hunt. An article in *American Hunter* talked of a place called Red Ives Peak, high in the headwaters country of Idaho's St. Joe River. Wright Byrom, an Army warrant officer and friend for more than two decades, agreed to try it for hunting season 1979.

Wright didn't have my kind of free time. I volunteered to go to northern Idaho a couple of weeks early and scout the area. Red Ives was spectacular, one of the last areas of northern Idaho not over-logged by the timber corporations. Towering cedar, douglas fir, and spruce climbed slopes and skirted meadows, giving elk and deer dark timber to hide in. The lush meadows provided ample feed. Endless beauty and endless bounty.

I set up our advance camp and hiked five hundred yards to a little knob overlooking a draw. Several elk were feeding at a natural mineral lick in the draw. A fallen Douglas fir offered an inviting place to have lunch and watch the elk. I settled on the log, opened a package of Canadian bacon, and sliced off a chunk.

After a few bites, I heard rumbling on my left. A bear came barreling out of the bushes, three hundred yards away. The wind was carrying my scent, and the scent of the Canadian bacon, directly to him. His nose twitched with the message: fresh meat, two kinds. I dropped my knife and the package of meat and pulled my .41-caliber revolver. It's not the sort of move you remember in detail. One minute I was having lunch, the next I was hefting a revolver, wondering about the odds of plugging a black bear with a pistol and doing enough damage to save myself. I didn't want to shoot the bear because I didn't need the meat, or the hide, and I didn't want to scare the elk.

The bear abruptly stopped, twenty-five yards away, and stood on his hind legs. His nose started working the wind again. Our eyes met for a few seconds. He dropped to the ground, turned, and ambled the direction he'd come from. I stood there for several minutes, gun in hand, jaw tight with anticipation, expecting a replay. Nothing happened.

Wright showed up a few weeks later. He couldn't believe I'd escaped the bear without firing a shot.

On opening day, that first year hunting in Idaho, I dropped a cow elk.

TWENTY-SIX

Grief can't be shared. Everyone carries it alone, his own burden, his own way.

—Anne Morrow Lindbergh

January 1986, Seaside, California

"Honey, I've been hurting right here." Fern was standing beside the kitchen table, patting her chest with the palm of her hand. She wasn't pale or feverish looking, but I side with caution.

"Let me take you to the doctor," I replied. "You know, we're not ten minutes from the base hospital."

"Ha. Oh, no mister. I'm not going to any hospital. I'm just telling you, I've had a little pain there." She turned away and busied herself with something by the sink.

Fern, now sixty-eight, had logged twenty-two years as a swimming instructor. How was I going to argue with her? I stirred more whipping cream and honey into my coffee and returned to my book.

Ten days later, I found her leaning against the doorway to our room, again patting her chest with her right arm.

"Same pain?" I asked.

"Yes, yes," she replied with a sigh. "But I'm all right. I'm going to sit down for a minute and I'll be fine. Just fine. Then I want you to take me to the PX."

"How about me taking you to the doctor and then the PX?" I asked.

She waved me away. "No doctor. I'm fine."

We climbed in our old Land Cruiser and motored over to the Fort Ord shopping center. Fern went inside to pursue her list. I stuck around the front and chatted with another military husband I knew. I wasn't that much help at shopping. This was a better place for me.

Fern finally emerged a half hour later, pale as onion skin.

"Vernon, I don't feel altogether well," she said.

"Let's go," I said. "I'm taking you to the hospital."

"No," she said emphatically. "No, I keep telling you I'm not going to any hospital. What I need is to go home and lie down. That's where you're going to take me."

I brought the Land Cruiser around to the front of the store, helped her in, and started for home. Not two blocks from the PX, Fern looked over at me, started to speak, and instead slumped forward. I cranked the steering wheel and made a U-turn, muttering at myself for not insisting Fern go to the doctor much earlier.

I slowed at red lights only long enough to see if there was any oncoming traffic and then blasted through. By the time I pulled up to the Fort Ord hospital emergency room, Fern was sitting up, seemingly semiconscious. I ran into the hospital and found an attendant at a counter inside.

"My wife . . . out here . . . come on," I said, or something close. I couldn't make complete sentences.

A trio of white-cloaked attendants were summoned. They rolled a gurney out to the Land Cruiser. When the door opened, she nearly fell out and couldn't get her hand up to stop herself. Still, she was awake.

A line of doctors examined her. First a lieutenant, then a captain, then a major. The room was abuzz with low voices. The words "heart attack" slipped out of the din.

"What's wrong with her?" I said, wanting to get their attention, wanting to help.

The major walked over to me.

"Are you her husband?"

"Yes. Can you tell me what's wrong?"

"Maybe a heart attack. But frankly, we don't know. We're going to take her upstairs for some tests. Why don't you give as much information as possible to the desk nurse and then come on up to the fourth floor."

By the time I arrived upstairs, Fern was full of tubes and wires, but was sitting up and talking. She was calmer than I expected.

"Vernon, why don't you go and get the kids? You know they will be showing up at our house for their Saturday visit. Might as well have them stop by here."

Fern was as calm and matter-of-fact as if she'd asked me to stop off at the store on my way home from work and pick up a dozen eggs.

Fifteen minutes after I returned to the house, the California portion of our clan started arriving: LaVerne and her two children, Larise and her child. All asked about Fern anxiously.

"When?"

"What happened?"

"What's wrong with her?"

"How long has she been sick, anyway?"

"Will she be OK?"

I answered each question a dozen times. We returned to the hospital together. Larise and LaVerne asked all of the same questions over again and Fern dismissed them all with, "I'll be fine in no time." The grandchildren eyed the strange surroundings silently. With a little imagination, it was the regular Saturday family gathering in a slightly different setting.

Ten, maybe fifteen minutes after we arrived, Fern grabbed her chest with one hand and clutched the nurse call button with the other. The nurse skidded into the room, looked at Fern, and shooed all of us out without so much as an exchange of words with her patient. We gathered in the waiting area in grim silence, sitting in those awful orange vinyl-covered chairs, disinterestedly poking at old, worn copies of *Reader's Digest* and the usual hospital waiting room religious publications that owe their distressed looks to nervous hands, not thousands of readings. Our grandchildren stood anxiously by, mostly silenced by our intense, unspoken worry. Eventually the nurse returned.

"Mr. Baker," she called quietly.

I followed her back to Fern's room. Fern's eyes were closed. A mask covered her nose and mouth, and there was no sign she was breathing save for the pulse of a respirator pump. I tried to take comfort in that mechanical breath.

The major I had talked to in the emergency room waited a discreet distance from her bed. He motioned to me.

"Your wife indeed had a heart attack, Mr. Baker, and now it appears she has had another. Or a stroke. We're not sure which. Unfortunately, she's in a coma. We will keep her under observation. I can't tell you any more at the moment. I'll be back to check on her throughout the weekend."

Fern never regained consciousness. We buried her a week later.

I kicked around our lonely house, pretended to work at the Red Cross and thought about Fern. I thought about the what ifs, such as what if I had insisted—and she had relented—about seeing a doctor sooner. We'd been together thirty-nine years and every painting she'd hung on a wall, every curtain she'd made, every box she labeled reminded me of who she was, what we'd had, and what I now didn't have. I involuntarily started to call her name when I went pawing through the kitchen, wanting to ask her where the extra salt was and whether we had any more beans.

An invisible blanket descended, suffocating me with lethargy. Most everything seemed pointless. I could pass hours sitting in a chair, thinking I was about to do something and instead drifting into a stupor. But this felt better than trying.

Months passed. One of the hunting gang talked me into going to Idaho again. We'd spent the early 1980s in Utah and Colorado and always struck out. No place had been lucky like Red Ives.

It was a change, a diversion, and hunting was an occupation that sent me back to the happiest parts of my childhood. Since my days wandering the Cheyenne prairie and the Medicine Bow Mountains, I dreamed of having a cabin in the woods.

Idaho was that dream. I appreciated the country more and more. The steep foothills reminded me of the parts of Italy I liked to remember. We found new hunting ground near St. Maries.

"How about a place to set up, like, you know, a permanent hunting camp?" I asked our local guide, a burly character named Kenny Organ.

"I'll do you one better," Organ replied. "I've got the key to an unfinished cabin down this road not a quarter mile. The couple doesn't live there and they are ready to sell."

It was a modified A-frame, set in a park of trees midway up a gentle slope. Raw and unfinished inside, it was perfect. As was the setting. Only a half dozen neighbors spread over several dozen acres, and the access road was the toughest mile of trail around.

My daughters balked at the move.

"What on earth do you want to live up there for?" they said. "We're here, your family is here. OK, the hunting is great, but all of the time? Look at this big house you've got down here."

I let them go on. In time, their own circumstances might help them understand what it was like, day after day, to stare at all of the evidence of what you lost. Years of losses had taught me to find a place to leave the memories and move on. In May 1987, I packed my truck and headed to Idaho for good.

As a kid, I had sworn I wouldn't chop another stick of wood or clean ashes out of another stove. And here, if I didn't do these chores, I had no heat. But I loved it.

I found a carpentry book and had fun trying to finish the inside of my house. When hunting season rolled around, I had the entire Benewah Valley at my door step.

Because I am a loner, I was in the area several months before I learned I was the only black man for fifty square miles. The newspapers told me other things people did not feel comfortable telling me—about the presence of the Aryan Nations compound north of Coeur d'Alene, in an upper-class white community called Hayden

Lake. A man named Richard Butler had built himself an enclave there, complete with a guard tower and a "Christian Identity" church.

Butler recruited all manner of neo-Nazis and got all of the attention he wanted merely by opening his mouth. He wanted the Pacific Northwest for a whites-only nation. In the early 1980s, some of Butler's followers formed a splinter group—The Order—and turned to greater violence, bombing a synagogue in Boise, robbing banks and armored cars, and killing people. A subsequent version of The Order bombed the federal courthouse in Coeur d'Alene and the home of a local Episcopal priest who led local antiracism crusades.

At first, the old fears crept in. Hayden Lake obviously was hostile. Nearby Spokane might be another Fayetteville. St. Maries might be worse. But no one bothered me. I kept to myself and people happily left me to that arrangement.

For the next three years, I puttered, painted, sawed, hammered, hunted and, most important, reflected and healed. When the memories got too tough I could walk in the woods for hours, letting the paths among the cool pines take over. Sawing and splitting wood until the sweat poured off my face, ran down my arms, down the small of my back, also had a way of cleansing that took my mind and body down to their basic elements.

From those bare rocks of the soul, I rebuilt for another day.

TWENTY-SEVEN

We love because it's the only true adventure.

—Nikki Giovanni

September 1989, Spokane, Washington

She sat two tables away, illuminated by the last golden wash of late afternoon sunlight. Her hands cupped under her chin. Blonde curls drifted toward her shoulders. Her attention was focused outside the window.

I counted on being able to eat lunch here, in the Spokane, Washington, airport coffee shop. I hadn't counted on seeing such a beautiful woman. And this when I only had an hour to catch an airplane to California to visit my children.

She eventually turned my direction. When I was sure she was looking directly at me, I winked. At that split second, her gaze had started to move on. Then her blue eyes stopped and came back and rested on my face. I winked again. She stared harder, but didn't wink back. Since she didn't frown, either, I decided to take a chance. I got up and walked over to her table.

"Good afternoon," I said. "May I join you? Sit down with you?"

"Sure you can," she said, in a cheerful German accent. "I've ... uhm ... been sitting here wondering what's wrong with your eye?"

"My eye?" I said. "Nothing's wrong with my eye."

254

"Well, when I was watching you over there, just before you came here, your eye kept fluttering." All of her "W's" sounded like "V's."

I started laughing, and laughed until tears leaked from the corners of my eyes.

"That's winking," I said. "I was winking at you."

She smiled broadly. "Oh," she said, "what's dis ... uhm winking?"

Her name was Heidy Pawlik, pronounced Pav-lick, she said. She was an interior designer who was born in Germany and lived in Bryn Mawr, Pennsylvania. I guessed her age at about forty.

Heidy was returning from an impulse trip out West. She did that, she said. Picked a place off a map and went to see it.

I loved watching the flash of her smile, the way her cheeks glowed and her eyes frolicked, as well as the lyrical sound of her voice. And she laughed freely and easily.

It was a most productive hour. I managed to get Heidy's address and telephone number before my flight was called. We parted, promising to stay in touch.

From the moment I returned from California we exchanged letters and phone calls. First there was the occasional chat or the casual card or quick note. It grew to a flurry. I received my biggest clue after returning from California at Christmas time. My house sitter left me a handwritten note by the living room telephone. "Heidy from Pennsylvania called, wanted to invite you for Christmas." I smiled at her thoughtfulness.

"Who is the woman that answered the phone while you were gone?" Heidy asked when I called. Did I catch a hint of jealousy? I wasn't sure. I also didn't play games.

"She's only my house sitter," I said. "My home doesn't have anything but a wood stove for heat. Someone has to be around all winter to keep a fire going so my water pipes don't freeze. So she came in to watch the place for me. There's nothing going on there."

Heidy changed the subject. "I've been thinking about us," she said. "All of these telephone calls are so very, very expensive. The phone bills are piling higher and higher. Maybe it's time we get a little closer together."

Not that the thought hadn't crossed my mind. It was the thoughts that went with that idea. Heidy was a well dressed woman of the city, accustomed to dependable electricity and heat, plenty of hot water, access to Macy's, and all of the other high-end places where she could pursue her favorite hobby: shopping. I live twenty-five miles from the nearest community of any size. The fact that it had a genuine supermarket with fresh produce that cost less than ten dollars a pound made the town remarkable for such a remote part of the world.

At that time, I didn't have an indoor toilet. Power outages are assured in my neck of Idaho. Snow leaves people stranded for weeks. I am never stranded because I'm content to do nothing more than make the two-mile round-trip walk to the mailbox. Getting out any farther doesn't do much for my blood pressure.

"I'll tell you what," I said. "I'll send you a plane ticket for next month, February. Say about the middle of the month. You need to get farther than the Spokane airport before you decide this is a place you want to spend time."

"Oh, it's no problem, I'm sure," Heidy replied. "I will very much enjoy coming to see you."

I wrote her a note with the airplane tickets, explaining that my only facilities were an outhouse. My attempt at fair warning backfired. Heidy wrote back to say, "I am so excited that you have an outhouse. We can sit out there with company and have coffee. I will really look forward to that."

Heidy figured an outhouse was a gazebo. I decided not to say more until she arrived.

I couldn't have picked a better time than February 1990 to test Heidy's will. An Arctic air mass dropped from the north to mingle with the moisture of a Pacific front. The skies whipped snow horizontally into the windshield as I drove to the airport to meet her. This would become the most difficult week in the history of romance. And the miseries of country living would drive Heidy away. I could feel it.

Heidy was laughing at the weather when she came off her plane. "Did you arrange this special for me?" she asked.

The trip home normally takes an hour and a half. After three hours we finally made it a little more than halfway—to Plummer, Idaho. I gave up and found us each a motel room. I can stand only so many hours of driving in a white-out. The concentration required to keep guessing where the road is grinds me down. Soon a guess about the shoulder becomes a trip into the ditch and the trouble triples.

Our dilemma would have increased if we made it as far as the turnoff by my mailbox. Even a four-wheel drive couldn't make the last mile this time of year, and I didn't want to pack her and her suitcases down the final goat trail in the dark. Heidy understood that much better when we arrived late the next morning.

A few yards beyond the mailboxes, on the final stretch of road, my neighbor—Duke Duplessis—waited with a sled and his team of malamutes and huskies. Big, white-bearded, and dressed in a red snow suit, Duke looked like a Santa who had traded reindeer for dogs.

"Oh, Vernon, they are so be-u-tee-ful," Heidy sang out. "So be-u-tee-ful."

I smiled and decided to score points rather than explain that practicality dictated the transportation, not my flirting heart.

The week was magic. We spent one of the last afternoons in the living room, me napping on the couch, her sitting directly under one of the skylights, drying her hair in one of those rare blue-sky winter days when the sun gives the illusion that snow is a beautiful winter coat, not a cold, driving menace.

"Hasie," Heidy said, calling me by her pet name for the first time. Hasie. Her big rabbit.

"Hmm," I half replied, drifting in and out of sleep.

"Hasie, I don't want to leave."

My heart danced a merry jig.

"Are you sure?" I asked. "Look at all of the snow. It's like this eight or nine months of the year. Sometimes more."

"Oh Hasie, I love this."

Heidy moved as many of her belongings as possible by mail, and I finally went, after spring thaw, to help her bring her car and other things west. Getting lost in the Philadelphia airport parking garage helped convince her that this was the correct move.

We lived together for three years. At first Heidy kept her car, drove the dirt back roads to town like they were the Autobahn, and kept her links to civilization. I shuddered when she finally told me she timed herself on the drive to St. Maries and was trying to beat twenty-three minutes. The curves on these back roads aren't banked for a Subaru traveling 65 mph. And logging trucks don't slow down for cars. More than one daring driver has met his end hooking fenders with the sixty-ton tractor-trailers.

Time and the overwhelming peacefulness of my mountain valley slowly won her over. Going to the mall became less and less important. The leather coats gave way to more practical wool; high heels were replaced by walking shoes.

Heidy hadn't spent much time with cook pot and cookbook. I taught her to cook, and she responded by permanently banning me from the kitchen. We narrowly averted one major incident of gastrointestinal disaster on a fishing trip our first summer together.

I was wetting a line in one of the small, unnamed tributaries of the St. Joe River, near Red Ives. Heidy was in the camper fixing dinner, including a salad. She spotted a jar of brightly colored condiments on the table and decided to stir them in with the tomatoes and lettuce. Thankfully she couldn't get the jar open. Those "condiments" were bright purple salmon eggs, specially treated to be fish bait, not salad garnishments. Although, I suppose, a soldier who has grubs for lunch in Italy can stomach most anything.

My daughters ventured to northern Idaho for a visit during the summer of 1993. When the introductions were over, they listened to Heidy tell stories about how I disappeared for weeks at a time each fall, about how I came back unshaven and dragging a 1,000-pound carcass into our kitchen. They invited her to avoid the agony and visit them during the upcoming hunting season.

My youngest daughter, LaVerne, called me when I returned from hunting camp that fall.

"Dad, why don't you marry that woman?" she asked.

"Why don't I what?" I asked.

"Marry Heidy. She loves you, she's a nice woman. You should marry her."

"Well, uh, I don't know," I said, stalling for time. "I guess I figured you might not like it."

"Come on, Dad. Why wouldn't we like it? You think about marrying her."

We found a little chapel in California to accommodate our families and went there in November and got married. The honeymoon? Frostbitten, at best.

In the seven days required to get to California, marry, and return, our corner of the world went polar. The man who was supposed to check on our house flaked out. When I walked in the back door, the lake on the floor communicated trouble; not half as much trouble as the wall of ice that extended from the second-floor balcony to the living room floor.

The frozen Niagara Falls was still growing. A pipe had broken upstairs, sending the water over the balcony. Meanwhile, the well pump had continued to send water upstairs, and continued feeding the frozen cascade. For a week.

"Hasie," Heidy said. "Do you think we can find somebody for the house cleaning?"

"Oh Heidy, out here we do our own house cleaning."

We laughed. We laughed all through our honeymoon. And still laugh.

When fame and spotlights came our way, people began looking for flaws in that honeymoon. Sure, Heidy's white and I'm black. I never thought of her as any particular color. I looked upon her as someone I wanted to get to know. When I finally began dealing with my anger and reflecting on my own agonizing experiences I realized that people of all races and walks of life had mistreated me. I also realized that people of all races and walks of life were quite good to me. Color doesn't determine how they will treat me. Their background, experiences, education, and attitude—things I can't determine at a glance—do. I began evaluating people the way I wanted them to evaluate me.

Heidy also is German, and that's striking, I suppose, because I fought the Germans in World War II. I jokingly tell people that I married the enemy. In the end, Heidy is an individual, not an ideology.

Put all of this together and the thing folks most want to make a big deal out of is where we live. They see a headline: "INTER-RACIAL COUPLE LIVING IN RACIST NORTH IDAHO." This sort of speculative worry is intensified by the fact that former Los Angeles cop Mark Fuhrman lives a hundred miles north of me, in Sandpoint, Idaho.

Nobody in northern Idaho makes much of this except those who live well beyond our little valley. It's not a sexy reality, but a peaceful one.

TWENTY-EIGHT

Happiness is good health and a bad memory.

—Ingrid Bergman

March 1994, Benewah Valley, Idaho

One telephone call threatened to permanently unravel our peace. "Where can we meet you next month?"

The voice was Daniel Gibran's, a professor from Shaw University. He was chief researcher on a study commissioned by the Secretary of the Army to determine why no black World War II veterans received the Medal of Honor, he said. The cases of black soldiers who received the Distinguished Service Cross were being reviewed on the chance that perhaps they deserved the Medal of Honor.

Gibran wanted to bring a Colonel John Cash and meet me in the nearest city served by a major airline. It was necessary to talk about that April day in 1945, those hills, that castle, Gibran explained, in order to adequately determine why men like me hadn't received the nation's highest honor for battlefield heroism.

Brilliant, I thought. Next there would be a study to determine why Southern states with large populations of impoverished blacks levied poll taxes. From there, perhaps a group of academics could investigate whether Ku Klux Klan founder Nathan Bedford Forest was racist. Anyone with an accurate memory of the United States, circa 1945, knew that black soldiers were measured by a different standard. After all, it took until 1991 for Corporal Freddie Stowers to become the single black World War I veteran to receive the Medal of Honor. Stowers led his company in the attack on a German-held hill, destroyed a machine gun nest, led the charge to a second trench line, was wounded, but kept leading until he was killed. His Medal of Honor nomination mysteriously went unprocessed for seventy-three years.

I still felt as if I had received my due with the Distinguished Service Cross. I needed no further recognition and didn't need the personal hell of recounting, detail by detail, the most traumatic, horrifying days of my life. Gibran was persistent.

The only reason to do this, I decided, was to let someone know that my men accomplished something significant. They deserved vindication. People, even if they were only researchers in some dusty academic dungeon, should know Runyon abandoned us, artillery officers doubted us, and we had embarrassed every white officer who claimed black soldiers didn't cut it. They should know the odds my men had faced and the recognition they were denied. I finally, reluctantly, agreed.

For two days, the following month, Heidy and I drove to Spokane early in the morning for hours of grilling and returned home in the evening. Gibran was an intense man, with dark hair, a dark beard, and dark eyes. He talked rapidly, asking acres of questions about the racial atmosphere of the country during World War II.

John Cash was a tall, quiet, likable black man with a distinguished graying mustache. A military historian, Cash asked about the war, my training, the battles, and the commanders. He was interested in what it felt like to be marching in my boots in Italy. He was interested in me as a person.

At some point in those two days, Gibran and Cash brought out top secret reports written by Runyon and other commanders from the 92nd Infantry Division about the Battle for Castle Aghinolfi. The repulsiveness of these recently declassified documents shocked me, although I had lived under the rein of the men who wrote them and was intimately familiar with their attitudes.

"As stated many times before, a few men do an excellent job, but the majority of negro infantrymen have no heart for combat and definitely have no desire to close with the enemy," Battalion Commander Raymond G. Sherman wrote in May 1945. "During the past eight months of combat in close contact with negro troops, I have tried every possible method to fight negro soldiers as infantry unsuccessfully.

"I am now completely convinced that the great majority of negroes [sic] cannot be made into good infantry soldiers or even satisfactory ones. They have on every occasion clearly demonstrated that they are entirely undependable."

Captain Runyon, my company commander, started by taking credit for any success we had during the battle for the castle, based on his sermons on teamwork and success. That pep talk must have been reserved for his white officers. My men and I never heard such words from him.

Then Runyon unleashed in the same vitriolic vein as his white brothers. He wrote, "In my opinion the average colored soldier loses all control of his mind when subjected to overhead mortars and artillery fire. I also learned that the colored soldier is for some reason or other terrified to fight at night. His imagination and fear overcomes [sic] his sense of judgment. The colored soldier wants to be led in battle, but usually it's a foolish officer who leads colored soldiers because invariably he loses half of his men."

Runyon inexplicably also complimented us, albeit begrudgingly at times. "After indoctrination he (the Negro soldier) loses his fear of enemy small arms fire. In fact, many men of Company C did welcome the opportunity to get into a small arms engagement with the enemy. They invariably could outshoot the enemy and were quite aggressive," Runyon wrote.

"I have been told that Company C led off on the Arno River Crossing, were largely responsible for the 370th Infantry success on Rocky Point on Main Ridge and I personally believe they contributed the greatest share (of the original 92nd Division) in the breakthrough to Massa. There are some real fighting men in that company and all in all they gave their best. I take pride in having served with Company C."

This schizophrenia, Gibran said, came from the fact that Runyon's original report was altered and backdated to fit the more racist views of his superior officers. Those officers, including General Almond, were determined that the official record show black men incapable of combat. Gibran and Cash delivered other surprises.

"Were you ever aware that you were nominated for the Medal of Honor?" Gibran asked.

"I wasn't aware of any of that stuff," I said. "I was a soldier. I did my job and stayed out of the political stuff."

"A clerk, Warrant Officer Robert Millender, recalls having prepared a Medal of Honor nomination for you," Gibran said. "Millender talked about it twenty years ago in an interview that we ran across. He said it wasn't the kind of thing he would forget, a black man finally was going to receive the Medal of Honor. Officers farther up the chain of command apparently blocked it.

"That's strictly against Army policy—every Medal of Honor nomination was supposed to go to the War Department in Washington, D.C., for final determination, no matter what commanders at any level thought of it," Gibran said.

"We were never told any of that kind of stuff," I repeated. "We did our jobs and stayed out of the politics. We knew those commanders didn't like us. But why shirk when somebody says you are no good? One of the greatest pleasures I get is proving people wrong. And we did."

The bombshells didn't end there. Runyon, they said, was nominated for the Medal of Honor for the Battle for Castle Aghinolfi by his white cronies at division command. When that was turned down, he instead received the Distinguished Service Cross. The man who huddled in the stable during the worst shelling while his soldiers fought it out, received the same honor I had. That cheapened the Distinguished Service Cross and it cheapened the sacrifices of my men.

The interviews with Cash and Gibran were the most difficult two days of my life, off the battlefield. All the prying and probing revived the memories I worked so hard to forget. It revived the guilt I felt over the men I lost and the men I had killed. It touched my anger over being treated like a dumb servant, who could do no right, in an Army of white gods who could do no wrong. This was not some cathartic experience as the purveyors of psychobabble might argue. It was a reminder of all the things that tore at my sanity.

I gladly went home to the middle of nowhere, to my wife, my woodpile, my dog, and my construction projects. I rejoiced in the fact that the house was still a mess from the broken pipe and the flooding. Working on it gave me focus and purpose and carried me away from the memories. At least temporarily.

Gibran called frequently during the next several months with questions for his study. Anytime I answered the telephone, Gibran opened with, "Have you made any money yet?" as if the prospect of the Medal of Honor, and all of the associated publicity, was something to revel in and profit by.

I tried to stay as even tempered and polite as possible. But it only exacerbated feelings that I was enduring this cross-examination, and reliving the hell, to no end.

I had plenty of other reasons to be skeptical. Since the end of the war, black leaders had called for investigations into the Medal of Honor question. Several of my soldiering colleagues—Spencer Moore, James Hamlet, and many others—pressed the issue for years. Sergeant Ruben Rivers's white commander, David Williams, fought to get Rivers recognition for his deeds with the 761st Armored Division in Germany. All for nothing.

In the early 1970s, an exchange of letters to the editor in *Ebony* magazine raised the call for an investigation into the matter again. Someone wrote to say I was dead and not to bother doing anything for me. I wrote *Ebony* to declare my status as a living, breathing soul and to ask for a retraction. The magazine never replied.

With that history, I could only surmise that black World War II veterans again were the focus of some fleeting attention. We were forced to relive our pain for more of the same cruel dismissal and disregard we had left Italy trying to forget.

An old soldier from the 92nd Division tried to soften my skepticism. Colonel Major Clark—who had the blessing or misfortune of being christened with a first name that corresponds to military rank—had served in the 597th Battalion, an artillery support group, and went on to rise to lieutenant colonel during a twenty-year career. Clark and I had talked occasionally over the years. He called me once after publication of a book about the 92nd Division, written by one of the white officers, who claimed I died on a patrol. Some months after Gibran first visited, Clark telephoned again.

He talked about a resolution being introduced in Congress to waive the 1952 deadline for bestowing the Medal of Honor on World War II veterans. He talked about other signs he thought indicated the Buffalo Soldiers might get their due. Still, there was no guarantee, and no hint of who might receive what.

Clark's gentle persuasiveness chipped away at my doubts. Time dragged on and reinforced them. I returned to wood cutting and hunting. A mountain lion helped take my mind off the medal and the memories.

I was returning to the house from a day on the elk trail late in the fall of 1995 when a growl startled me. I spun around to find a mountain lion crouched twenty feet away. I stood still. A mountain lion can't see you well in the woods if you don't move. Since he was upwind, he also couldn't smell me.

A minute, perhaps two minutes, passed with us locked in a stare-down. All these years of hunting and I had never come this close to one of the big cats. His light green eyes held me breathless.

Eventually, the lion's tail began to twitch. One careful step after another, the lion started to circle me, to get downwind where he could smell me.

I turned with each of his first five or six steps to make sure he didn't have a chance at the back of my neck. Then I realized that once he got a whiff of me, I was lunch. I shot him. He weighed 162 pounds, three pounds less than me. For months, we enjoyed mountain lion chops, roasts, and tenderloins.

As I started to think about getting the mountain lion hide out of the freezer the following spring, almost two years to the day after Daniel Gibran first called, an NBC News reporter name Joe Johns telephoned.

"I'd like to talk to you about your receiving the Medal of Honor," Johns said.

"Nobody's told me I'm actually going to receive it," I responded. "All I've heard about is this study."

"The Secretary of the Army is supposed to announce it soon," Johns said. "You and six other black soldiers are going to get the medal. The other six men are dead."

My head spun. The old memories taunted my carefully constructed peace of mind.

Johns also wanted to meet us in Spokane. He was the most generous among the interviewers. He rented us a motel room, one that even accommodated our dog Lucky, so we could rest during the two days of interviewing instead of making the 130-mile round trip from home to Spokane each day.

It was a ride on the continuing roller coaster of hope and disappointment, through no fault of John's. He called one day to say the interview was going to run and then called a few days later to explain another delay. News executives were waiting for some event. Like all the other efforts relating to the medal, this one baited with hope and hooked with disappointment.

Other calls for interviews started pouring in. News magazines and newscasts were talking about the Shaw University study—the one Gibran and Cash were involved with—and about how racism kept the American military from recognizing the sacrifices of the black soldier in World War II.

General Almond's final report on the failure of black troops in World War II, "was remarkable, not only for its thoroughgoing racism, but also for the white leadership's rejection of its own personal responsibility," the Shaw study said. "The report possibly constitutes the only instance in American military history where all of the top commanders of a division placed the blame for failure completely on their soldiers, rather than accepting responsibility themselves."

As a result of the Shaw study, the cases of ten black soldiers, including me, were reconsidered. In order to ensure fairness, the story of our deeds were stripped of anything that would identify us or our race and submitted to an Army review board. The cases of ten white soldiers who already had received the Medal of Honor also were submitted as part of a blind comparison.

All ten of the white soldiers were reconfirmed as worthy of the medal. Seven of the ten black soldiers were selected for the Medal of Honor—myself and six others, just as Johns had said.

I was stunned. It didn't seem possible, after more than fifty years of denial. For my men, for all of the other black soldiers who served this country for more than two hundred years, this was welcome news, recognition well deserved.

As for myself, I wasn't sure why I was selected. I was a soldier, a warrior. My country sent me to battle and I did what I was asked, for all I was worth. That was enough.

For months, I lay awake at night trying to figure out why this was happening and why it included me. And what my nineteen comrades would make of it.

TWENTY-NINE

When thou art above measure angry, bethink thee how momentary is man's life.

—Marcus Aurelius

Spring 1996, Benewah Valley, Idaho

The letters began pouring in, often addressed only with *Vernon Baker, St. Maries, Idaho.*

"Dear Mr. Baker:

I saw the story of your heroism on TV and it really upset me that the white prejudice during that time was so brutal to you and the other black veterans who certainly deserved meritorious awards. It just inflamed me. I well remember that vicious war and prayed many of my friends through it.

Ann Avery
Phoenix, Arizona"

"Dear Mr. Baker:

Congratulations and thank you. We are a nation of 265,000,000 different people, not a single one braver than you. God Bless You.

Larry Jennings
Tulsa, Oklahoma

P.S. My father was killed at Anzio. He would have been proud to have saluted you."

"Dear Mr. Baker:

I am a 50-year-old white male who salutes you and your comrades in arms for the sacrifices you made on behalf of our country... I applaud your refusal to bury the discrimination you dealt with before, during and after your service. I believe we've made progress, but I know we've got a long way to go and I'm glad you dealt with it in the principled way you did.

Dennis C. Edmiston
Decatur, Georgia"

People from around the world wrote and called to apologize for the way the nation treated the black soldiers and to heap us with accolades. Even my former son-in-law called from the Virgin Islands. I was astonished at the outpouring.

I'm not sure there's a major newspaper or television show that didn't come to our house. Churches, chambers of commerce, universities, and veterans organizations called, held ceremonies, and honored me in every possible way. I was grateful for the sentiment.

But there were days I felt as if a bulldozer equipped with television cameras and lights plowed through our living room. The peace and quiet I'd found in the backwoods of northern Idaho was a memory.

By September 1996 Congress waived the 1952 deadline for World War II soldiers to receive honors. President Bill Clinton signed the legislation and called for a White House ceremony the following January. Demands from the media increased. I wondered where my elk hunting season was going. Then I wondered where it had gone.

Not long after New Year's 1997, on the clearest winter day in months, a young white Army captain and his driver appeared at my door.

"Captain Mark Jackson, 437th Military Police Company, and this is my driver, Specialist Jason Luhrs," the dark haired man with intelligent eyes said. "We're here to brief you on the next few days and on your trip to Washington, D.C., for the Medal of Honor ceremonies."

When the Army decided to right a wrong, it spared nothing. Pentagon officials combed through hundreds of files to choose military escorts for myself and the families of the other Medal of Honor recipients. The caliber and qualifications of men they chose was unheard of for this sort of duty. My escort commanded a military police company in Fort Belvoir, Virginia.

The astounding moments kept unfolding. A white captain was sitting in my living room, waiting to serve my every need. I was unfairly cool to him at first, a bit suspicious, considering the Mark Jackson I came to know. My suspicions were a throwback to my military days, not only dealing with white officers but with the white military policemen who had harassed me in Italy.

Captain Jackson read my unease, I know, but carried himself as if I were the most congenial person he'd ever met. He and Specialist Luhrs hauled in firewood, shoveled snow, and carried my luggage—not just to the car, but all the way. A white captain followed me, a black man, through airports, dragging my gear.

Alexandra, Heidy's daughter and now my stepdaughter, flew from Germany to join us for the trip to the White House. We stopped in the Spokane airport and lunched at the table where Heidy and I met eight years earlier. A television reporter came by to chat. She asked me what had changed since I fought in Italy. That was easy. Fifty-two years earlier a white woman wouldn't have dared sit at the same table with me in a public building and interview me.

The whirlwind intensified. I soon sat next to General Colin L. Powell in the Cosmos Club in Washington, D.C., talking about Army life.

"I came along at a time when most of the barriers were down in the Army," Powell told me. He kindly credited the efforts of my generation and earlier generations for the change.

"While I was privileged, I will never forget those who went before me and those who were willing to serve their country, which was not willing to serve them," Powell said, leaning across the couch and grabbing my arm to show how much he meant it.

In all of the awards, all of the ceremonies, all of the honors this country has belatedly bestowed on black soldiers, none felt as overwhelming and uplifting as those words. Colin Powell went all the way, he became the top general in the country—chairman of the Joint Chiefs of Staff. Think of the loss to this land if racism had kept him from serving this country as he has served. Think of the other Colin Powells who could have enriched our lives and contributed so much if we had opened the door sooner.

By the next morning, I was backstage with President Clinton preparing for the Medal of Honor ceremony. President Clinton was sincere and treated me like a regular guy. I liked him. He didn't ask me about the war, thankfully. But he and the media were fascinated by my encounter with the mountain lion.

Within minutes of our private meeting, I stood with the families of five of the posthumous recipients under the chandeliers of the White House East Room. There was the son of Sergeant Edward A. Carter, the widow of Private Willy F. James, Jr., the oldest sister of Sergeant Ruben Rivers, the niece of First Lieutenant Charles L. Thomas, and the widow of First Lieutenant John R. Fox.

A military escort waited in Los Angeles until the last possible minute, in case members of Private George Watson's family could be located and flown to Washington, D.C., to accept his medal. To no avail. In the end, Sergeant Major Gene McKinney, the first black to become the top noncommissioned officer in the Army, accepted the medal for Watson.

I refocused on the room. It was packed with a blur of big wheels and dignitaries. When President Clinton placed the medal around my neck, I guess I cried. Newspapers ran photographs of me standing there with tears running down my face. I don't think they knew why I cried. I didn't cry for myself. I had made peace with the anger that burned my soul years earlier. I cried for the real heroes—those men I left behind on that hill, that day in April 1945. I saw their faces, their questions, their determination, their hopes and fears. We knew we were fighting for a country that didn't appreciate us, and yet we were proud to fight. President Clinton said we Medal of Honor recipients "were denied the nation's highest honor, but their deeds could not be denied." Those words describe my platoon and all of the black men who have valiantly gone to combat in every war this country has ever fought.

I felt the loss of those men, and I felt the loss of my children. Like Private Watson, I had no blood relatives to stand with me. My only living sister is incapacitated by a stroke. And four of the most important people in my life, my daughters, were absent from this moment, this pinnacle of my life.

I remembered a time when one of my daughters called from Germany, even though she was twenty-one, and asked my permission to marry. That closeness evaporated. We don't talk anymore—and haven't for years. Something happened after Heidy and I were married. I try to understand it, try to understand that my life with another woman is difficult for them because they may see Heidy in the place of their late mother. I think they measure one woman against the other and find themselves dissatisfied.

This is not a case of one person being better or worse, or of Heidy replacing Fern. I still love their mother, and I don't for a day regret our thirty-nine years together. This is a case of me going on with my life, with my need for companionship, for love, for sharing difficult days and joyous days intimately. I cannot face down these memories alone.

I hope my children are happy. I hope they are raising their children the way Fern raised them. And I hope they know that I love them, that beyond any medal, any ceremony, any accolades, or any accomplishment, I am proudest of them. Nothing can fill the holes in my life created by losing them.

After the White House ceremony, we were whisked off to a luncheon at Fort Meyer, Virginia, where a galaxy of generals' stars lined up to shake my hand. Five decades earlier I couldn't get them to return my salute.

A quick meal. Quick speeches. Back to the bus. Within an hour I was on my way to see our names added to the Medal of Honor wall in the Hall of Heroes at the Pentagon. General Robert Foley, one of two Medal of Honor recipients still on active duty, gave me a glimpse of the camaraderie I might have known if any of my fellow medal recipients had lived.

The days were exhilarating, but exhausting. I am not one for the spotlight, not one for running such a gauntlet. I dislike the attention, the questions, and all the ceremonies. I do it to honor the men who fought with me, to repay a debt to them I cannot ever repay.

The morning after the White House ceremony, we moved to Arlington National Cemetery to give our last respects to Sergeant Edward A. Carter. His family paid to have him reburied here. Carter fought three years for the right to go to combat and then had to relinquish his sergeant's stripes in order to go into battle. The Army required as much to ensure he did not command any white troops.

Church bells sent out eleven chimes as Heidy, Alexandra, and I wove through the rows of white tombstones in the cold January wind to Carter's grave site. Far up an asphalt lane, a team of six flawlessly matched draft horses clopped in perfect rhythm to the clack of the wheels of the caisson they pulled. Three ramrod-straight soldiers from the 3rd U.S. Infantry Regiment sat, one behind another, on the left-hand horse of each pair.

A separate mounted soldier accompanied the caisson, which bore Carter's body. Eight soldiers, also clad in dress-blue uniforms, brought up the rear, marching two abreast. As the caisson drew by, the honor guard surrounded the silver, flag-draped casket. They drew it off with white-gloved hands, methodically side-stepping in unison, one stride every four seconds. They turned and, with carefully measured marching steps, brought it to the top of a tree-lined rise.

A chaplain gave the usual homily about life and death. But he also talked of an Army that wasn't open to all. From beginning to end, the wrongs of fifty-two years were acknowledged.

The full-military-honors included the traditional gun salute. Taps wept from a bugler's horn. And we wept.

I walked back across the cemetery, leaning on the arm of Mark Jackson, not because of physical fatigue, but emotional exhaustion. At that moment, when the last waver of taps was swept into the wind, I was filled with loneliness. I longed for impossible companionship—for my men, for the other Medal of Honor recipients.

I was the only man among the black Medal of Honor recipients to survive to see this day. I was one of only two men in my platoon to live to see this day and the other man, Napoleon "Dandy" Belk was too sick to come and share the moment. For all the friends and family, I could not turn to one man who had been there that day, or who had been in equally extraordinary circumstances, look him in the eye and share a handshake that says, "I know your hell."

The cold wind picked up across the snowy cemetery and sent me walking faster, past a hundred of the thousands whose last honor was being buried here. A shiver came over me, much like the shivers of the days, two years earlier, when people started talking to me about April 1945. This was a shiver of loneliness that went beyond my fellow soldiers.

Why? Why was I chosen? I know of nothing extra special in my life or my story except for the people around me, from my grandfather to those soldiers who went with me to Castle Aghinolfi. Why shouldn't Private Watson or Lieutenant Charles Thomas or Sergeant Carter have lived for this moment? I cannot fathom it, but I continue to probe the question.

As we left Arlington National Cemetery, we passed the grave of Audie Murphy, the actor of "To Hell and Back" fame who also earned the Medal of Honor. My loneliness intensified. His gravestone pushed another point home. We were heroes from long past. Our moment, all that we stood for, was gone.

It's not the regret people may assume. It is the wondering of this: what could black soldiers have accomplished if even one had received the Medal of Honor fifty-two years earlier? How much earlier would there have been a Colin Powell, a black sergeant major of the entire Army? Would I have had the opportunity to fulfill my dream of becoming the sergeant major of even a battalion? Would there have been enough acknowledged black heroes that the Army would have allowed me to fight in Korea, to prove, once again, that soldiering didn't depend upon the color of my skin?

Before the week ended, I would stand before a display in the Museum of American History that talked of the 442nd Infantry Division—the Japanese-American unit. The man at the heart of the display, Private First Class Sadao S. Munemori, died April 5, 1945, in the mountains near Castle Aghinolfi. Private Munemori took over when his squad leader was wounded by withering fire, charged two different machine gun nests, and destroyed them with grenades.

The Germans easily discovered him, followed his every move with other machine guns and grenades. Still, Munemori nearly reached the safety of a shell crater and two companions, when a German grenade bounced off of his helmet and rolled toward that shell crater. Private Munemori leapt into the blizzard of bullets, ran and threw himself on the grenade. His comrades lived.

Nearly a year after the battle, Private Munemori's mother was presented with the Medal of Honor for his deeds that day. He was the only Japanese-American, the only Nisei, to receive the Medal of Honor in World War II.

Here was yet another man whom I owe and cannot thank. What could we have shared if he had lived until this day? Would I be here if he had not died protecting my right flank?

War does not resolve such questions. It only raises them.

EPILOGUE

*The human heart does not stay away too long from
that which hurt it most. There is a return journey to
anguish that few of us are released from making.*

—Lillian Smith

April 6, 1997, Forte dei Marmi, Italy

A beautiful black woman with sad eyes sat on the flowered couch
near the lobby windows in the Hotel Eden. Here was one more
tragedy of the war, one more wound, wanting to be healed. Which is
one reason I returned to the battlefields fifty-two years after the fact.

"Can you help me?" Raffaella Ricci asked through an interpreter.
"I'm searching for my father. His name was Ralph Jill. He was a
Buffalo Soldier of the 92nd Division—the Signal Corps—when you
were here.

"He and my mother dated. He left with the other soldiers, in
October 1945 but was to return to marry my mother. I was born of
their love in December 1945."

She paused, brushed aside an errant lock of hair and looked at
her own twenty-seven-year-old daughter, who sat beside her. They
beamed into each others eyes.

"After he left," Raffaella continued, "my grandfather sent my
mother to Switzerland to live, and there I was born. But my grandfather would not allow my mother to marry a black man. When my

278

father came back in 1947 or 1948, he went to my grandfather and asked for my mother. My grandfather told him that both my mother and I had died with my birth. Then he sent my father away."

"I'm sorry," I said. "I do not know this man, Ralph Jill. We had very little contact with the Signal Corps. I was an infantryman, a rifleman. Do you know anything more about him?"

"My father, I think, was born in Harlem. They say he was tall, about two meters, and couldn't walk through a normal door. He worked on the telegraph and was an artist. My mother said he arrived with something on his sleeve. Maybe he was a man of position?

"He stayed in Pietrasanta, at the Deposito Luisi, a marble factory used by soldiers and refugees. He wrote to my mother after he left, and sent photographs. But my grandfather demanded she send them back."

Raffaella paused for breath, her eyes watering, her cheeks patchy and puffy from the tears that gathered there. She opened her purse and pulled out two photographs. One was of a dark, curly-haired Italian woman with a baby on her lap. Obviously the child was Raffaella and the woman was her mother. The other photograph depicted them sitting on a blanket outside with two other women, who also were holding babies. Perhaps it was the first picnic of summer.

Raffaella pulled her own daughter close and looked at me questioningly, as if to say, "You are a Buffalo soldier, you must know my father."

"I'm sorry," I repeated. "I don't know of this man—your father. What does your mother say? Is she still alive?"

Raffaella shifted uncomfortably on the couch as she listened carefully to the interpreter and then shook her head. She pulled at her daughter again, as if there was some way to bring her closer, to gain more reassurance.

"My mother, Assunta Ricci, is still alive. She knows more, but she will not tell me. She does not want me to find my father. He had a girlfriend in the United States, too, I guess. When he came back to see my mother, he was already married and had another daughter. I think his girlfriend's name was Doris.

"I have written the White House, the Italian consulate, everyone. I don't want any money or anything like this from him. I just want to know my father."

Raffaella Ricci stories cover the globe. In the course of war, many people are casualties of circumstances, not weapons. I could not help her with her father, but I could sympathize with her loss and her search for an end.

I, too, want to close wounds and answer the questions of World War II. Some wounds will not heal, some questions will not find answers. Even with a Medal of Honor, I remain haunted.

I came to Italy imagining one last reunion with Giovanna. Despite the help of newspapers, police, and Italian secret service agents, I did not find her. There was no chance to explain, to apologize, to reconnect.

Thousands of people embraced me—the towns of Montignoso, Massa, and Cararra, the cities of Pietrasanta and Florence, even the president of Italy. It was a homecoming more incredible than any lost soldier could long for.

Yet, I came to Italy imaging one last important march. I planned to retrace my steps to the castle, search for the place where each of my nineteen men took his last breath—those places are indelible in my memory. I planned to pay homage to each man's soul, apologize, thank him, and make our peace. Perhaps I owed a similar apology to the two young German lads in the tank, I reasoned.

I was not prepared to meet my ghosts.

On April 4, 1997, the day before my pilgrimage, I visited Castle Aghinolfi from the German side of the lines. The invisible hand squeezed my soul. We were far worse off than I had realized fifty-two years earlier. The Germans had more of an advantage and tougher defenses than we knew. Not only were they hitting us with mortar rounds from the castle, but there was a German mortar battery behind us that we had missed in our charge up these hills. The ravine was deeper than I remembered; the distance to the castle greater.

We never had a chance. And yet we did it.

I had stayed after Captain Runyon left, because I wanted the Buffalo Soldiers to have the respect and acknowledgment we deserved. I wanted to disprove every white commander who claimed black soldiers only melted away. We did that—we proved that we are fighters. But the price was too high. Nineteen of my twenty-five men died, and still there was no appreciation. I should have realized that would be the result before I committed these men to their deaths.

I had suspected Captain Runyon wasn't coming back that day. Standing at that castle in April 1997, I saw his retreat differently. If I had been in his boots, I too would have left. Abandoning the field at that point was the prudent move. He wasn't a Buffalo Soldier, a man who lived under the accusation of always running. He was a white man; he could leave with honor when the odds were overwhelming. We were Buffalo soldiers; we had to fight to the last man to retain any shred of dignity.

Despite my passion for my men, I cannot better explain why I cannot honor them—the heroes who didn't retreat—by remembering their names. I know it paints me harsh and distant. It has its price. It is a regret that I cannot resolve but will wander the ghostly battlefields of Italy, of my mind, and will always visit me.

I do not welcome these memories, but I do not shun the responsibility of carrying them. We did the best we could—and a hell of a lot better than anyone believed we could. We fought fiercely and proudly for a country that shunned us, and we kept fighting because we knew the price of allowing Nazi fascism to rule was far greater than even what we endured. Every time I see a child smile, get to listen to a symphony play, or freely choose a book to read I know we made the right decision.

War, however, is the most regrettable proving ground. For the sake of my nineteen comrades, I hope no man, black, white, or any color, ever again has the opportunity to earn the Medal of Honor. War is not honor. Those who rush to launch conflict, and those who seek to create heroes from it, should remember war's legacy. You have to be there to appreciate its horrors. And die to forget them.

APPENDIX

Six of my fellow black soldiers received the Medal of Honor posthumously for their deeds of valor in World War II.

Private George Watson, 29th Quartermaster Regiment: Enemy bombers severely damaged Private Watson's ship—the Dutch steamer *Jacob*—near New Guinea on March 8, 1943. Instead of saving himself, the Birmingham, Alabama, native went after several other soldiers who could not swim and pulled them to a life raft. The exertion exhausted him, and Private Watson was dragged down by the suction from the sinking ship. Private Watson's widow died in November 1995, just three months before the White House ceremony bestowing the posthumous Medal of Honor on her husband. His body was never recovered. Private Watson is memorialized in the American Battle Monument Cemetery in Manila. He originally received the Purple Heart posthumously for his bravery.

Sergeant Edward A. Carter, Jr., 12th Armored Division: When the Germans started pouring bazooka and rifle fire on the tank where he was riding on March 23, 1943, Carter jumped down and tried to lead a patrol of three other men across an open field near Speyer, Germany. Two of the men were killed and the third man was seriously wounded. Carter sustained five wounds but kept going. Eight enemy soldiers went after him. Carter killed six and captured the other two. He retreated, using them as a shield, and obtained valuable information from them on the location of other German troops. Sergeant Carter was born in Los Angeles and raised in China by missionary parents. He originally received the Purple Heart and the Bronze Star for his actions. He died in Los Angeles in 1963. Sergeant Carter was reinterred in Arlington National Cemetery in January 1997.

Private Willy F. James, Jr., 104th Infantry Division: Private James was the lead scout during an attempt to capture a vital bridge near Lippoldsberg, Germany, on April 7, 1945. This Kansas City, Missouri, lad was the first American soldier to draw enemy fire in this battle and was pinned down for more than an hour. He used the time to observe enemy position in detail. James managed eventually to get back to his platoon where he helped work out a plan of attack, and then led the charge. Private James was killed by a German machine gunner a short time later while attempting to go to the aid of his fatally wounded platoon leader. He is buried in the American Battle Monument Cemetery in the Netherlands and originally received the Purple Heart and the Bronze Star, posthumously, for his valor.

Sergeant Ruben Rivers, 761st Tank Battalion: Sergeant Rivers was first wounded November 16, 1944, when his tank was hit and disabled near Gueblin, France. Sergeant Rivers refused medical treatment and took over another tank. He fought for another three days, again and again refusing morphine or evacuation. "I see 'em, we'll fight 'em," he radioed after refusing a direct order to leave the battlefield. When his company's tanks had to withdraw, Rivers stayed to provide covering fire. His tank was eventually hit, killing Sergeant Rivers and wounding his crew. Sergeant Rivers was one of fifteen children born to a Tecumseh, Oklahoma, cotton farmer. He received the Silver Star while still alive and the Purple Heart posthumously. He is buried in the American Battle Monument Cemetery in France. His white commander, Second Lieutenant David Williams, immediately nominated Rivers for the Medal of Honor. His paperwork disappeared after he turned it in. But Williams continued to fight for more than five decades to win recognition for Rivers.

First Lieutenant Charles L. Thomas, 103rd Infantry Division: Germans wounded Lieutenant Thomas as he was riding in an armored car, leading a force to capture Climbach, France, on December 14, 1944. Lieutenant Thomas helped his crew get out of the armored car and was wounded in the chest, legs, and left arm. Although he was in intense pain, Lieutenant Thomas directed the setup of antitank guns and started returning enemy fire. He then briefed a platoon leader before allowing himself to be evacuated for medical treatment. Known to his family as "Uncle Charlie," Lieutenant Thomas was born in Detroit. He received only the Purple Heart for his bravery in France. He died in 1980 and is buried in the West Lawn Cemetery in Wayne, Michigan.

First Lieutenant John R. Fox, 92nd Infantry Buffalo Division: When U.S. troops were pushed out of Sommocolonia, Italy, on December 26, 1944, Fox and other men volunteered to stay. They staked out the second floor of a house in the village to direct American artillery fire on the advancing Germans. As the Germans closed in on the house, Fox insisted that the last volley of shells be dropped directly on top of him. After an American counterattack, Fox's body was found along with 100 dead German soldiers. An Ohio man, born in Cincinnati, Fox was an avid horseman. He met his wife, Arlene, when riding near Dorchester, Massachusetts. His daughter, Sandra, was only two when her father died. He originally received the Bronze Star and the Purple Heart for his bravery. Lieutenant Fox is buried in the Colebrook Cemetery in Whitman, Massachusetts.

ABOUT THE AUTHORS

Orphaned at age four, **Vernon J. Baker** was raised in Wyoming by his grandparents, in a town with just a dozen other black families. During adolescence, he spent two years at Father Flanagan's Boys Home in Omaha, Nebraska. He graduated from high school in Iowa, worked as a railroad porter, fought to join a segregated Army, and was sent to Italy with one of the few all-black regiments to see combat in World War II.

Mr. Baker fought in Italy, earning a Purple Heart, Bronze Star, and Distinguished Service Cross. He was one of the most highly decorated black soldiers in the Mediterranean Theater. On January 13, 1997, fifty-two years after Mr. Baker's World War II military service, President Clinton presented him with the nation's highest decoration for battlefield valor, the Medal of Honor.

Mr. Baker stayed with the Army, lived through its desegregation, and became one of the first blacks to command an all-white company. He joined the Airborne along the way and made his last jump at age forty-eight.

After retiring from the Army, he spent nearly twenty years working for the Red Cross. Today he lives in northern Idaho with his wife, Heidy.

Journalist **Ken Olsen** also grew up in Wyoming. He is an award-winning writer for the Spokane, Washington *Spokesman-Review,* which featured his widely hailed series on Vernon Baker. His free-lance efforts include essays published in the *Left Bank* series of literary anthologies produced by Blue Heron Publishing Co. He also is coauthor of a winter guide to Yellowstone National Park. Mr. Olsen and his faithful dogs live in northern Idaho.

SELECT BIBLIOGRAPHY

BOOKS

Buck, Pearl S., *Of Men and Women*, New York, John Day Co., 1941.

Forbes, B. C. and Sons, *The Scrapbook of Thoughts on the Business of Life*, New York, Forbes Inc., 1989.

Haedrich, Marcel, *Coco Chanel: Her Life, Her Secrets*, 1972. Publisher unknown, as reprinted by Rosalie Maggio in *The Beacon Book of Quotations by Women*, Boston, Beacon Press, 1992.

Mowat, Farley, *And No Birds Sang*, Boston, Little, Brown & Co., 1979.

Robinson, Marilynne, *Housekeeping*, New York, Bantam Doubleday Dell, 1980, as reprinted by Rosalie Maggio in *The Beacon Book of Quotations by Women*, Boston, Beacon Press, 1992.

MAGAZINES

Giovanni, Nikki, *Reader's Digest*, New York, 1982.

ARCHIVES

Center for Military History, Washington, D.C.

INDEX